TO MOSCOW—AND BEYOND

By Harrison E. Salisbury

TO MOSCOW—AND BEYOND

THE SHOOK-UP GENERATION

AMERICAN IN RUSSIA

STALIN'S RUSSIA AND AFTER

RUSSIA ON THE WAY

TO MOSCOW–

ILLUSTRATED

AND BEYOND

A Reporter's Narrative

HARRISON E. SALISBURY

HARPER & BROTHERS *Publishers* NEW YORK

Some of the material in this book first appeared, in
different form, in the *New York Times*.

Library of Congress catalog card number: 60-7537

For Julia and Tom

Contents

A portfolio of photographs taken by the author follows p. 114.

TO MOSCOW—AND BEYOND

I

A Walk Through Moscow

THE MAY SUN splashed fire on the gold domes of the Kremlin churches just visible over the crumbling rose wall of the Kitai Gorod. Theater Square was bustling with Sunday traffic. From the open window of my Hotel Metropole room I caught the scent of purple lilacs in the pleasant park outside.

For five years I had not been in Russia. Now I was back in Moscow on a spring day so bright and warm that it was drawing all the inhabitants of the city out of their winter-sealed rooms. People sat on park benches or strolled lazily, letting the sun heat their blood and set it tingling again after the long Russian winter. As I stood at the window and watched the people surge in and out of the square, pushing up toward Manezhny Ploshad and on into Red Square, I thought it was time I went out and walked again in Moscow. It was time to join the ebb and flow of citizens on the wide, crowded sidewalks, to loiter around the wall boards and the stalls of the street vendors, to listen to the Russian voices and the Russian talk, to hear and see what the streets could tell me of the changes that had come to Russia and its people in the long period that I had been away.

Moscow . . . a transit town, Vasily called it. A city of people coming and going. Nowadays a million strangers passed through it every day. So it was said. That was not the Moscow I first knew. I first saw Moscow in the fading afternoon light of

1

a wartime winter's day, a day when the chilly corridors of the Metropole Hotel were candle-dark by 3 P.M. Moscow was a city beleaguered then, thin, gaunt, and wolfish under cotton-padded jackets and sheepskins, a city that stumped along in felt boots, squeaking on the hard-packed snow, a city that moved with shoulders bowed and heads bent under the burden of war. Only when the fiery comets of the salute guns on the Kremlin walls tore the blacked-out skies in victory salutes were eyes raised and shoulders lifted. But only for a moment.

Wartime Moscow possessed a weary bravery that lent color to the brutal grayness of the city and the life of the people, the queues, the cold, the hunger, the heartbreak, the tragedy, the markets where men or women sold, bit by bit, the heritage of a lifetime for bread or a scrap of meat, where old *Pravdas* fetched ten rubles a copy and peasant women rested their haunches on *sumki* stuffed with fat rolls of rubles that grew fatter as the war went on.

That was the Moscow I first knew. Then, as now, I lived in the Hotel Metropole; and as I walked through its corridors today I recognized almost every stick of furniture. Here was the same heroic portrait of Lenin and Stalin on the third-floor landing, the life-sized nude in white marble (banished to an obscure corner after an unfortunate incident with a vodka-bemused army officer), the creaking elevators, the floor clerks and their gossip.

I had not returned to the Metropole without some trepidation. Here I had lived and worked in the suspicion-laden days of the cold war's worst period. Here I had watched the growing madness of Stalin's last years of terror. In my baroque room, with its great draperies, I had felt the shadowy tentacles of the "doctors' plot" reach closer and closer. From the front windows of the Metropole I had watched a blue sanitary truck cart Stalin's body from the Kremlin to the Hall of Nobles across the Square, there to lie in honor while the endless throng of

Muscovites, some sobbing and some cynical, passed to view it. And here I sat as Beria's security troops drew tight around the inner city the steel ring which held Moscow in his power during those strange times.

I had left Moscow in October, 1954, with a sense of deep relief. Already, with Stalin's death and the "collective leadership" of his successors, the atmosphere of Moscow had lightened and a new spirit was abroad. It was too early then to be certain how deep this new course would run and what would be its final destination, but it was clear that Russia had broken with the horror of Stalin's final epoch and that the changes long stifled by the dictator's dead hand were coming with startling swiftness. The outlines of the new Soviet tendency had been visible before I boarded my airplane to depart Moscow. Nonetheless I was more than happy to leave Russia, to leave behind a country where I had known the chill of terror, the shadow of suspicion, and the blackness of tragedy.

Now five years had passed in which I had only arm's-length knowledge of Russia. For five years Stalin's heirs in the Foreign Office had refused me a visa to return on grounds that I had slandered the Soviet Union in my reports about the country. For five years I had watched Russia from afar. I had read *Pravda* every day, studied the torrent of new books, speeches, and publications. I had talked with returning travelers and argued with the Russians who came in increasing numbers to the United States on missions of several sorts.

But there is no substitute for one's own eyes. As Mr. Khrushchev likes to say: "Seeing is better than hearing." It is also better than reading. Now, thanks to the kindness of Vice Premier Anastas Mikoyan, I was back on Russian soil again, back in the Moscow to which I kept returning although each time I left I thought I would never come back. I was eager to pick up the threads of the past, to trace them into the present and try to make out if the future had some pattern. I knew that five years had changed Russia. It had changed the world. The grim wounds of the cold war in Korea and Indochina had healed into ugly scar tissue. Fear of hot war was less, but doubts for the future were greater. Sputnik, the revolutionary Soviet probes into space, the shift of power from planes to intercontinental rockets, the emergence of China—these were only some of the problems which had caused my desire to return to Russia to mount higher and higher.

There were the unsolved mysteries of the past. What was really happening in those last years of Stalin's life and did we still have secrets to unravel about the manner of his death? Was it true, as I had heard, that the Jews for some unfathomable reason were still being oppressed? I had every reason to believe that terror was no longer being used as the principal instrument of state policy. But I did not know how this was spelled out in human relationships; whether, for instance, I might now at long last meet any of my old friends of wartime days.

And over and above all were the mysteries of the East. The truth about Soviet-Chinese collaboration or, as some insisted, the growing signs of conflict. I did not know whether I might manage to get to China. Half the foreign correspondents I knew had been trying to get to Peking. I proposed to try as well. If I could not get into China, I would go as far East as possible. I wanted to see Siberia and the grandiose projects which the Soviet counted on to transform that amazing subcontinent from a land of prisons and ice to the national workshop and bread basket. Perhaps I might manage to penetrate Mongolia or even North Korea.

I could not guess how far I might be permitted to travel. But even if I never left Moscow I already knew that I would return to America possessed of a knowledge of the main streams

of Russian thought and feeling and aspiration more vivid than
any I could obtain from the printed or the spoken word.

I arrived in Moscow just before the great May Day holiday
and was caught up immediately in the festivities. It was easy
to see that Moscow had changed more deeply than I had expected. More deeply, indeed, than many Russians themselves
realized because they had seen it all happen piecemeal. To me,
returning after long absence, the impression of change struck
with landslide force. I saw it in the hubbub and bustle at the
airport, the roar of the arriving and departing jets, the staggering park of TU-104's on the airport apron. I saw it in the
welter of construction which transformed the Cheremushki
prairie into an unknown city, gashed with new highways,
studded with new apartment houses, boiling with bulldozers
chewing at the ragged edges of the open fields. I saw it in the
gaiety of May Day, the banishment of masses of tanks and
guns, the absence of a fly-past, the hula hoops and balloons of
the sports clubs, the youngsters who turned Red Square into
a village fete, playing London Bridge Is Falling Down and
dancing the polka.

And the Metropole had changed. Not the décor. Not just
brighter lights. It had something to do with the spirit—the
rough-edged jokes of the big blonde breakfast waitress, the
smiles of the room maids, the greeting of Mrs. Grey, the administrator, who looked up from her eternal textbooks to say:
"You are one of ours. It is good to have you back."

In the long Stalin years the Metropole was inhabited by a
curious clientele—four or five correspondents like myself,
survivors of a riotous band of wartime days; a few tobacco,
cotton, or fur buyers who slipped in and out like shadows; a
handful of minor diplomats occupied with bridge and whisky.

There were endless delegations—Rumanian peasants; German Communists; English trade unionists, chattering like spar-

rows; Uzbek women, clad in rainbow silk and diffidence. The atmosphere of the hotel in those days was somber and often mysterious.

Today as I stepped into the lobby two American youngsters, wearing blue jeans and T-shirts, scampered past me. They raced ahead, skirting mountains of luggage and darting among the tourists, most of whom seemed to be speaking English. On the sidewalk in front of the hotel I smiled at the militiaman, an old friend of mine, and almost immediately was surrounded by youngsters clamoring for *moneta* and chewing gum.

At the curb eight or ten new cars were drawn up and around them had gathered a considerable crowd. There were a sleek 1959 all-black Chevrolet Impala, a cream-and-green Ford station wagon, a gray Jaguar sports car, a red Renault, a tan Mercedes, and several Soviet cars. The Ford wagon attracted the biggest crowd. I noticed an elderly countryman wearing an old-fashioned Russian cap with patent-leather visor and high leather boots. He stopped and fixed his weathered eyes on a baby-blue sedan.

"Ah, those Americans," he said to a companion. "What automobiles they are making. Remarkable machines!"

"But, *dedya* [uncle]," his companion interjected. "Look at the insignia. This isn't an American machine. It's a Russian Volga."

"Humph," muttered the old countryman with a shake of his head. "Ours . . . theirs . . . it's all the same thing, more or less."

The same thing, more or less—it seemed to me there might be more profound truth in the countryman's remark than he realized. Not only in the sphere of chrome-decorated cars. In other things as well. The whole scene had a kind of unreality about it—the American cars, the throng of Russians, the bored, indifferent militiaman.

The night before, I had returned to the hotel at midnight.

The crowd of Russians was as big then as now. They were clustered around three Americans and a kind of sidewalk forum was in progress. Questions were going hot and heavy. What was American education like? How much does an American engineer earn? Do American women work? How much does an American apartment cost? What has become of Shirley Temple?

I stopped to listen.

"What about your unemployed?" I heard a youngster ask. "We hear that you have three million out of work."

"No," an American voice replied. "It's about five million."

The crowd was silent for a moment, startled at the unexpected frankness.

"How do the unemployed live?" a Russian finally asked.

"They get unemployment benefits . . . pay. It runs about twenty dollars a week," the American said.

"You mean a man gets paid two hundred rubles a week for not working?" a Russian said.

The American nodded. More bewilderment. Pay for not working. Who could believe that?

"But here," said a Russian loudly, "the workers own the means of production and its products."

Another Russian voice cut in: "Do you feel you own the products of your production?"

There were snickers. A Russian asked: "Why is your economy so fruitful?"

The American replied that it was because it was to the interest of the businessman to produce large quantities of good products at cheap prices and to pay good wages since this assured him of good production and of purchasing power to buy his products.

"I think," the American observed, "that your picture of American industry and American capitalism is very much out of date and behind the times."

"Yes, indeed," one of the Russians said in a voice of sudden comprehension. "That must be it. The picture we have is that of the old days, not of the present time."

A young man who said he was an electronics engineer from Riga asked me why Americans were so interested in Soviet education.

"Why is that?" he asked. "We think that our education has many faults."

I told him we wanted to take what was good from the Soviet system and use it in ours.

"What is the chief difference between the two systems?" he asked.

American students, I explained, have greater freedom of choice. They select subjects for themselves and study what they want.

"Yes," the young man agreed. "And here the professors tell us what to study. What is the advantage of your system?"

"We think it teaches the student to think independently and reason for himself."

"Of course," the young man said. "That is very good. Students must think for themselves."

The sidewalk forum was a change indeed. I remembered so well the old days. One morning on my way to the old Foreign Office, across the square from the Lubyanka prison, I had seen an old woman swathed in black shawl and sheepskin coat, lying on the narrow path that had been trampled down between the high snowdrifts. Apparently she had dropped dead. People on the street hurried on to work without more than a glance at the body. No one stopped. No one spoke. It was as if the body were not there.

I asked a Russian about the incident. "We don't like to get involved," he said. "If you stop in the street a militiaman will come along and ask you what you are doing there. It is better not to stop." There was some law, he said, against crowds in the street. Groups of more than three persons were prohibited.

I thought of this as I strolled on this pleasant Sunday around the Square. I noticed a pretty blonde girl, perhaps a University freshman. She was wearing red ski slacks and a form-fitting blue sweater. Five years ago she would have attracted indignant stares from women and rude wisecracks from men. Russian women did not wear slacks, trousers, or pants. Such garb was considered indecent. Today the only glances the girl drew were those which her figure attracted.

I looked at the people: a woman with a red balloon; three little girls with butterfly nets in red, yellow, and blue; peasants with string bags; city couples in their Sunday best; a breathless blonde girl clutching a small bunch of *landushi,* lilies of the valley (Landushi—that was the name of the song which was the rage of Moscow, a popular love song bereft of ideology). At the subway entrance gypsies were selling jonquils, crimson tulips, and white lilacs. An artist with a tan beret had set up his folding chair and easel and was placidly sketching the crowd. Five old women stood in a row, their arms filled with masses of *cheremushki,* the fragrant white blossoms of bird cherry.

There was a casualness about the crowd which was new to me. It reminded me of a sunnier climate, lighter temperament, something more Latin than Slav. Across the street there was a sidewalk queue, a crowd waiting for an airport bus to take them direct to planeside for the jet service to Leningrad. TO LENINGRAD—55 MINUTES, 105 RUBLES the sign said. It looked as though the wonderful old "Red Arrow"—the Moscow-Leningrad express, with its mahogany and brass wagons-lits, its diplomatic couriers, its faded atmosphere of international intrigue—was doomed as surely as were the "Twentieth Century" and the "Broadway Limited."

For many years I had taken a particular walk through Moscow at irregular intervals, always over the same streets, past the same buildings and, often, I suppose, through the same crowds. It had come to possess a certain meaning for me, a way of measuring change against change, of taking the city's pulse and temperature. Just before Stalin's death I had made this walk and had been struck by the terrible isolation in which I lived in this city of four or five million human beings. For hours I had strolled in the crisp February air. Not once had I spoken to another person and not once had anyone spoken to me. It was like passing through the city as a ghost, unseen, unheard, unnoticed. In those days Moscow walked with narrowed eyes. Moscow wanted no word with a stranger.

After Stalin's death I walked the route several times again. On one such walk I saw the first notice of a Wagner concert a few weeks after the dictator's demise. Wagner had been banned in Russia for twenty years. On another walk I had watched for the first time people strolling in Red Square, casually and unhindered by the police.

I decided today to walk my route again and match the new Moscow against the old Moscows I had known—wartime Moscow, cold-war Moscow, Moscow in Stalin's terror, and Moscow in the first glow of post-Stalin relaxation.

I turned up the narrow lane between the State Historical Museum and the Lenin Museum which leads into Red Square. Here once stood the most holy of the Moscow shrines, the Chapel of the Iberian Virgin with its wonder-working ikons. It had vanished in 1930, demolished so that tanks and military vehicles would have more free access to Red Square. In my time the spot had been marked with the famous text from Marx: "Religion is the Opium of the Masses." It was carved in red stone on the wall of the Lenin Museum. But this disappeared after Stalin's death. Now the lane was a shoppers' thoroughfare leading up to GUM, Russia's biggest department store, facing the Kremlin.

Beside the State Historical Museum I watched a bustling

man in a blue French smock set up a small table and folding chair. As he busied himself he called in a strong carrying voice: "Kremlin tickets! Get your Kremlin tickets here. Three rubles. Citizens, get your tickets for the Kremlin excursion."

Kremlin excursions! Stalin must be whirling clockwise in his tomb.

Beyond the Historical Museum militiamen were putting into place metal barriers to channel the great files of visitors which form up to pass through the Lenin-Stalin Mausoleum. Here was a flock of pigeons being fed by a covey of small girls, pigtailed, hair-ribboned, and wearing white Sunday dresses. Around the circle of girls was a circle of camera fans. Pigeons have become a Moscow passion since flocks of them were brought in for the Youth Festival in 1957. Now in many streets there are feeding stations, each with an old woman selling grain to be fed the birds; pigeon hotels, great communal birdhouses set up in parks on quiet side streets; and strict laws to protect the birds. Chauffeurs complain gloomily that the penalties for running over a stray pigeon are more harsh than for hitting a pedestrian. As I drifted on down the Square, a broad-faced Kazakh militia-man came up with a smile and said: "Citizens, you will have to feed the pigeons later. We have to clear the area for the Mausoleum queues." Suddenly I glanced up and felt for a moment that I had been transported into the nineteenth-century Russia of Tolstoy, Tchaikovsky, and the czars. Coursing into the Square came a glittering troika, harnessed to three dapple-gray horses with flowing white manes and dancing hoofs. The sun sparkled on the silver embossment and polished black harness. At the reins was a coachman garbed in plum livery in the old Russian style. Two well-dressed men sat in the troika. The equipage whirled through the center of the Square, paying heed neither to the automobile traffic nor to the curious stares. It raced past the Mausoleum and Spassky tower and slowed for a moment before St. Basil's mad and beautiful

turrets. Then it turned sharply and, horses prancing higher than
ever, flew back the way it had come, disappearing at the far
end of Red Square.

Whence came the troika? Who were the men who sat so
stiffly? Who was the proud coachman with his plum uniform
and his silver whip? I do not know. No one in the Square knew.
For a moment there was a curious silence among us all. We
held our breaths in wonder. Then a clatter began as each exclaimed to his neighbor. I walked on, thinking of Gogol's
prophetic lines: "Russia . . . flying onwards like a spirited troika
that nothing can overtake. . . . The spectator stands still, struck
dumb by the divine miracle. . . . What mysterious force is
hidden in this troika, never seen before? Russia, whither flyest
thou? Answer! She gives no answer. . . ."

Whither was Russia bound? Whither, indeed. I had given
half my adult life to the question. The fate of our age and, no
doubt, of future ages depended on the answer. It was the central
question of our times. And this was what once more had led
me back to seek an answer. On this beautiful spring day I was
searching anew for signs and portents.

Beside the Spassky gate I hesitated, half-tempted to break the
ritual of my walk and join the stream of citizens going inside
the Kremlin. The first time I had passed through the gate my
propusk had been checked by seven security guards. Today I
paused at the gate to see if it was really true that anyone
could freely pass through the ancient wall and stroll the fairy-
tale streets where Russia's history is graven in stone and
preserved in mortar and brick. The young army lieutenant and
his wife ahead of me paused and asked an attendant with a red
arm band. "May one just walk in freely?" the officer asked
with deference. "Of course," the guard replied in a tired voice.

So it was true that the Kremlin was a tourist attraction and
not a citadel of secret terror. I continued my stroll around the

faded pink walls which no longer seemed so grim and frightening. On the grassy banks beside the Tainiye (Secret) Tower I found small boys rolling downhill and girls gathering yellow dandelions and plaiting them into coronets for their hair. Lovers dawdled, and a mother and her child were sunbathing in the warm air.

I followed the Moskva River embankment to the great Borovitzky gate, oldest of them all, and turned up Kalinin Street. Here was a little secondhand bookstore where after Stalin's death I first saw the works of Ivan Bunin displayed. Today I hardly glanced at the shop because my attention was caught by an outdoor book fair on the plaza of the Lenin Library across the street. It was thronged with people, poring over books, few of which could have been published five years earlier. I saw Sherwood Anderson's stories, Sinclair Lewis' *Babbitt*, William Saroyan's *The Adventures of Wesley Jackson*, Charles de Gaulle's war memoirs, the works of Anatole France, Graham Greene's *The Quiet American* and *Our Man in Havana*, Hans Christian Andersen's *Fairy Stories*, a collection of Sholem Aleichem, translated from the Yiddish, a volume of Gerhart Hauptmann, Lope de Vega's dramas, and Jules Verne's *Mysterious Island*. There were books by Romain Rolland, Stendhal, Victor Hugo, Dickens, Mark Twain and Karel Capek. Some I did not recognize—Charles Roberts' Indian stories and *John K. Youngblood* with an introduction by Paul Robeson. One was straight out of the pages of *American Boy* magazine in the days of my youth—James Willard Schultz's *The Mistake of the Lone Bison*.

One of the books which was selling like hot cakes was called *Unseen Light*. It was a science-fiction thriller in a Broadway setting. As I walked up Kalinin Street I saw ads on the billboards for Arthur Miller's *A View from the Bridge*, for an Austrian industrial exhibition, for the American ice show *Holi-*

day on Ice, for the Paris Symphony and for the Moscow State Symphony playing a program made up exclusively of non-Russian works.

The pent-up demand of the long Stalin years for anything foreign was bursting all bounds. The pendulum was swinging hard to the other extreme.

Often as I walked along the street I halted to snap a picture or jot down a note. It was obvious to all that I was a foreign journalist. But no longer was this a barrier to conversation. Instead, it was an invitation. My walk became a progress from one chat to another. First, talk about American books and authors. Then, surprise that an American would be carrying a Japanese camera. Inquiries from peasants for directions around the city. Approaches by young boys who wanted to practice their English. Another youngster who wanted to talk German. A boy at the book fair who shyly wondered if I had any American books I could spare. No longer was Moscow a silent city. It was getting to be a chatterbox.

The route I followed up Kalinin Street had been famous in Stalin's time. This was the way he traveled, coming and going from the Kremlin to his *dacha* on the Mozhaisk chausee outside the city. Often I had seen his cavalcade sweep down narrow Arbat Street, roar through Arbat Square with singing tires and on down Kalinin Street to the Kremlin. A special system of traffic lights flashed all red several minutes before Stalin's limousine appeared. Special details of traffic militia stood duty night and day to divert all traffic aside for Stalin's car. Plain-clothes men were so thick on Arbat Street they sometimes pushed the shoppers off the sidewalk. No one was permitted to live in an apartment along this route without a double security check.

Now, as I walked up Kalinin Street, I saw only one or two traffic officers. It was a peaceful, normal scene. The same thing had been true several mornings previously when some col-

leagues and I were jaywalking across the street just before
9 A.M. We were going to call on Georgi A. Zhukov, chairman
of the State Committee on Cultural Relations, whose offices
are in a rambling old mansion at the head of Kalinin Street.

As we got to the middle of the street we were held up mo-
mentarily by a big limousine. I knew by the amber fog lights
that it was a government car. Glancing up, I was startled to see
Nikita Khrushchev sitting next to the chauffeur on the front
seat. He was driving to work and obviously had timed his arrival for 9 A.M. (Stalin's day began at 3 P.M. and often ran until
3 A.M. or 4 A.M.) Khrushchev's car moved at normal speed and
had no cavalcade. It was followed by a single brown Pobeda
with three or four security men. Stalin always was preceded by
two specially built security cars and followed by one or two
more.

This, it seemed to me, was typical of the style of post-Stalin
Russia. Relaxation, a de-emphasis of the police and security.
There was much more to the picture than could be crowded
into a single stroll in the city. And yet I felt the walk had
served to fix and clarify for me some of the main tendencies in
Khrushchev's Russia.

Just as the Moscow streets in Stalin's day unfailingly bared
the harsh outlines of its rigidness, its xenophobia, its sterility,
and its terror, so now the streets reflected an inner ease and
security which Stalin's Russia never possessed.

No doubt Russia was not merely a gay stroller, a troika out
to see the Sunday sights, a patron of the new, the bright, and
the foreign. Beside the posters of the American shows and the
French music, there were advertisements for lectures on
Marxism, courses in nuclear physics, and an announcement of
the meeting of the local society of atheists. I had seen no police
agents and none, I believed, had followed me. But at least one
of the young men who stopped to talk to me slipped away
quickly with a remark that "It's dangerous." The people looked

well dressed in their Sunday clothes and there were foreign foods in the shop windows—Bulgarian peas and tomatoes, Chinese canned fruit, Hungarian sausages. But I would never mistake Kalinin Street for Main Street in any American town.

Not everything has changed in Moscow, I said to myself as I rode down the escalator of the Smolensk Metro station to take the subway back to the hotel. The Arbat does not rival Fifth Avenue and the old apartments in the *pereuliki* or side streets look five years more dingy than when I last saw them.

No, not everything had changed. But much had. Very much. And the changes were in the right direction, changes toward a better life for the Russians, less tension, less strain, less force. They were changes which we as Americans could only welcome. But where would these changes take Russia and what were the motives of the new leadership in carrying them out? These, I thought, are the questions to which I must apply myself by probing as deeply as possible into sensitive and critical areas of Russian life and thought.

II

The Decline of a Police State

ONE MORNING after I had been back in Moscow a
couple of weeks the telephone rang. A voice said in Russian:
"Is this Gospodin Salisbury?" I said yes. The Russian chuckled.
"Good," he said. "I was sure it was you. This is your old friend
Sergei Petrovich."

Sergei Petrovich is not his real name. Not that there seems
now to be any good reason to give him a pseudonym. But in
such things habit tells me it is better to err on the side of caution. He was an old friend of mine from the days of World War
II, one of my oldest friends in Russia. I had not seen him in
fifteen years, and I was pleased and startled that he should
know I was back in Moscow.

"I saw you on Gorky Street the other day," he said. "At
least I thought it was you. So I decided to call the Metropole
and make sure."

I met Sergei several times. We lunched and talked just as
we might have in any other capital of the world: London, Paris,
or Rome. And this was what was so unusual: the normality of
our meetings. I had hoped that I might find it possible to see old
friends in Moscow, to establish once again some ordinary human
contacts with Russian people. But I had not been at all certain.
I remembered only too well what had happened when I came
back to Moscow in 1949. I had a number of Russian friends
during the 1944 days. We joked about the police then, but we

17

did not let it keep us from going to each other's homes, from joining in parties and get-togethers. A good many Soviet-American romances flourished at that time.

When I returned in 1949 I tried to meet some of the Russians I had known best. I telephoned but they did not answer. I left messages. I sent a note or two. Nothing happened. Sooner or later I saw one or two on the streets. They turned their eyes away from me and walked more rapidly.

I soon understood the trouble. Those were horror-haunted days, even worse than I realized then. Nothing was more dangerous for a Russian than contact with a foreigner. In the dwindling little "international colony," the small group of foreign correspondents and the Russians who worked for them as translators, secretaries, couriers, cooks, maids, or chauffeurs, hardly a week went by without a disappearance.

What happened we seldom knew. Only a detail or two. The person had been called to the offices of the Interior Ministry. A policeman had rapped on the door in the early morning hours. The victim was taken away. That was all. Inquiries were fruitless. It was generally believed that questions only harmed the victim by earning him a harsher sentence in the labor camps.

This was the kind of thing that was commonplace in 1949. There was the case of the Russian girl, married to an English RAF man who had returned to England. As a kind of protection to her the British Embassy gave her a clerical job. One night her brother telephoned, very upset, and wanted her to meet him. She kept the rendezvous on the steps of the Bolshoi Theater immediately after the evening performance of "Swan Lake." Two Embassy men went with her, for they were suspicious of a trap. A few minutes after 11 P.M. a car pulled up and the girl's brother stepped out. A moment later two strong-arm men materialized out of the shadows. Before the diplomats could move, the girl was lifted into the car and whisked away. There was nothing to do but lodge another futile protest with the Foreign Office.

Small wonder that my Russian friends in 1949 had nothing to do with me. They would have been insane to act otherwise. And I had observed that after Stalin died Moscow residents did not let their guard down with foreigners. The government made many gestures. It declared an amnesty and released thousands of prisoners from the labor camps. Beria and his principal henchmen were arrested and executed. The dreadful "troikas," the three-man administrative courts of the MVD, were abolished. The troikas had sentenced men and women to death or life imprisonment without trial. Even before I left Moscow in 1954 the first of the "rehabilitations," the restoration of the good name of Stalin's victims, had begun. There were rumors of more to come.

But the Soviet attitude was still "wait and see." Too many times there had been relaxations under Stalin, only to be followed by new and more horrible violence. The people in Moscow in the first years after Stalin's death behaved a little woodenly, a little as Russia had reacted to the great reforms of Alexander II, the freeing of the serfs, and the end of the censorship after the long years of tyranny under Nicholas I. Like the Muscovites, I, too, had been skeptical. As late as 1954 I had been in eastern Siberia. I had seen the enormous regions where the police were supreme, where the land was MVD-run, where the labor was state prisoners condemned to what was called in the obscene euphemism of the Stalin days "corrective labor."

There in the east, no one had heard that the police regime had come to an end. There in the east, terror was still the force which ruled the country. I saw the great concentration camps with their barbed-wire barricades, their watchtowers, their tommy-gun guards in almost every east Siberian and sub-Arctic city which I visited. There was no attempt at concealment. The institutions were too big for that. And I saw the hideous results

of the brutal system on the victims—the seventeen-year-old
boys, drunk and unconscious on the wooden sidewalks, the in-
describable boredom and despondency, what the Russians call
skuchnost and *poshlust,* which settled over the countryside
like a miasma. Drink was the only escape they had from a
reality which no courage was great enough to face.

Small wonder that Muscovites were slow to accept the validity
of government declarations that terror had ended. The police
state, as they could see, still existed despite the pleasant pro-
testations of the new rulers.

But when I returned to Moscow in 1959 I found this changed.
Moscow and its citizens now regarded the end of the terror as
real. They believed this because they had seen with their own
eyes the cutting back of the police power. They had watched
their surviving friends and relatives come back from the camps.
They had tested the abolition of the special police powers in
the courts and they had seen the terrible camps closed down.
Everyone knew of high police officers who had been arrested
for their crimes, and everyone knew of the famous ballerina
and her Enoch Arden dilemma. (She had been married to a
high MVD general. He was arrested. She thought he would
be shot or given life exile in Siberia. So she married a famous
army general. Now, to everyone's consternation, the MVD
general had been set free and returned to Moscow.)

These are the changes which explain why my friend did what
he never would have dreamed of doing in the old days—called
a foreigner, an American journalist, in that hotbed of police and
provocation, the Hotel Metropole, and talked with him freely
on an open telephone line.

Perhaps this does not sound very impressive either as an act
of political courage or as evidence of deep change in the Soviet
state. But it is only one of a thousand pieces which make up
the mosaic of the decline of the police state in Russia.

One day, for example, I chanced to encounter five different

persons who had at different times been victims of Stalin's
political police. Each now is free and occupying a position of
some consequence. One man for many years was a Soviet
diplomat. He was a man of prominence, ability, and prestige.
Suddenly he was recalled to Moscow. His friends saw him a
time or two. Then he vanished. Not until Stalin had been dead
more than two years did he reappear on the scene, somewhat
more quiet, somewhat more serious than before. Today he is
no longer a diplomat but he occupies an important state post.
Few of the persons with whom he comes in contact know that
he spent four or five years in a Siberian labor camp.

Another man is an important Moscow editor. During World
War II he had been a correspondent for *Izvestia*. Later he went
into one of the Moscow ministries. About twelve years ago
he disappeared without trace. He was an old friend of mine.
When I was in Moscow previously I had tried to learn what
had become of him. No one knew. Or was willing to say. Three
years after Stalin's death this man bobbed to the surface. Today
he looks much older; his hair is thin and gray; he has put on
weight. At first glance you might take him for a comfortable
bureaucrat who had gradually broadened at the beam with the
passing of the easy years. Only if you knew his history would
you understand your mistake.

A third man now works as a translator for a Moscow publishing house. Many of his associates know that he spent a year
in the hands of the police because he is one of half a dozen
former police victims who work for this organization.

The other two men whom I met that day are much more
prominent. I ran into them at a Kremlin reception. One is
Pyotr L. Kapitza, the nuclear physicist who spent several years
under house arrest in his villa at Zvenigorod, just outside Moscow. He, like several of his fellow physicists, refused to work
on the hydrogen weapon. Some of the others were sent to
Siberia. Kapitza was merely deprived of his laboratory, cut off

from contact with his fellow workers and confined to his home. The other man is Andrei N. Tupelov, the famous aircraft designer who produced both the TU-104 and the TU-114. Tupelov was jailed during the 1930's. I never have understood what the charges were. Probably no one knows what was in the minds of the secret police at that time. But Tupelov for several years was confined to a laboratory which the secret police established out in Siberia. There he worked at his designs and, indeed, turned out plans for several aircraft which were put into production. Today, Mr. Tupelov is not only an honored figure in the Soviet Union. He is one of the closest of Mr. Khrushchev's personal associates.

There are so many released political prisoners now scattered through the Soviet Union that it is quite impossible to keep any count of them or what they now do. I met many of these men whose histories I happened to know. I probably met many more whom I had no way of recognizing. No medals and no badges of merit are worn for service in Siberia.

But everyone knows someone who has come back. And often it is a relative who has long been absent.

"All I know is that several friends of mine have come back and two who came back are working in my office," a middle-aged woman told me. She thought her experience was fairly typical.

It is not only individuals who have returned. Stalin deported whole populations to Siberia. Now many of these peoples have been permitted to return to their former homes. This is especially true in the Baltic states. Tens of thousands of Estonians, Latvians, and Lithuanians were shipped to Siberia by Stalin— some before and some after the war. The survivors of these purges have now been permitted to go back to their homes. So have thousands of Ukrainians and minor nationalities which were almost wiped out, like the Kalmuks. Volga Germans who were deported to Tadjikstan and Siberia from the Volga and

Ukrainian regions, because of fear that they might be disloyal during World War II, have begun to return to their homes. And the tiny tribes in the Caucasus which Stalin wiped off his maps in anger, eradicating the names of their towns and principalities and shipping the people to the far north and far east, have returned to their mountains.

No one has attempted to total up the number of persons restored to decent living in the years since Stalin's death. No lists have been published. No announcements have been made. However, a special effort has been made to place Stalin's victims in positions at least as good as the ones they would have held had their careers not been cut short by arrest and exile.

The presence of so many former prison-camp inmates in important posts seemed to me to give an inner toughness to the fabric of Soviet society that it did not formerly have. These men are not easily frightened. They have few illusions about the nature of the Soviet state. They often work with an idealism which has nothing to do with the worn bureaucratic traditions of the contemporary government and party apparatus. They form a real barrier to the rise of a new police power.

It may be that Georgi A. Zhukov, chairman of the Soviet State Committee on Cultural Relations, was exaggerating when he said that there is no longer a single political prisoner in the Soviet Union. But he was not exaggerating much.

There is no doubt whatever, for instance, that the great Vorkuta labor camps in northern European Russia which were the scene of strikes in the summer of 1953 are now closed. The coal is being mined by ordinary civilian labor. Several hundred Vorkuta camp guards have been given jobs driving taxicabs in Moscow. They are not a prepossessing lot. They do not know the city well. They are likely to overcharge and cheat. Moscow citizens are not very pleased with this addition to their labor force.

When former Governor Averell Harriman visited Karaganda

last summer he found that a big workers' housing project was being erected on the site of one of the old concentration camps. Karaganda for years was synonymous with secret police. A great coal and metallurgical complex in eastern Kazakhstan, it was one of the worst of the Interior Ministry institutions. Now it is being run on a civilian basis.

Fifteen years ago, when I first visited Novosibirsk, the metropolis of western Siberia, there was near the center of the town a great area of prison barracks surrounded by barbed wire and closely guarded. Last summer I found that this horrible sight had vanished. I saw no evidence in any of the Siberian regions which I visited that labor camps were still in operation. Even the Kolyma gold fields, in the remote Maritime provinces off the Sea of Okhotsk, are said no longer to be run by prison labor. And the Russians invited an American inspection team to Kamchatka to satisfy itself that prison labor was not being used in the crab-meat industry.

Mr. Khrushchev boasts that he has reduced the number of policemen, both secret and ordinary, by a very large number. Just how large he does not specify. Such figures cannot be obtained by casual observation. I saw as many traffic police on the Moscow streets as before. There seemed to be even more speed cops on the Soviet highways. The number of highway police per vehicle in the Moscow area must be the highest in the world. However, the special military units of the Interior Ministry have been cut back substantially. In Beria's day the Interior Ministry had its own infantry, artillery, tank corps, and air force. Now most of these units have been incorporated into the regular army. The border patrol force has been put under separate command. MVD troops, with their characteristic red and blue caps, no longer march in the great Red Square parades.

A determined attempt is being made to transform the police from an object of public contempt to one of public respect. Great use is made of the image of Felix Dzerzhinsky, "Iron

Felix," the fanatically devout Polish Communist who under
Lenin's direction founded the first of the Soviet police agencies,
the Cheka. Dzerzhinsky was an avenging agent against all the
early enemies of the Communists whether they came from the
right or the left. But no one ever accused him of corruption
or use of the police power for any end other than the service of
the Revolution in its desperate years of trial.

For years Dzerzhinsky's name was seldom mentioned. Now
it has been brought forward as a symbol to glorify the purged
police. His statue has been erected in the center of the square
outside the Lubyanka prison which has long borne his name.
Someone, no doubt an employee of the MVD, places fresh
flowers at the base of the monument each day. Biographies of
Dzerzhinsky and collections of his writings have been issued.
And at the sprawling camps of the MVD troops, several of
which still exist on highways just outside Moscow, I saw
portraits of "Iron Felix" erected over the blue-painted wooden
camp gates as a kind of ikon.

The direction of the police has, of course, been placed in
new hands. There has been a good deal of tinkering with the
police setup. In the initial period after Stalin's death the "collective leaders" were determined that no one would use the
police to establish himself in personal power, and this was the
basic crime charged against Beria.

The police function was split. The ordinary domestic police,
the firefighting forces, the traffic officers, all the housekeeping
police, were placed in the hands of a veteran police officer,
General Sergei Kruglov. The secret police, espionage and
counterespionage, were put under a committee attached directly to the Council of Ministers and headed by General Ivan
Serov. In 1960 the national MVD—ordinary police administration—was abolished and its functions turned over to the individual Soviet republics.

However, once Khrushchev consolidated his personal power
he put in his own personal nominees to handle the two arms

of the police. For the regular police he picked a man named
Dudorov, who had had no police experience. He was a building
specialist, an administrator. Apparently his chief qualification
was his lack of previous ties to the police. Later on Khrushchev
removed General Serov from the State Security Committee
(the KGB) and put in his place Alexander N. Shelepin, who
had been the head of the Communist Youth organization. Here,
too, Mr. Khrushchev was seeking a new symbol as well as a
new executive director. Shelepin is one of the young turks, a
group of young Communist Party officials who have advanced
rapidly under Khrushchev's tutorship. He is only forty-one
years old.

Shelepin has made a strong effort to restore the reputation
of the security forces. He has sought to rebuild the police on
a somewhat different basis and, particularly, to establish close
connections between the police and the Young Communist
League, which still is a reservoir of young and enthusiastic
cadres.

It was feared by some Russians that once Khrushchev had
consolidated his power he might, like Stalin, seek to rely on
the police to run the country. This has not happened. Khrushchev has been careful to maintain a close balance of security
forces. He seems consistently to reject the use of the police
power as a major implement of government. None of his political
opponents have been executed or formally exiled, although
the obscure posts to which they have been relegated may seem
like exile to the victims. His reluctance to utilize force suggested
to me that he personally may have suffered more seriously at
the hands of the police power during the Stalin epoch than has
been revealed.

The Soviet army continues to watch carefully against any
new rise of police influence to a point at which it might again
intervene in army affairs. This concern was very apparent before

the downfall of Marshal Georgi K. Zhukov. But it seems to be shared by his successors.

Serov, I was interested to note, has not passed out of the picture as many have supposed. Although his name is seldom mentioned he is usually present at all important state occasions. He is a Deputy Chief of Staff of the Army, serving under Marshal Sokolovsky. There are those who say that Serov's background was primarily an army background rather than a police background. They equate his removal from the State Security Committee with a reduction in army control over State Security functions. A more likely hypothesis is that Serov is a security man who spent most of his career in army security and has gone back to this function.

Yet it should not be supposed that fear and terror has completely vanished from Russia. Or that the police no longer interfere in the affairs of the ordinary Russian citizen.

The police still keep a vigilant eye on foreigners and particularly on their contacts with Russians. From time to time they interfere in a brutal and arbitrary fashion.

A tourist I knew in Moscow met a Moscow University student on the street. The boy wanted to practice his English and attached himself to my friend. They spent a pleasant day together and, late in the evening, went to the Leningradskaya Hotel for a farewell drink in my friend's room. Hardly had they gotten there when there was a rap at the door. A policeman asked the student to come with him. The next day the boy turned up briefly. He said he had been taken to a station house, questioned for an hour, and let go with a warning not to see the American again.

An American couple with whom I was acquainted went on an excursion not far from Moscow with a Russian friend they had met in an art gallery. He, too, was intercepted by the police and warned he would be "in serious trouble" if he did not leave the foreigners immediately. Another American made the acquaintance of a young Russian writer who invited him to his cottage outside Moscow. The American spent a pleasant afternoon at his friend's cottage and arranged to come again. The following Sunday the American went to the suburban railroad station, bought a ticket, and boarded the train. Before the train could leave, two plain-clothes men appeared, ordered him off the car, and told him the suburb was off-limits for foreigners. He never saw the writer again.

This kind of activity reached something of a peak in the autumn of 1959, after the U.S. Exposition had closed and the great summer rush of tourists had slowed to a trickle. There had been the same kind of "clean-up" activity by the secret police after the Youth Festival in Moscow during the summer of 1957. Apparently, the police feel it necessary to show their teeth after a period in which—because of the large number of foreigners in Moscow or because of some foreign policy consideration—they have relaxed their vigilance somewhat.

The curse of the foreigner's life in Russia used to be the plain-clothes men. They usually were not much bother in Moscow except to the military attachés. But when I went on a trip outside Moscow I never knew what kind of surveillance I would encounter. Sometimes, to my surprise, I would visit a provincial town and never see a single undercover agent. Other times, as in eastern Siberia, they swarmed over the landscape. I have even found them hiding behind bushes in a park.

This year, however, I encountered no surveillance in Siberia. I wandered around towns by the hour, snapping pictures (always likely to arouse a security agent's suspicions), and could not have been more free from scrutiny. When my colleague Max Frankel was in Siberia a few months earlier he reported the same thing—complete absence of observation as far as he noticed.

Nor was I aware of being watched in Moscow. Indeed, only

once did I catch a glimpse of one of the old sleuths who used to hang out at the Metropole Hotel. This was a young man who always looked as though he had just gotten out of bed. Perhaps this was his professional disguise. His eyes were sleepy and his hair was hopelessly tousled. He had followed me a time or two in the old days and I had caught him at it. After that he always looked embarrassed when I chanced to see him huddled in the service doorway of the Metropole, waiting to pick up the trail of another victim. One day last summer I was standing outside the Metropole and saw him again, sleepy as ever, peering out from his old lair. He did not notice me and I turned away. The next time I looked he had vanished, no doubt hot on a trail.

But I did have the experience of being shadowed on several occasions. Most of these occurred in Leningrad. A number of men with the unmistakable appearance of shadows hung around the Astoria Hotel. I knew from the military attachés that Leningrad security was extremely sensitive about the water front, probably because the great atomic icebreaker *Lenin* was then in the last stages of construction at one of the Neva shipyards. Perhaps there also were other things which they did not want the attachés to see while out strolling along the Lieutenant Schmidt embankment.

So it was not entirely a surprise to discover myself being picked up by a rather careless young sleuth in the Hermitage art gallery and then to notice that shadows stayed on my track as long as I walked along the Neva embankment. But it was unusual to discover sleuths making their reappearance when I wandered around many other parts of the town, along the wonderful canals and the monuments of the glorious Petersburg past.

In Moscow the more sophisticated residents are aware that foreigners are still under the watchful eye of the security services. They know that if they have something to do with foreigners they run the risk of being called in for interrogation.

Yet some Russians are completely blasé to this possibility.
Several Russians who work for a ministry which deals with
foreigners had a gay party with a friend of mine in a Moscow
restaurant. The restaurant closed at 1 A.M. and they proposed
to adjourn to his apartment for a nightcap.

The American warned them that he lived in a foreigners'
apartment and that there was a policeman at the door.

"We know," the Russians said. "So he'll report us and they'll
call us in and lecture us. But what can they do? Just talk. Come
on. Let's go."

This is the essential internal change which I found in Soviet
society. Five years ago no Russian would have thought of
making such a proposal unless he was completely naïve or
acting as an *agent provocateur*. Today they know they cannot
get into serious trouble for such conduct.

The name of Leon Trotsky used to make Russians blanch.
Sometimes, when I felt extremely angry with a Russian, perhaps
a guide showing me a provincial museum, I would deliberately
introduce Trotsky's name just to see my victim squirm. Trotsky's
name is still not often mentioned. But one day when I was in
casual conversation with a young man in a provincial town he
mentioned Trotsky in a discussion about books. Another young
man made a joke about his physical resemblance to Trotsky.
A third said, "We have begun to talk about Trotsky a little but
we still don't write about him." Another said he thought that
books would be written and published about Trotsky "in another five years or so."

While Russians may still display fear in contacts with foreigners, they are much more at ease with one another than they
were. They know that the day of the poison-pen letter writer,
the day of the informer, the day of the secret indictment has
come to an end. Few Westerners can appreciate what this
means, for they have not lived in a society where for years a
single anonymous denunciation could tear a respectable, hard-

working man away from his family and job and condemn him to spend the rest of his life in a bleak mine beyond the Arctic Circle.

I got a curious whiff of the macabre world which Russia used to be. One evening a knock came at the door of my Metropole Hotel room. I was out but my son, Michael, answered the door. It was a middle-aged man of nondescript appearance with a bulky package done up in brown paper. He handed it over, saying, or so Michael thought, that it was for me. I came in a little later and examined the mysterious packet. It was a monument to Stalin's Russia, the Russia of the poison-pen letter, the secret police, the interrogation, the destruction of human character under the grinding wheels of these evil forces.

How it came into my hands I cannot guess. Whether it was intended for me or someone else there is no way of ascertaining. It was a collection of *papki*, cardboard Russian files, in which were gathered hundreds of letters, affidavits, receipts, forwarding notices, ministerial acknowledgments, legal papers—heaven knows what wasn't in that file.

From this documentation could be pieced together the story of a man who, as far as I could figure out, had been a young high-school teacher out in Bashkiria on the Volga before World War II. Apparently he was pursuing his simple life quietly and obscurely when, about 1938, someone (whose identity he did not still know after twenty years) submitted an accusation of wrongdoing on his part. An interminable interrogation followed. It wound up with the man being convicted and sent to a Siberian work camp. During the war he volunteered for the front and was permitted to go. He served, obscurely but well. At the end of the war he returned to his old town on the Volga and took up his life again. But now the old charges came back to dog him. New accusations were made. He fought his way clear of them; but slowly, as I could see from the petitions and letters, his own balance was affected. Soon it was he who

was writing the accusations to one official after another. If he
did not get action from one official, he wrote a denunciation
of the first man to the second, with copies to the Party Secretary,
copies to the MVD, the MGB and anyone else who came to
mind.

The whole monstrous process was spelled out in interminable
detail—the young schoolmaster, the false charge, the ruined
career, the rehabilitation, the new charges, the growing in-
sanity. Finally, the victim was the center of a web of accusations spinning out in all directions and tangling up echelon
after echelon of officials. It was all there. The naked bones of
his horrible story reflected the case history of Russia under
Stalin. I turned the yellow pages with increasing sickness and
disgust. This is what Stalin's state had reduced men to.

And now what had happened since Stalin's death? The
Bashkir schoolmaster could no longer get satisfaction. No
longer did men cower and whimper at his charges. His letters
went forth in a widening circle. But not always did the ministers,
the party secretaries, the police bother to reply. He was now
classified as his own original accuser should have been long
years ago—as a crank, a crackpot, a nut.

Perhaps, I thought, the fact that the great file had been delivered to me was evidence of the twisted mind's despair of
any longer extorting attention from Soviet officials. Casting
about for some new outlet the man may have heard of me, a
foreign correspondent, and deposited his precious file, accumulated page by page over the years, in my possession hoping that
I would at last right the wrongs and bring his enemies to
justice.

This might indeed be the case. But it was time, I thought,
to bring at least this illness to an end. I did not bother to see
if my Bashkir friend would show up to retrieve his precious
papki. I quietly deposited it in the wastebasket—and hoped
that some devout chambermaid in the service of the MVD

would not salvage it and start the process all over again.

A man who has lived long in Russia, and whose judgment on Russia's internal affairs is more valid than that of most foreigners, told me that in his opinion the most important change in Russia since Stalin is not the change in the attitude of Russians to foreigners.

"This has occurred, of course," he said. "Russians are much more willing to have dealings with foreigners than they were. You have seen this yourself. But this is not so important as another change: Russians have stopped being afraid of each other, and this is the big thing."

My friend, I believed, was right. Certainly there were still Russians whose conditioning through the long years of fear had not worn off. But, generally, they were beginning to treat each other like normal human beings. And, in the process, acting more and more like human beings themselves. This was the new tone of Khrushchevian Russia. Clearly, the police state had not entirely vanished; but it had been decidedly weakened. And if the weakness was to prove permanent, the implications were far-reaching indeed. If Russia no longer was to be ruled by the knout, or the fear of the knout, the whole system must undergo radical change. New motivations, new incentives must be provided. Force and decree would no longer suffice. A Pandora's box of problems would be opened, most of them new both to the rulers and the ruled. It well could be that Russia stood at the threshold of a new and exciting phase of history.

III

Sometimes You Can't Tell a Russian from an American

OFTEN LATE AT NIGHT during the Stalin years I would walk the streets of Moscow. Night after night at the Central Telegraph Office I would write my dispatches after *Pravda* came out, perhaps at 2 A.M. or 3 A.M., then put the story through censorship and dictate it to London. Finally, I would make my way back to the Metropole Hotel through the dark and narrow Moscow pereuliki. No one but myself was abroad at the hour except, of course, the eternal militiamen at the principal intersections and here and there a white-aproned *dvornik*, or concierge, sweeping the pavement with a long-handled witch's broom. But, of course, I was not the only one awake in Moscow at that hour. I would see a light in a window and, peering through the flimsy curtain and over the barricade of geranium plants, I would see a gray-haired old grandmother standing at a kitchen stove, cooking kasha or boiling borscht. I would see the old *babushka* standing there, her face drawn in weariness and her limbs trembling with exhaustion, cooking at 3, 3:30, or even 4 A.M.

I understood only too well what lay behind this curious, sad spectacle. In the isolation of those days I did not get to know many Moscow apartments. But I did know a few. And I knew how the people lived and why the grandmother was cooking tomorrow's meals at three in the morning.

34

I knew, for example, one flat which I think was fairly typical of that time. The building had been fashionable in 1906. That was the year when a well-to-do family (with whose survivors I was acquainted) first moved there. Not a rich family, not nobility, just comfortably well off. A man and his wife, their boy and girl, a couple of servants. It was an eight-room apartment on a street not far from the Arbat. The building was decorated in glossy white and green tile with a frieze of Russian *bogatiri*, or legendary knights, over the entrance. The man and his wife were liberals, strong sympathizers with the Revolution. He was an engineer, she an artist. They threw themselves into the revolutionary cause with enthusiasm. In those days of 1917-18 the apartment was much too big. They could not care for it. Two sisters of the husband and an old aunt came to live with them. Only one servant stayed—a hard-working, loyal countrywoman.

Gradually over the years the space which the family occupied in the apartment contracted. By the time I knew them the husband was long since dead. His wife, now elderly, lived with her daughter and two grandchildren in one room. The son and son-in-law were both dead—one, I believe, in a concentration camp; the other in the war. The two aunts occupied a second room with the old servant. All were feeble. One sister was mildly demented; the other was blind. The rest of the apartment for many, many years had been occupied by separate families. One room belonged to a woman doctor, her husband, and two small children. Another was occupied by a woman given to drink and a succession of lovers. She had her twelve-year-old son with her. A middle-aged factory worker and his wife occupied another room. He liked to drink on Saturday night and usually brought three or four friends home to share the vodka. I don't remember who occupied the other rooms. I know there was at least one other elderly woman whose mind was not quite right. In all, close to twenty-five persons lived in this flat—not counting transients.

The life of these people was sheer horror. Long since, each had gotten on the other's nerves to the point of hysteria. Winter was the worst season. Their being cooped up night after night led to incredible disputes over the rota system for sweeping the corridor, over whose turn it was to use the kitchen, over who was responsible for the filthy toilet. Nothing in the apartment or in the building had been repaired for years. Most of the apartments were papered with old *Pravdas,* glued to the walls by the occupants to replace the broken plaster. The war with rats and cockroaches was endless.

This is how most people in Moscow lived up to the most recent times. Certainly, there were families who had better or larger living quarters. But for forty years or more most of them lived in squalid communal flats.

It was this scene that came to me when I drove in from the Moscow airport through the endless blocks of new housing which have turned the flat wastelands of the Uzhny Zapodny region into a different country. In these square miles of new apartment buildings, 200,000 or 300,000 Muscovites have found a place to live in the past two years. And in two other great new Moscow housing regions an equal number have received flats.

When I inspected these new buildings closely I readily saw that what the foreigners had told me about the shoddiness of construction was not exaggerated. Nowhere else in the world, I am certain, will you find new buildings faced with pleasant tan-colored ornamental tile—with great safety nets jutting out at the second story to catch the falling tiles so they will not beat out the brains of passers-by.

I laughed when I heard the diplomats' children chanting on the way to school: "Yaroslavsky is falling down, falling down." Indeed, the brand-new building where the youngsters lived out on Yaroslavsky chausee, now called Prospekt Mira (Peace

Street), *is* falling down. It cracked right down the middle last summer. The embarrassed housing bureau of the Foreign Office had to order the diplomats out posthaste before the whole structure collapsed, scattering hi-fi sets, freezer cabinets, bathroom fixtures, washing machines, driers, electric blankets, electric egg beaters, and electric can openers, so painfully imported over such vast distances at such vast expense by the foreign tenants, out onto the Moscow pavement.

People say that the mass of these new buildings will constitute the Moscow slums of 1965. They are right. Moscow's chief architect calls much of the construction inexcusably bad. He also says that the building program is just a drop in the bucket. Only if the program can be hugely expanded and continued ceaselessly for ten years, in his opinion, will Moscow break the back of its horrible housing problem—the accumulation of forty years of neglect, waste, and incompetence.

All this having been said, I cannot think of any Moscow resident being anything but pleased at the prospect of moving into one of these new apartment houses, no matter how many tiles tumble from the walls.

"My wife and I and our two children live in one room in a little wooden building on a courtyard," my friend Alexei told me. "My wife and I have lived there ever since we were married, before the war. I lived in that room with my parents before they died. I have lived in that room as far back as my memory goes. I cannot remember when anyone spent a kopek to repair the building or to paint a sliver of wood in it. Would I move into one of the Uzhny Zapodny apartments? You bet I would. Let it fall down. At least it would be something new in my life."

I found a curious little musical playing in Moscow. It was written by Dmitri Shostakovitch, and it was being performed by the Operetta Theater, an organization devoted to cheap middle-European concoctions. Why Shostakovitch chose to write for this theater I cannot understand. But he did. He took as his theme the new Cheremushki housing development. As operetta it was trash, as production it was a jumble, as entertainment a bore. But as a sociological document, *Cheremushki* fascinated me from beginning to end. Shostakovitch has made up a kind of fairy story about Cheremushki. Never have buildings been so beautiful. Never have colors been painted so bright. Never have neighbors been so happy (once the bad wolf of the corrupt manager has been put in his place). All this is not the real Cheremushki. But it faithfully represents what Cheremushki means to Moscow and its citizens. It is Moscow's daydream of what Cheremushki is.

When I heard Khrushchev tell Vice President Nixon, during their argument in the kitchen of the American model home at the U.S. Exposition in Moscow, that in Russia "we build for our grandchildren" whereas the United States builds-in obsolescence so as to have a new market for houses in twenty years, I could not help chuckling. I am sure this remark brought a laugh to many Muscovites. They have no illusions as to the permanence of the new housing. They would like it to last longer— certainly. But they are used to watching buildings turn old before their time. It is just as hard for a Muscovite as it is for a foreigner to walk down a street and tell at a glance whether a building is two years old or twenty. Both look pretty much the same.

But this did not keep the Muscovites from pulling every string they could to get into Cheremushki. Priority was being given to the people who occupied the worst housing. This had given rise to a new Moscow racket. Well-informed citizens were paying premium rents and a bribe to the superintendent to rent rat-infested basement flats, because people who lived in quarters like this were being given first choice at the new housing.

The vast increase in new housing, of course, has instigated a whole sequence of events. People need new furniture to go with the new flats. They need curtains, kitchen equipment, rugs, beds, lamps, refrigerators. Many of them want to dispose of their big, old, dark, overstuffed, ornate furniture and do a complete job of redecorating. Furnishings that were adequate for one room will hardly do for a new two-room- or three-room-and-kitchen flat—rooms that are much smaller than the single room of the past. Some of them will not even hold the huge wardrobes so dear to Russian taste and tradition.

Inevitably this caused a series of minor crises. Soviet production is not geared to consumer goods. It is not geared to quick changes in models, types, or styles. Khrushchev has been talking for three or four years about the necessity of getting clean, new, simple, modern furniture on the Scandinavian style. It is hard to say whether he is motivated by considerations of taste or considerations of economy. But, either way, it is a step in the right direction. Only now, however, is the needed furniture beginning to come into the shops; and the supplies are woefully inadequate.

Only after the Premier himself had made sarcastic references to the orange, pleat-and-tassel, silk lampshades which have dominated the Moscow scene for generations did it finally occur to the lampshade producers that their product could be made in other colors, other materials, other sizes, and other shapes.

In my years in Moscow I was a great shopper. I didn't buy much; but I toured the stores, week after week, checking goods and prices. I thought then and still think that there is no more sensitive barometer of Soviet economy than the flow of goods into the stores, the shortages, and the new products. When in 1950 I found that more and more aluminum pots and pans, copper samovars, and copper wire were appearing in the stores I became convinced that Russia did not expect the Korean War to spread into the European theater. One of the first signs of the easier policy of Stalin's successors was the appearance in the stores of flour for sale in unlimited quantities. Flour had been

rationed since before the war. At first the housewives could
not believe the storekeepers; they were sure it was a trick. So
day after day they queued up to buy flour, certain that the
supply would soon be exhausted. They filled every bag, box,
and barrel they could lay their hands on with flour. But the
government understood the housewives. It poured more and
more flour into the stores. Finally, the women gave up. Flour
sales dropped to nil. The women were convinced that flour had
arrived in the stores to stay.

Three or four Moscow jewelry stores were always included
in my shopping tours. I never failed to marvel at the treasures
I found in these stores. Sometimes it would be a great diamond
of three or more carats (a little flawed and yellowish but still
a big diamond). It would be priced at, perhaps, 40,000 rubles.
I have no idea who bought those diamonds. Peasants, I suppose,
to hoard in a little hollowed-out space under the loose brick
in the stove. There were aquamarines as big as ice cubes and
almost as pale. These usually turned up at the Samosvet store,
the store which sold semiprecious stones from the Urals. Old
garnet jewelry, obviously the treasure of the "former people,"
was common. Occasionally I saw a delicate pair of earrings
with pearls. Now and then there would be a real treat—a
genuine piece of Fabergé, perhaps a small bouquet of flowers,
made of precious stones. But more likely a less attractive piece,
made for the Moscow merchant trade—a dragon stickpin with
tiny ruby eye, a locket decorated with amethyst and rose quartz.
Very rarely a piece of beautiful enamel, colored like a summer
garden, a relic of the old Imperial Enamel Works.

Of all the consumer goods on sale in Moscow, my favorite
item was an emerald. Not an ordinary emerald. A big beauty.
An emerald big enough to choke a small pony. I have no idea
how many carats it weighed, and less idea where it may have
come from. I suppose there have been bigger emeralds in the
world, but I never had seen one. This little proletarian bauble

was modestly priced at 144,000 rubles. It was kept in an ordinary showcase along with a conglomeration of other gems, including some seedy diamond engagement rings, solid gold watch fobs, and a massively intricate and elaborately engraved gold sewing basket which undoubtedly once had graced the boudoir of a stout and handsome Moscow matron.

I used to go every week to the jewelry store to see if the great emerald was still there. It first appeared sometime in Stalin's last year. When I left Moscow in the fall of 1954 it was still on display. I thought it would prove as permanent as the Moscow winter.

But on my return I found that the emerald had vanished. I could not even get a clue to what happened to it. The clerk at the precious-stones counter whom I had gotten to know well during my weekly shopping excursions had been changed. Another girl was in her place, a girl who either had never heard of the emerald or didn't care to discuss it. What could have happened to the great stone? It hardly seems credible that a peasant hoarder bought it. Nor is it likely that some on-the-make commissar purchased the gem for his wife or sweetheart, for commissars are usually long on power and short on cash. Besides, ostentation would not further a Communist career. Russia does have artists wealthy enough to indulge in such whims. An author like Mikhail Sholokhov or Konstantin Simonov, a playwright like Nikolai Pogodin, or a painter like the elder Gerasimov would have the money to buy the stone. But somehow I cannot imagine anyone from Russia's artistic life investing in a symbol so gross and grand. Authors and playwrights and painters—even ballerinas—in the Soviet Union are well paid, well fed, and well housed. But there is a limit to the kind of conspicuous expenditure which they would consider wise.

I suppose I will never know who bought the great emerald. But my guess is that it now adorns (in secret) the mountainous bosom of the wife of some Red Army general, recently retired after long years of service in occupied Germany. During those occupation years his wife (like the wives of many occupation officers) made many a trip, or so I fancy, back and forth between Berlin and Moscow. Each time I see her bringing back suitcases bulging with German nylons, French lingerie, English woolen, and even such luxuries as American electric razors, American girdles, jazz records, and other items of inestimable value in the Moscow gray market. Year by year the stacks of rubles in the old brown suitcase tucked back under the bed of their Moscow apartment would grow and grow. The question would arise more and more urgently—what to do with the mountain of currency. There is a limit even to what the wife of a general can buy—the dacha in the country, the heavy furniture which once graced a fine flat in St. Petersburg, the encrusted dinner service, the silver peacock, a Repin for the wall. All of this was possible, but still the bundles of rubles would bulge as the years rushed past. I used to see such stout and vigorous matrons following the same trail I followed from jewelry store to jewelry store. They all knew the great emerald. I had seen them eying it. I heard a matron one day asking the salesgirl about a fat amber brooch which shared the tray with the emerald. And I saw the glitter in her eyes as the girl lifted out the tray. Her eyes were for the emerald and not the brooch. On another day I saw the woman again. With a little embarrassed chuckle designed to convince both the salesgirl and herself that, of course, her interest in the emerald was sheer curiosity, she casually asked to inspect it. The girl cast a quick look around the store, a look in which there was excitement and even, perhaps, a little fear—for this stone cost more than she would earn in twenty years of clerking. Then she removed the stone from its velvet curtain. With a hot greed that could no longer conceal itself, the woman took the stone into her hands. I could see her struggle with her passion and the reluctance with which she put the stone back, the resolution with which she inwardly swore that she would not see it again. Perhaps this woman was the general's wife of my imagination. I could see her taking the train back to Berlin. Then, the months of anxiety, sharp as a knife, as she waited her next visit to Moscow, imagining what might happen to the stone, seeing in her mind's eye the wife of some other general, perhaps another woman such as she who delved in the black market, slipping back to Moscow ahead of her and buying the stone.

The time must have come when she could restrain herself no longer. It would not have been time yet for her semiannual vacation in Moscow, but she could not wait another day. She went, I imagine, to the general with a trumped-up story about the children or her aging mother. She was blind with worry. She simply had to go back and see if they were all right. And the general, slow and stiff, at first resisting and then giving up with a shrug of the shoulders. Women! What could you do with them when they got a notion in their minds? Writing out the application for the pass, sending an aide to pick up her ticket, going down to the dismal Bahnhof to see her off in a compartment on the special Red Army train, then going back to the Officers Club to drink a few vodkas and eat some *zakuski*, some of those fine pickled mushrooms and the fresh caviar which had just come in from Russia, to gossip with his fellow generals and complain a bit about women and their ways, in the knowing and cynical fashion of a man who knows utterly nothing about the ways of women.

That, I imagine, was how it happened. She arrived in Moscow at midmorning. She had to fight a temptation to rush direct to the Stoleshnikov to see if the emerald was still in the store. But first there were things to do. She must go to the apartment and see if all was well, see if that idiot girl from Kostroma, that stupid Natasha Dmitrovna, had things in order. And, of course, she must pull out the big brown suitcase from under the bed and extract the enormous rolls of rubles and transfer them into her fine West German *sumka*. It would have been late afternoon before she arrived at the store, breathless but seeking in every way to conceal her excitement. She would not go directly to the precious stones counter. First, she would look at the watches and the silverware. Then, unable to restrain herself longer, she would shoulder up to the crowd that always surrounded the valuable jewelry and push forward, using her elbows. She would raise herself on her tiptoes. Yes. It was still there. *Slavo bogo*. Thank God. No one had bought it.

But, of course, having finally bought the great emerald (and I could fancy the excitement that caused—the store's manager, coming a-running, the word quickly spreading from salesgirl to salesgirl, the bookkeepers emerging like white worms from the back room to peer and stare, the flutter of gossip among the customers, the salesgirl so nervous she could hardly write out the slip, the manager taking over at this point and writing it out himself, the cashier with trembling hands counting the stout bundles of rubles, counting them again, counting them a third time, finally reaching for her rubber stamp and stamping the receipt paid, just as she did for all the other sales of the day), what could she do with it? Could she wear it? Not likely. I could not imagine her appearing in public with it. Not even the greatest general's wife would feel her position so secure that she would flaunt this czarina's jewel in public. Show it to her husband? I doubt very much whether she would have the courage to do that. He would not be so stupid as not to understand the danger her act involved.

No, I thought, that emerald at this moment is reposing in the same brown imitation-leather suitcase where the rubles used to lie.

Well, that may not be the fate of the emerald. But I do not believe my imagination has led me far astray. Soviet society has progressed to the point that this symbol of conspicuous display can enter the trading system and be offered for sale. It can be worshiped by Soviet citizens in whose breasts beat the same covetous desires as in bourgeois society. It can even fall into the hands of a woman as stricken with pride of property as any Moscow wife before the Revolution. But not yet can she flaunt her pride in the faces of her sisters in this transitional society where property may be coveted and possessed but displayed only with caution.

The disappearance of the unusual emerald made me ponder. Moscow had traveled a long way, it seemed to me, from that pure spirit of egalitarianism which burned in the hearts of the makers of the Revolution. And the emerald is a measure of the distance which Soviet society had moved. It had still some distance to go before we could speak of the triumph of bourgeois mores in Russia. But it was moving rapidly.

For the present, a passion for possession is more tactfully cloaked in some other garb. It is better, for example, to be a numismatist, specializing in gold and silver coins of the Roman Empire. Or a gemologist with a taste for unusually cut sapphires and rubies. Or a collector of gold enamel snuffboxes or mother-of-pearl fans.

For hoarding purposes anything is preferable to the ruble. Shortly after Stalin died the jewelry stores began to sell small gold discs. They were supposed to be used for making gold teeth. You could buy these discs at a price which was about three times the world price for gold. This was expensive, but to many Russians it seemed a worth-while investment. I did not find the gold discs this time. But I did find platinum discs, the same size and, I suppose, for the same purpose—priced, of course, at about three times the world price for platinum, and still regarded as a good investment by the Russians.

Perhaps this makes Moscow sound more bourgeois than it really is. But Moscow has been subjected to some strange and unusual influences in recent times, and most of these influences have been introduced by the government itself.

Take the Dior fashion show, for example. It is the last thing you would expect the proletarian state to introduce of its own free will. Yet the government invited the Dior firm to come to Moscow and gave it a free hand in showing what it wished. Dior came, and did not compromise an inch. Dior presented exactly the same show it gave in Paris. The same strange, skeletal models, with their death's-head faces, spinal walks, and operatic gestures, demonstrated the clothes. The Wings of the Soviet Air Club, where the show was held, was daily drenched in "Diorama," "Miss Dior," and other Dior perfumes. A hi-fi system softly played the latest music from Paris and New York.

There were only eight hundred seats available for each performance. Moscow women literally fought for tickets. Most of them went to women in the clothing industries and their friends. But there were many young actresses in the stands and a good many girls who looked like the daughters of prominent Soviet officials.

How did they react? I saw girls who were starry-eyed. They sketched the first half-dozen models, and then forgot to sketch as the haze of Paris elegance wafted them into dreams that never could be fulfilled. Nor was it only young girls. There were sharp-eyed women, dressed in good taste, women who either remembered how Paris dressed or had access to Western patterns, whose eyes were as dewy as those of the youngsters. I saw white-smocked ice-cream girls watch with bulging eyes, and mechanics whose jaws dropped.

I asked one middle-aged woman, probably a seamstress, judging by her white blouse and well-tailored skirt, what she thought of the show. She gave me a cryptic glance. "I think— a lot," she said, and turned away.

A saucy-looking blonde in cheap blue print dress and cheap

red sandals was helping a Russian photographer who was taking pictures for a Soviet magazine. He was bubbling with enthusiasm.

A beautiful English model came down the runway in a marvelous red silk gown.

"Wonderful!" the boy exclaimed.

"Terrible!" the girl replied. You could almost see her comparing her sleazy dress, probably her best, with the gorgeous creation on the model.

"How do you think Moscow women will like these styles?" I asked her.

"Not much," she snapped.

"Why?"

"They're too extreme."

"Don't you think they're pretty?"

"They're pretty but they're not for Moscow."

I sympathized with her, but I thought she would feel different if she had a chance to dress like the lovely models.

The Dior girls came and went. They were in Moscow only ten days. They put on their show, let themselves be photographed against the walls of the Kremlin and beside St. Basil's Cathedral. Then they went back to Paris. What did they leave behind? Much more than a memory. Within a week or two you began to see girls on Gorky Street wearing imitations of the more simple Dior styles. Spike heels appeared, dreadfully expensive, in the new House of Shoe Styles. The demand for sheer Western nylons became greater than ever. On the bathing beaches Russian girls began to wear dressmaker suits, of good quality, form-fitting, rubberized silk.

The Dior people negotiated at great length with the Soviet cosmetics industry with a view to licensing Russia to produce Dior cosmetics or, more appropriately, to sign a management contract for the Dior firm to modernize the Soviet industry. Whether anything will come of this, in the end, it is hard to say. But the fact of the negotiations is what counts.

For when all is said and done, why did the Soviet government invite Dior to Moscow? Not just to give the daughters of the ministers and the rising young actresses a thrill. And certainly not to embarrass young movie technicians with their boy friends.

No. Dior was brought in because the government wants to take the Russian woman out of her flowered print and give her a chance to look like her Western sisters. Why? Because, I would guess, the Russian woman wants to look like her Western sisters and the present Russian government can see no reason of policy why she should not. Neither puritanism nor emphasis on heavy industry is going to divert the Russian woman much longer from the heritage of her sex, the right and opportunity to look just as pretty as she wants to.

Already Moscow has made a long step forward in this direction, longer, perhaps, than many Americans realize.

At a diplomatic party last summer some Swedish businessmen were congratulating Mr. Mikoyan on the fine appearance of the Moscow citizenry. They were surprised to find Muscovites so well dressed.

Mr. Mikoyan beamed. Consumer goods is his field.

"Yes," he said, "it's true. Our people do look much better. Their clothing has improved. In fact there are times when you can't tell them from Americans."

He turned to me. "Isn't that true, Mr. Salisbury?"

I was happy to support Mr. Mikoyan.

"Yes," he said. "Today when you see them on the streets you can't always tell the Russians from the Americans, especially in the summer."

I was walking down Gorky Street the day after this talk. I saw a good many youngsters who fitted his description, boys in slacks and sports shirts, girls in light summer dresses. They would have passed without notice in any American town. This

was a change. I could remember the day when I was able un-
erringly to distinguish a Russian from a foreigner just by a
glance at his shoes. Indeed, this was the first place a Russian
looked when in doubt as to who you were.

Now this was no longer a certain test. I had even seen Russian
boys with Ivy League clothes and close-cropped American
college-style haircuts—a far cry from the floppy sailor trousers
and skin-shave pates so common a few years ago.

So Russians were going to look like Americans. What next, I
wondered. Cola? Even that, possibly. Or so it appeared after
Mr. Khrushchev was introduced to cola at the U.S. Exposition.
He still didn't think cola was the greatest; but the whole Presidium drank it with relish. Mr. Mikoyan had been trying to
introduce it for some time. He already had lined the principal
streets with red-enamel soft-drink vending machines just like
the cola machines he saw in America.

If cola came, I wondered where the line would be drawn.
TV dinners? Mikoyan saw those in America and liked them.
Popcorn? Bubble gum? Who could say?

A man from the Soviet Foreign Office was criticizing me one
day not long after I returned to Russia.

"It seems to us," he said, "that you are making it sound as
though Russia is getting more and more like America. We don't
like that. Russia is Russia and America is America."

Perhaps so. But it seemed to me that if this was the way he
felt he had better take the matter up with Mr. Khrushchev, Mr.
Mikoyan, and the Presidium. They were the ones who were
putting the American spin on the Russian ball. Not me.

IV

A Sentimental Journey

IT WAS EARLY AFTERNOON and the train on the suburban railroad was only half-filled. In the seat ahead of me were two middle-aged women. Each wore a faded straw hat and was burdened with a variety of parcels, some wrapped in old newspaper, some tucked into two bulging string bags. From their conversation I judged they were going to visit their sister and her husband in the country. Across the aisle were three young girls in calico dresses. Ahead of them was a man with gold pince-nez reading a mathematics journal. Typical passengers on a typical suburban line.

The sun was bright and the day was pleasantly warm. The train passed through a region I had known extremely well five years ago. We paused briefly at the Serp and Molot (Hammer and Sickle) station. This was, I remembered, a factory located on the outskirts of Moscow. But no longer so. In five years the city had marched out into the country on the stilts of the long-handled building cranes. We rode on and on through an area which I recalled as almost open prairie. Now it was thick with new apartment buildings, buildings under construction, and new factories.

Soon a beggar appeared at the end of the car. He wore a raveled gray army overcoat. One pants leg was tucked up at the knee and he hobbled on a single crutch. As he made his way ahead he sang in a mournful, nasal voice. There was a nostalgia

50

about his song which seemed to bring the breath of Siberia and the begging columns of prisoners right into the sunny railroad car. Rubles fluttered into his out-held cap as he stomped forward slowly, his voice quavering in false notes.

I dropped a handful of change into the cap and sat back, staring out the window. This was truly a journey into the past. How many times I had ridden the suburban train to Saltikovka. And I could not remember once when there had not been a beggar on the train, sometimes two or three. And always, as today, the Russians gave generously, although they knew as well as I that this was a way of life—a quite profitable way of life. Almost my first impression of Russia was Astrakhan during the war. It was winter and bitter cold. Snow was falling in the early evening as we went for a stroll in the city. Crossing a bridge with the wind biting fiercely at our coats and snow pelting our faces, we encountered a blind violinist with a woman to guide him, playing for alms in the January blizzard.

Russians had a compassion for beggars which was deep and mystic. It would, I thought, take more than forty years of Communism to disturb these deep-flowing currents of Russian feeling.

Looking out the window I saw that we had finally left the city behind. Here was the countryside as I remembered it, small villages at frequent intervals, pasture land and small forests. There is a lovely little onion-domed church and cemetery in Nikolievka, the village just before Saltikovka. I often walked to this village church and spent a quiet hour browsing about. Today I was happy to see it again, looking as perky as a village bride. The dome was bright with new blue paint, and the building shone fresh white with grass-green trim around the doors and windows. I remembered the cemetery as an obscure ruin of decaying tombstones and underbrush. Now it was spreading out over the surrounding lands and the ground was raw with the scars of new-dug graves. I knew that one of the real short-

ages of Moscow was cemetery space and that this had led to
scandals—cemetery superintendents taking bribes to exhume
old graves and sell the plots at fantastic prices to bereaved relatives unable to find a place to bury their loved ones. Many
Muscovites, I had heard, were going out of the city to find
burial places and escape this ghoulish racket. Apparently,
Nikolievka was one of the spots they had found.

The next stop was Saltikovka, only two or three minutes away.
I found myself as excited as a child. What would it be like?
Was it really the next station or had I miscalculated? Was the
market still there? Would I find the dacha unchanged? And
what of Dedya Petya and the others I had known? An almost
uncontrollable eagerness came over me as the train pulled into
the Saltikovka station. Half the passengers seemed to be getting
off. I glanced out the window. Indeed, it was Saltikovka, and a
Saltikovka which appeared little changed. There was the gate
to the market and people thronging to and fro. There was the
little row of shops at the point where the Ryazan highway
crossed the railroad. All bright blue under a new coat of
Ukrainian paint. Beyond the tracks a new brick building, possibly a store. Otherwise Saltikovka station was just as I had
preserved and crystallized it in my memory: the same mud when
I descended from the wooden railroad platform; the jumble of
pedestrians straggling across the railroad tracks right at the
point where the train once killed a man, tossing his crumpled
body a hundred feet away; the notices in purple pencil and
rusty ink tacked to the telephone poles around the market
entrance—"Pleasant room and ½ porch for rent for the summer,"
"For Exchange: two rooms in dacha for room in Moscow," "For
Sale: new dacha, four rooms, garden"—Russia's substitute for
the want-ad columns. And around the ads stragglers from the
Moscow train, looking to see if the room or cottage they were
seeking was available. I glanced around, half-expecting to be
approached by the elderly man with the neat spade beard

whom I knew from the old days, the local real-estate broker
who was always ready to find a buyer, a seller, a renter—for a
fee, of course. But today, at least, he did not seem to be present.
Perhaps he was busy showing a property to a client. His activ-
ities were strictly illegal but necessary if life was to go on in
the way Russians liked it to go.

The reason why Saltikovka was such familiar ground to me
was that for several years, several of the worst Stalin years, I
rented a dacha in the village and spent much of my time in the
summer and a bit at other seasons in the pleasant little community.

There had been a time when I knew, by sight, half the people
here in the farmers' market. I wondered whether I would recognize anyone today: the smiling Mongol who used to sell
bulochki, those wonderful Russian rolls that are the first cousins
of hot cross buns; the wizened old lady who sold religious
medals and pictures and kept a collection of ancient ikons and
religious books in a gunny sack which was concealed under the
folds of her wide black skirt; the old crones who sat all day
beside their piles of sunflower and dried watermelon seeds,
cracking and eating them without cease, not even interrupted
while they tumbled a water glass of seeds into a newspaper
cornucopia for the occasional customer.

I pushed my way into the market place, and the years fell
away. It was as though I were still living in the blue-painted
dacha on Dachnaya Street and had come down to the market
on this pleasant Sunday noon to see what there was for sale.

True, my smiling Mongol friend was no longer there with his
basket of hot buns. In his place there was a bosomy blonde with
a smiling red face who looked something like the big warm
buns she kept closely covered in her linen-shrouded basket. The
little old woman with her collection of ikons was gone, dead,
no doubt, for she had been well into her seventies when she last
bade me godspeed in a quavering voice. But in her place was a

woman who could have been her sister. She had a great copper samovar—big, battered, and possibly a century old. She spoke in a hoarse whisper, begging me to buy it. I was tempted for a moment. But it was an ugly samovar and there was nothing I had less use for. The old *semichki* ladies were there—all in a row, sitting and spitting out the seeds as they had a hundred years before and would, I felt sure, a hundred years hence.

Piled up in great heaps were plaster-of-paris cats, bigger than life-size, gaily splotched with turquoise and saffron, carmine and black. The big ones sold for twenty rubles. Small ones with blue and pink bows around their ochre necks were five rubles. There were piggy banks made to look like great toadstools and miniature Russian stoves; rainbow-colored *matushkas;* stacks of fitted wooden rings made like the Kremlin towers; pink paper butterflies on wheeled sticks; papier-mâché tablets, decorated with deers' antlers; wooden lacquer spoons; wooden boxes (neat and practical for sending parcels through the mail); a newly varnished bedside washstand; a mahogany table, badly scratched; an old wooden plane; stacks of old iron.

There was a man selling ax handles. A man selling rake handles. A man selling slatted blinds made of fragrant new pine. A boy selling a red-and-white collie. A half-dozen women with pink-nosed white rabbits in baskets. An old woman with a fat live goose cuddled under her arm. An old woman with a brace of ducks under her shawl. Chickens and more ducks and billygoats. But no little piglets. It was past season for them.

The market stalls were overflowing with the summer vegetables—gray-green *kabochki,* or squash; yellow onions; stacks of small leaf lettuce; pink new potatoes; white fragrant garlic; piles of bruised cherries, juice staining the wooden counters; small green crab apples, wormy as ever; tender little carrots and yellow turnips; white parsley roots; mushrooms—the big pink ones, the twisted yellow ones, the *podsosni* (under the pine trees), and the *poddubni* (under the oak trees)—all a little dry and small because of lack of rainfall; great big white country eggs, twice the size of the city ones and only a ruble apiece; barrels of new cucumber pickles, swimming in brine and fragrant with dill.

No. The market had changed very little in the time I had been away. In the little shops which surrounded the open bazaar, however, the stocks of consumer goods were better than I remembered them. Now you could buy almost the same goods in these little shops as in the stores on the Petrovka. Here were the new, shiny, aluminum pots and tea kettles I had seen on Gorky Street (not the dull, cheap finish in which all Soviet aluminum used to be turned out). Here were bolts of dress goods, cotton and wool and silk, as good as those in the shops on the Sretinka. People were jamming the hardware store to buy a new packaged disinfectant. On the shelves were bright china sets in a dozen patterns.

I felt at home in the market place. The people were the same as ever—*dachniki* strolling in their Sunday costumes (as customary, some of the men in lounging pajamas and some of the women in dressing gowns). There were the usual beggars lolling close to the market entrance—some of them the same I had known five years ago. And here was a sign forbidding "hand" trading, or the sale of seeds, dogs, chickens, and goats—prohibitions which the militiamen in their market station showed no sign of having read or intending to enforce. Outside the market, music blared from the little drygoods store; it had added a line of phonographs and records. There were taxis and a busy bus service to take passengers from Saltikovka market two miles down the Ryazan chausee to the workers' textile settlement of Balashikha. This was new. In my day you walked from Saltikovka to Balashikha, unless you had a bicycle or could beg a ride on a passing collective-farm truck.

It was a prosperous and contented community that I found myself strolling through. There were more cars on the Ryazan

road than in the old days and more young men with motor-
bikes, some with their girl friends tucked on the seat behind. In
the years I had known Saltikovka there had been quite a building boom. People, many of them retired army officers, came
out from Moscow, got the village soviet to allot them a plot of
ground, and then built a cottage, often with their own hands
or with a little help from one of the local carpenters.

Saltikovka, many years before, had been a serf village belonging to a wealthy Moscow family. In the late nineteenth century it had begun to be popular as a summer resort. Middle-
class Moscow families spent the summers in rustic villas under
the tall, straight pine forests. The village was still regarded as
a summer resort although there was hardly a cottage or house
in the community that was not occupied the year around. Fast
and frequent electric train service made it a popular spot for
Muscovites fortunate enough to get a cottage here. The summer
houses almost invariably had good old-fashioned Russian stoves
of the Dutch oven type. The first thing a family did when it
won possession of one of the houses was to winterize it. Actually,
Saltikovka was suburbia, or as close to it as Russia had been
able to get.

Each house had its own plot of land; and in the years when
I had my dacha, people were busy planting fruit trees, setting
out raspberry bushes, and putting in strawberry plots. Before
this the plots had been planted almost entirely to potatoes and
cabbage. But now almost every inch of space in each yard was
devoted to fruits and berries. Of course, there was also a plot
for potatoes, usually in the rear. Most of the residents had
chickens or geese. Just as many goats as ever were tethered
along the road to take the best advantage of what the Russians
liked to call "God's grass."

The orchards had grown wonderfully well since I last saw
them, half-concealing many of the houses. Each house had its
carefully maintained wooden fence—a necessity if the goats

and chickens in search of "God's grass" were not mistakenly to find it in a neighbor's garden. The chickens, I was pleased to note, were still wearing daubs of yellow or blue or crimson on their behinds so the owners could identify their own without too much argument.

None of the streets of Saltikovka, of course, was paved. I had watched, in the last two years of my Moscow stay, a road crew of two men (occasionally augmented by a third) busy themselves with the task of laying an asphalt surface on the old cobbles of the Ryazan chausee. Each morning they would chop wood, heat a fire under their caldron of tar, and by noon, if the fire was going well, the tar would be liquid enough to spread on the road. They worked steadily, day after day and month after month; but when I left Russia, only half the distance of the highway from Balashikha to Saltikovka market had been asphalted.

Now, it appeared, the task finally had been completed. But when I walked up the road I was pleased and somehow reassured to find that at least one quarter-mile stretch of the highway near the Saltikovka pond still displayed the hundred-year-old cobbles, innocent of tar.

I was even more pleased, however, to find the pond filled with water once more, and around its grassy shores the same crowd of bathers—many of them out from Moscow for the day—that I used to see. The last time I had come by that way, the pond was only a mud bottom; it had been drained a year previously for the construction of a bridge which was still unbuilt.

Now the bridge was finished, the water had accumulated again, and the pond seemed gayer than I remembered. Every boat in the little blue boat station had been rented out. Muscular young men in swimming trunks were competently colliding their boats with those of shrieking young women, some of whom wore good-looking one-piece suits. The young women were doing their best to pretend they could not manage their boats in order to make it easier for the young men to ram them.

I found a little change at the Vodipad (waterfalls) restaurant: an outdoor lunch-stand beside the small dam and spillway at the foot of the pond. No longer did the Vodipad sell vodka. Vodka is the target of a government temperance drive. Now the Vodipad did a rushing business in great foaming *krutki* (mugs) of strong beer. A dozen men, several with elaborate tattoos of blue and red, sat quaffing their beer. Many of them ostentatiously broke a raw egg into the krutki "for fortification."

I turned off the highway beside a small roadside food stall and started down the rutted lane which led in the direction of my old dacha. This road always became impassable after a heavy rain. I remembered how we had tried to persuade the village soviet to make some repairs, but they refused. Their argument was that if the road were left impassable the foreigners would finally go away and leave the village in peace and quiet. It had worked, in a sense. At least there were no more foreigners left in Saltikovka, and the road was in just as bad shape as it had been. I wondered what the dachniki with cars did about it. Probably made a detour or left the cars at home. There still weren't enough automobile owners in Saltikovka to constitute a real pressure group.

The lane ran beside a meandering small stream. There were the same sulky herds of geese which had been there the first afternoon I saw Saltikovka. Here was the place where the angry dachniki had dug trenches across the road in the vain hope that this would cause so much general indignation that the authorities would be compelled to fix the road. And here was the pleasant green-painted dacha with whose owner I used to chat. Once he had given me the most beautiful strawberry plants I had ever seen; I was glad to see that his strawberry patch still flourished. And here, at the corner, was the house of the man who tried to steal the village well. He had put a fence up around the communal well and tried to appropriate it for

his own use. But the angry dachniki compelled him to restore
free access to the water. Five years had not caused his property
to deteriorate. He had built a higher fence around his orchard,
but now the trees were taller yet and heavily bowed with a lush
crop of apples. The would-be well-thief was prospering.

But now I had reached Dachnaya Street. Halfway up the
hill was the dacha itself, still blue but faded now to a pastel
color. The sapphire and amber glass that we had installed
around the porch windows (acquired from the Ministry of
Railroad Supply which used the glass for its railway signal
system) was still there. And I could see a man in pajamas
lolling in a front-yard hammock. So far as the eye could detect
little had changed. I might just now be returning, not from a
five-year absence, but from a two-hour trip to the market.

Not everything was the same, however. I saw a little tow-
haired girl playing outside the *obshchezhitiye,* the rough communal barracks at the foot of the street. I guessed correctly
that she was little Nadya, now eleven instead of six. Where
would I find Dedya Petya, I asked her. She looked as though
she wanted to run away but finally managed to say: "He's
dead." She did not know exactly when he had died. Later I
learned that it had been two years ago. His wife had died a year
before that.

Dedya Petya was as kind a man as I had ever known. He had
been a railroad worker but was retired and worked for the
Dacha Trust as a watchman. He was a tall, straight, handsome
man with a fine beard. I sometimes brought him coffee for his
wife. She thought it helped her heart, which was very weak.
Dedya Petya was a serious man. He took his watchman's duties
with gravity. Once, when a drunken workman broke into the
dacha and stole a few small things, Dedya Petya's anguish was
painful to see. He wore a neat cotton padded jacket, summer
and winter, and a fine pair of high Russian boots. He kept his
old railway man's cap with its semi-military visor. As he walked

under the tall straight pine trees with a great silvery ax in one hand, he at once called to mind a character in an old Russian folk tale.

I had told myself before I went to Saltikovka that the chances were that I would not find Dedya Petya. Nevertheless I had brought a can of coffee under my arm and also a good warm woolen shirt which he could wear in winter under his padded jacket. I was too late with my presents.

I looked at the field around the barracks. Just as always. A large patch of potatoes. A smaller patch of cabbage. Across the grassy lane I saw a man coming away from the well with a pail of water balanced on each shoulder. Many and many a pail of water I had pulled up from that well and carted up the lane for the garden in the dry summer weeks. There was the brick house that the pleasant, lame army colonel had built right across from the dacha. I had watched every stage of that process, from the year when the colonel and his wife lived in a little shed in the rear until the great day when they moved into the completed first floor of the brick house. I had seen them set out their orchard in the rear. The colonel and I had waited turns at the well with our pails of water. Now, I saw the colonel's wife standing in the doorway of the house. She looked gray and old. I glanced about the colonel's garden. The fruit trees had not prospered. Some had been winter killed; others were spindling, unlike those of the well-stealer down the lane. I saw the two iron beams jutting out of the second floor of the house. These were destined to be the supports for the little second-floor balcony which, as I could see, the colonel had never built. I was very much afraid that Dedya Petya was not the only one of my old friends who no longer lived in Dachnaya lane. The colonel, too, it seemed sure, had not survived the five years' absence. He never had been strong. I did not know what the trouble was with his leg—some war injury, I supposed. Perhaps there were other wounds, less visible.

Slowly I walked up Dachnaya lane. There were more changes at my old dacha than I had taken in at first glance. The apple and pear trees had vanished. So had many of the shrubs. But most of the roses were still there. I looked next door at the house of the Balakirovs. It looked to me as though the fruit trees and shrubs had made only a short journey. The Balakirov place was flourishing. Where once had been a grassless yard and small potato patch now were fine apple and pear trees. There were shrubs leading up to the front path. Perhaps I was mistaken; but I remembered the frequency with which the Balakirovs' goat had managed to get into our garden, always when we were not at home, and the dexterity with which the Balakirov chickens managed to thrust aside the boards which we erected to keep them from scooting under the fence.

Life was going on in Saltikovka. Not exactly the kind of life that Americans have in their suburbs. More like the life in a summer colony in the 1880's. I would be surprised if Saltikovka had more than one or two persons who drove their cars in and out of Moscow each day. Certainly, ninety-five per cent of them commuted on the electric railroad, walking twenty minutes or half an hour to and from their homes. The houses had electric lights (although they were apt to go off during a bad storm). They had outdoor privies. There wasn't a dacha in town with indoor plumbing or piped water. Everyone used the community wells, winter and summer. There was no supermarket, no delivery services, no hamburger joint, and no juke boxes. The food in the market was good, but it reflected the seasons of the year. In summer you could buy almost anything at Saltikovka. But in winter it was a desperately plain fare of potatoes, cabbage, and root vegetables.

Still and all, I knew that given a chance there was hardly a family in Moscow which would not move to Saltikovka tomorrow if it could get a house and a plot. People would put up with what seemed to them minor inconveniences for the sake of a place of their own, a place where they could latch the gate at night and close out until morning all outside life.

Houses in Saltikovka were almost impossible to rent and expensive to buy. The better ones sold for 150,000 or 200,000 rubles or even more. This was out of reach for most Moscow citizens. What they dreamed of was getting a plot allotted by the city council and putting up their own houses. I had often watched it done. This took several years, and it was costly too. The materials easily ran to 25,000 or 30,000 rubles. Labor was expensive if you did not do it all yourself. But it was worth it. Once the house was built it was yours—yours to have and to hold, to live in, to keep, to pass on to your children, to sell in time of great necessity or to rent.

The state would help a person build a house. There were loans at nominal interest with twenty years to repay. And now it was getting easier to obtain the materials needed to build a house. During my time there, the favorite source was the storehouse of a factory. Rare indeed was a dacha which had not been built at least in part with materials illegally drawn from some state warehouse. Now the hardware stores and the building-construction stores were fairly well stocked.

In my years in Moscow I had counted Saltikovka the most pleasant experience I had. There I had gotten close to Russian life and had met Russian people. I knew a little of how they lived. But, even so, the Saltikovka years had been cold-war years. The people were friendly but not intimate. I knew them to say hello to. I watched them work and play. I listened to conversations more often than I participated in them.

Saltikovka still seemed to me more pleasant than any part of Moscow, even though I missed my old friends. I turned back down Dachnaya Street, deep in thought about the times I had spent there. As I walked along slowly, in reminiscent mood, I saw a woman picking her way across the rutted tracks and the rough bridge that ran over the little stream where the geese liked to graze. She was middle-aged and wearing, not a country dress, but a well cut dark blue silk dress more suitable for a diplomatic reception in Moscow than a country road.

She came up to me a little out of breath and flustered, and I saw that she was wearing a big, expensive, and rather old-fashioned diamond brooch at the collar of her dress. She stumbled through an apology and asked me if I had not lived a long time ago in Dachnaya Street. Indeed, I said, I had lived there. Just as she thought. She had often seen me in the old days passing up and down Dachnaya Street. But in those times—she hesitated for the right word—she had just not thought to speak to me. But the fact was she had noticed me walking today and decided she would speak to me this time. She hadn't wanted to ask me about this before, but she had two brothers and a sister in the United States. She had not heard from them since before the war. She didn't want to bother me, but was there any chance at all that I might be able to look them up?

She had only the address of one brother, who had last been living in Pittsburgh. But if I could find him she was sure that he would know about the others.

The words tumbled one after the other in her excitement. I assured her that I would be glad to help. "Thank God," she said. "Here is my name and my address and telephone number in Moscow. If you find out anything, anything at all, please let me know. I will be so grateful."

I left her with eyes sparkling and walked on back to the Saltikovka station. There was no doubt about it. Life was better in Saltikovka than in the time I had spent there. In those days, the last of the Stalin days, there was not a resident in Saltikovka who would have come up to me with such a request. True, it was a little thing, just a simple human inquiry. But that was precisely what they could not do in the Stalin days. The dates which the woman mentioned told the whole story. Not since 1940 had she heard from her family abroad. Not since

1940 had she dared to hear from her relatives in America. Now she approached an American in broad daylight on an open lane in Saltikovka. God knows how many babushki standing behind the shutters of their cottages had seen her. But now this made no difference. It was not only the material life of Saltikovka which was better. The first small steps had been taken toward a better life of the spirit.

V

The Tragedy of the Jews

I WAS SITTING in a quiet book-lined apartment in the Arbat quarter of Moscow. The windows were open, and outside I could hear children playing in the courtyard and shouting back and forth in the cool shadows of the summer evening. I was talking with an old friend of mine, a Jew, about what it was like living in Moscow during the "black days." The black days were the days from late 1948 until Stalin's death in March, 1953, when a secret but deadly anti-Semitic policy was being pursued by the Kremlin.

"Was it worse in those days," I asked, "than back in the 1930's during the great purges?"

I had lived in Moscow during the "black days." But much of what was happening in that time I had learned about only later on. And much, even now, was still concealed from me. One of the purposes of my return to Moscow had been to try to obtain some sense of perspective on the Stalinist persecution of the Jews and to try to seek out the reasons for the continuing prejudice and discrimination against Jews in Russia.

My friend had no hesitation in replying to the question which I put to him. "It was worse during the 1940's," he said. "It was worse because it was all secret. You did not know exactly what was happening. Sure. Your friends disappeared. There were rumors. God knows there were rumors. People lost their jobs. People went into exile. But why? Why? That was the question.

No one ever knew why, and this was what made the terror so much worse."

I thought of this conversation one night when I found myself in a shabby little hall on Komsomolskaya Square. It was the Club of the Railroad Workers. The program that evening presented the singer, Zinovi Shulman, in a concert of Yiddish songs. A hush spread over the room as the buxom blonde announcer in her flowered silk gown came down to the footlights.

"The next number will be a song based on a poem by Itsik Fefer," she said. The audience gasped. People leaned over to whisper to one another. When the song was over, Mr. Shulman, his faded coattails fluttering, took bow after bow. It seemed as if the audience would never tire of applauding.

Mr. Shulman appeared embarrassed. He knew, of course, that the applause was not for him but for Fefer, the Red Army Colonel, Young Communist official, admirer of Stalin, poet— and Jew who was executed in 1952 as one of the secret victims of Stalin's ferocious anti-Semitic phobia.

Finally, Mr. Shulman was permitted to continue. He sang a number or two. Then came another sensation. It was a number called "Home." The audience applauded before he sang and then afterwards for a long time. Again Mr. Shulman mopped his brow and balding head in slight embarrassment. For again the applause was not for his voice. It was for "Home." Home was the homeland, Israel.

Could this be it, I wondered? Could this be what it is really all about, this persisting anti-Semitism which stains modern Soviet Russia like ink that never quite washes off the guilty hands of the government? Could it be the heritage of a tradition and a tie to a land and people beyond the sea? I well knew the sensitivity of the Communist rulers toward even the slightest and most sentimental foreign association. After all, good Soviet citizens had been sent into exile under Stalin for no reason other than the fact that they had received a letter from a relative in New York.

To be sure, Khrushchev's Russia is not Stalin's Russia; and anti-Semitic manifestations are not what they were under the old Generalissimo. But the virus as I could see was still there, ugly and persistent, forever coming up to the surface. Kill the Jews and Save Russia! The old anti-Semitic cry of the Czarist pogroms had not been forgotten. I had heard it muttered on the street and I expected that I would hear it again.

The mournful little concert at the Railwaymen's Club was, certainly, a kind of petty act of contrition for the crimes of the past. It was one of thirty or more Yiddish concerts which were given in Moscow during a few months after the one hundredth anniversary of Sholem Aleichem's birth was formally celebrated in the spring of 1959. The audience at the concert interested me. Almost all were Jews. Outside of a dozen foreigners including two ladies from Brooklyn, the people seemed to come from the middle levels of Soviet society: managers of stores, department heads in government offices, doctors, teachers in middle school, engineers. They were middle-aged and often accompanied by a younger son or daughter in the twenties or early thirties. The younger people often did not understand Yiddish. The songs were translated for them by their elders.

"Before Stalin's last years," a Jewish friend explained to me, "many of these people would not have regarded themselves as Jewish. Take myself for example. I grew up in the 1920's and early '30's. I thought of myself as Russian, not Jewish. Then, after the war I found that it did not make any difference what I thought about myself—I was a Jew on the books. I was a Jew to the director of the institute where I worked. Very well. I became a Jew to myself."

Nowhere in the world, I was assured, was there less anti-Semitic feeling than in Russia from the mid-1920's until the eve

of World War II. The days of the Czarist pogroms and of the
Jewish Pale of Settlement seemed to have vanished forever.

Of course this was not quite true. There had been a sub-
stantial vein of anti-Semitism underlying the 1930 purges. The
joke: "You're not a Trotskyite and you're not a Jew, so why
were you arrested?" had a good deal of validity. And I never
believed the common story that active anti-Semitism was re-
introduced into Russia by the Hitlerites. I remembered too
vividly the wartime rumors in Moscow that the Jews were
"getting out." I had heard too many tales, complete with nasty
details, of how "the Jews saved their skins" by crowding onto
the evacuation trains that took so much of Moscow's population to the east. "The Jews are bribing the railroads and carting
off their gold"—this was the kind of rumor that ran like wild-
fire through the Moscow streets in October, 1941.

How did those stories start? Did Stalin encourage them? I
wondered then and I wonder now. I know that when I got to
Moscow early in 1944 the aftereffects of the anti-Semitic outburst were still visible. People still told how anti-Semitic sentiment was permitted to course through the city unchecked. It
was not for two years, not until November, 1943, that the late
Alexander Shcherbakov, wartime propaganda director and
party boss of Moscow, called in his party underlings and curtly
informed them that anti-Semitism was not a government policy.
In other words, for two wartime years, 1941-43, the Party organization of Moscow proceeded on the theory that anti-Semitism
was the government policy. Accident? I hardly believe so.

"What everyone overlooks in discussing anti-Semitism under
Stalin," a friend who has lived many years in Moscow told me,
"is that anti-Semitism was popular. People liked to believe bad
things about the Jews during the war. After the war even if
Stalin had wanted to stop anti-Semitic sentiment it would not
have been so easy."

But, as abundant evidence now shows, Stalin had no desire

to halt it. Unknown to the outside world, anti-Semitism had become the secret policy of the Stalin regime. Even I, living in Moscow, with my ear to the ground, watching every clue that came along, even I was never clearly aware until after Stalin's death how far and how official this policy ran. I saw the signs, the symptoms, the telltale marks. But I never saw the whole picture. Even now I could not clearly establish the motivation. And that, of course, was what made the terror so deep to its victims.

"The difference between the terror of the 1930's and that of the 1940's was this," one man told me. "In the 1930's you had to be important to be arrested or shot. In the '40's it made no difference. Anyone could be arrested. Literally anyone. One day a little Jewish watch repairman was arrested. A few days later he was executed. Why? No one knows. To this day no one knows. I don't think the police knew even then. His name just happened to be on a list. Maybe it was confused with another name. In any event, he was shot."

Today many people assume that the anti-Semitic outrages occurred only in the last weeks of Stalin's life, at the time of the so-called plot of the Kremlin doctors. But Stalin had been carrying out secret persecution of the Jews on a wide scale since 1948. And the truth is that Stalin's anti-Semitism first showed its terrible face at least ten years earlier. So many tragedies have beset Russia's Jews in more recent times that few people remember the victims of that earlier era. But if you go back to the late 1930's, you find that Stalin was singling out the same kind of victims then as he chose later: Yiddish writers and poets, Yiddish scholars, leaders of the Jewish community, officials of the Birobidzhan settlement in the Far East, members of the Jewish Bund (the Jewish socialist organization which never got along with the Bolsheviks), not to mention the many, many old Bolsheviks who were numbered among Stalin's opponents and who happened to be Jewish.

From what source did Stalin's venom against Jews stem? Was this one of the early manifestations of his schizoid personality? Did he transfer to the Jews his hatred and fear of the Trotskyites simply because Trotsky was Jewish and the international wing of the party included many Jews? Perhaps we will never be able to get to the bottom of it. But the fact is that the parallels between 1938 and 1948 are striking. In 1938 the Jewish publishing house in Moscow was closed. So was the Jewish newspaper. Jewish communal organizations were dissolved. The ties between the American Joint Distribution Committee and its Russian correspondents were severed. So were the connections between American Jewish philanthropists and the Jewish agricultural colonies which they had assisted in the Crimea and the north Caucasus.

Indeed, had it not been for the coming of World War II, perhaps there would have been no need for a new purge in 1948. Perhaps the Jews would have long since been suppressed. But war did come and with it the need for rallying all elements behind the patriotic effort. A Jewish Anti-Fascist Committee was organized. Jewish cultural organizations were revived. They were encouraged to establish contacts with their religionists abroad, particularly in the United States, and in every way to stimulate support for the Soviet cause.

Thus, as can now be seen, the stage was set for Act Two.

One other point has always interested me. This is what role, if any, was played by the late Lavrenti P. Beria in crystallizing Stalin's anti-Semitism. The anti-Semitic moves of 1938 coincided with Beria's rise to power. Now, there is a curious thing about Beria. In Georgia, where he was Party Secretary, he had posed as the friend of the Jews. There is still in Tbilisi today a Jewish cultural museum which he founded as part of an effort to stimulate the national cultural consciousness of the Georgian Jews, who had been violently discriminated against by the Czarist regime. Beria helped the Jewish communities of Georgia economically as well. Many Georgians will tell you that Beria himself was half-Jewish. And an unusual number of Beria's highest lieutenants in the NKVD were Jewish. This was in line with standard police policy of using minority personnel on the theory that they would be more trustworthy in dealing with Great Russians. But it was in sharp contrast to the strict anti-Semitic personnel policy which had long since been established in the Foreign Office, the Foreign Trade Ministry, the highest organs of state planning, the Red Army High Command, and other Soviet bodies.

Whether it was inspired by Beria or not, the fact is that when anti-Semitism was revived as a policy in 1948 the principal victims were the very Jewish cultural and social leaders who had been instructed by the government to form the Jewish Anti-Fascist Committee in 1942.

No one to this day knows how many persons died during the postwar anti-Semitic purge. One group of twenty-four persons was executed on August 12, 1952, on charges of Jewish nationalism and conspiracy with foreign states to detach Soviet territory (the Crimea) from the Soviet Union.

Itsik Fefer was one of the men executed. He had been one of a group of twenty-five who were secretly tried between July 11 and 18. Only one of the twenty-five survived the trial. She was Lina S. Shtern, a physiologist and member of the Soviet Academy of Sciences. She was sentenced to a life term of imprisonment and released, of course, after Stalin's death.

But these were only the more prominent among the persons who lost their lives in the anti-Semitic outburst. Hundreds were arrested in the drive. We still do not know the fate of many of these persons. Many, of course, died in the Siberian camps. In addition to the principal trial in Moscow, there were others. One was held in Birobidzhan. It is likely that trials were held in the Ukraine. Many Jews were shipped to Siberia without trial at the orders of the Interior Ministry three-man courts, the notorious "troikas." The roll of victims included most of the distinguished names of Jewish intelligentsia.

What touched off this outbreak? No one really knows yet for certain. The ostensible reason for the involvement of the Jewish Anti-Fascist Committee appears to have been some discussions which occurred at the end of the war concerning the possibility of using the Crimea as an area for Jewish settlement. The Crimea had been depopulated by Stalin, who shipped most of the Tartar residents out to Siberia as punishment for their readiness to collaborate with the Nazis during the occupation. The idea of setting up Jewish colonies in the region probably was suggested by the fact that there had been Jewish colonies there before the war. The project was discussed officially. Solomon Lozovsky, the old Deputy Foreign Commissar, was an advocate of the plan and so were some of the Anti-Fascist Committee members. They paid for their talk with their lives. There is no evidence that any conspiracy was involved in the Crimea talks. The question was raised in normal government channels and apparently came up in the Politburo. Stalin did not agree to the plan. What the other Politburo members thought about it is not known, except that Khrushchev has stated that he opposed the scheme.

Some Moscow Jews believe that the overt cause for the anti-Semitic campaign in the autumn of 1948 lay in the reception accorded to Mrs. Golda Meir, Israel's first minister to the Soviet Union. She was received tumultuously by Moscow's Jewry. When she visited the Moscow synagogue 10,000 persons crowded the street outside, unable to get into the temple. For days after she took up residence in the Metropole Hotel, a queue of Jews formed outside her suite. There were hundreds of persons in the line.

"I am sure this triggered it," a Moscow resident said.

I have always thought the theory had a certain plausibility. The year of 1948 was a year of extreme sensitivity in Moscow.

This was the year of the break with Tito and the sealing of the victory of Mao and his Chinese Communists. It was a year of Berlin crisis, of grim cold war, of threats of hot war, of deep and desperate suspicions. In such an atmosphere the demonstration of the Moscow Jews could easily have been seized upon by a paranoid ruler as evidence of their loyalty to a foreign state.

Certainly stories circulated among the Russians in Moscow at this time such as: "Did you see the Jews in the street? Their Messiah has arrived. They are laughing at us now. They think they have their own country." This and similar remarks were typical of Moscow's street reaction to the Meir incident.

Certainly within no time at all the secret campaign against the Jews was thrown into high gear. All over the country Jewish institutions were closed—the Yiddish theaters in Moscow, Birobidzhan, and Minsk, the Yiddish publishing houses, the newspapers, the cultural organizations. Within a month there was not a single Jewish institution, except for the synagogues and prayer houses, left in the country. The press blossomed with attacks on "homeless cosmopolitans" who were depicted in *Krokodil* cartoons with bulbous and elongated noses. Jews were quietly dismissed from their jobs or transferred to the provinces. They were arrested in the Ukraine and shipped to Kazakhstan. Those who had survived the Nazi terror in the Byelorussian marshes were shipped to Siberia.

"No one who was not a Jew in Moscow in 1948 knows what it was like," a man told me. The internal passport of each Soviet citizen specifies his nationality: Russian, Georgian, Ukrainian, or Jewish. This man decided to "lose" his passport. He tore it up and flushed it down the toilet. Then he applied for a new one at the local police station. He put down his nationality as Russian. Fortunately, a routine police check did not disclose his deceit. He received his passport as a Russian.

"Many of us did that," he said. "It was a matter of self-preservation. The word *Jew* is not on my passport today. But

I feel more Jewish than in the days when it was there."

Some, of course, could not protect themselves so simply. They were prominent and were known to be Jewish. The more prominent they were, the more quickly they lost their jobs, particularly in cultural and intellectual fields.

The campaign against "homeless cosmopolitans" had been publicly launched by Ilya Ehrenburg. Mr. Ehrenburg's parents were Jewish, but he himself has savagely criticized Jews who did not place Soviet nationalism before their Jewish culture. But whatever else he may be, Mr. Ehrenburg is a man of courage. The day came when one of his colleagues rose in the Soviet Writers Union and called for the expulsion of a long list of members—all Jewish.

Mr. Ehrenburg rose.

"There is only one thing wrong with that list," he said. "You have omitted one name."

"What name is that?" asked the sponsor of the proposal.

"Mine," said Mr. Ehrenburg and sat down.

Perhaps because of this quixotic action, the Jewish writers were not expelled as a body, although many, individually, fell victim to the campaign.

Elsewhere Jews found few protectors. Moscow State University announced proudly that it was a citadel of *Russian* culture. What this meant became clear when the rolls were purged of Jewish professors. Even today the University has only one full professor who is Jewish. At the Academy of Sciences there is a long-standing tradition of anti-Semitism dating back to Czarist days. Here a purge of the Jews was also carried out. However, the Jewish predominance in mathematics and physics was so great that it was not possible to dismiss them all without wrecking the departments.

This was the real background against which the scenario of the better-known Kremlin doctors' plot of 1953 was presented. In the 1953 case, Jewish doctors in the Kremlin hospital were charged with plotting to poison and do away with the Soviet leaders. They were said to be acting at the instigation of the British and American intelligence services, which transmitted their orders through the American Joint Distribution Committee. In the weeks before Stalin's death, Jews were being arrested all over the Soviet Union. It was obvious that a new and even greater terror was in preparation. Stalin, it is said, was planning to exile all Russia's Jews to Siberia. But Stalin's death averted this fresh disaster. The plot was denounced, its victims (except for a few who had died in prison) were freed and their good names restored.

In the years that have followed, the government has painstakingly overhauled all the old records. It has notified family after family that the husband or brother or son was unjustly accused and executed. Surviving Jews, along with other victims, have been repatriated from Siberia. The works of the Jewish writers who were shot have been reissued in new editions (in Russian translation) with thoughtful and reminiscent prefaces.

But in all of this something is lacking. There has never been any public acknowledgment of the anti-Semitic outrages of the Stalin era. Khrushchev did not say anything about the anti-Semitic bias of Stalin's mania in his famous "secret" speech. No lists of "rehabilitated" victims have ever been published. Literary articles discussing the victims carefully avoid specifying the manner of death, although the date is always a give-away and sometimes the death is called "tragic" or "untimely." The Yiddish publishing house has not been re-established although occasionally there have been hints that it might be. No works in Yiddish have been brought out except for a small memorial edition of the works of Sholem Aleichem which sold out in Moscow the day it appeared in the bookstores. The bulk of the edition apparently was designed for "show" sales abroad. In contrast, the collected works of Aleichem are being brought out in Russian in an edition of 225,000. No Yiddish theaters

have been re-established despite the continuing success of the
Yiddish concerts.

None of the existing proscriptions against the Jews has been
lifted. They are still not admitted to the Foreign Service school.
They are not accepted in the higher military schools. They
find constant difficulty in getting admitted to universities, especially Moscow University. The admissions policy of the spe-
cialized institutes appears to vary from school to school, but
discrimination is more likely than not.

Khrushchev's party may not discourage Jewish careers but
it does not encourage them. No Jew has risen to high party
rank under Khrushchev. The one Jew in the Presidium, Lazar
M. Kaganovich, has vanished. Most Jews, however, regarded
him as anti-Semitic; and he described himself as a Russian,
not a Jew. No Jew has risen to a post of consequence in
the propaganda apparatus. There are many Jewish writers
on both daily and monthly publications, but none is the editor
of a prominent newspaper. The number of Jews of cabinet rank
is infinitesimal.

In religious matters there is persisting and open discrimination. The Jews have fewer and poorer houses of worship than
other faiths. They are permitted to train few rabbis. They have
fewer printed materials and find it difficult to obtain articles
needed for services of worship. Maintenance of dietary laws is
difficult because it is hard to get the special foods, particularly
for holidays. Kosher slaughter facilities are rare. Two Moscow
restaurants now serve traditional Jewish dishes, but they are
not kosher.

Nor is this all. There have been ugly manifestations of anti-
Semitic spirit by the populace. Many of these outbursts have
occurred in the Ukraine, where Jewish houses of prayer have
been closed in some localities by the authorities and Jewish
cemeteries have been desecrated. Repeatedly in the past year
Ukrainian provincial papers have carried both anti-Jewish

articles and articles which are thinly veiled anti-Semitic prov-
ocations. And in the Moscow suburbs a small Jewish house of
prayer was burned down, apparently by a band of neighborhood toughs.

What does Mr. Khrushchev think about this? Why is it that
his government does not act resolutely to bring anti-Semitism
to an end and forthrightly condemn the outrages of the past?

There are many persons, both in and out of Russia, who believe that fundamentally the trouble is that Mr. Khrushchev
himself shares the anti-Jewish attitudes so common to the
Ukraine where he spent most of his boyhood and youth. Some
Russians insist that Mr. Khrushchev must be cautious because
of the underlying popularity of anti-Semitism in Russia. They
say that the repudiation of the Kremlin doctors' plot was not
popular, that Moscow had been only too ready to believe the
worst of the Jewish doctors.

"Everyone in those days could tell you of a drugstore which
they knew had been padlocked because the authorities discovered the Jewish pharmacist secretly mixing poisons in the
medicines," a friend of mine said. "Everyone had a father or a
brother or a cousin who had died because a Jewish doctor
deliberately bungled an operation or gave a wrong diagnosis."

In all of this, it seemed to me, one could sense the terrible,
terrible need of Russia for a scapegoat, for some one or some
people on whom to pile the blame and the guilt for the horrors
of the Stalin epoch. This, I thought, must be what gave popular
appeal to the anti-Semitic lie. And this was what made it attractive to the government. I remember riding with a taxi
driver on the Sadovaya the April day in 1953 when it had been
announced in the morning papers that the Kremlin doctors'
plot was a fraud and a frame-up.

"Those *svoloch!*" the driver said. "They got away this time.
But their day will come. We will get those yids!"

Perhaps there is something to the theory that the government must move slowly. At the time of the Hungarian uprising, it is said, there was a sudden, frightening rise in anti-Semitism. Once again the Jews were being blamed for Russia's troubles.

It does not seem logical to me, however, that it is fear or considered public policy which motivates Mr. Khrushchev's lack of frankness on the Jewish question. It is not as though he had never spoken about the Jews. He has commented a good many times. But each time his remarks sound muddled and an anti-Jewish bias shines through.

Only last summer he made the curious statement that the day might come when Jews would be permitted freely to leave the country. This seems a most dubious proposition to me. I don't know how many Jews are left in Russia. Mr. Khrushchev puts the figure at 2,000,000, possibly on the basis of the 1959 census. This seems low. Most authorities think the total is closer to 3,000,000. There were 4,500,000 or 5,000,000 Jews in Russia before the German invasion which, of course, struck hardest at the traditional areas of Jewish settlement.

I have not the smallest doubt that if the Soviet government were to permit free emigration tomorrow that 75 to 80 per cent of the Jews would leave the country. That would not have been true two decades ago. But the anti-Semitic policies of Stalin and his successors have taught the Jews of Russia that their government regards them as enemies of the state and their fellow citizens regard them as inferiors.

The truth is that Mr. Khrushchev, just as Stalin, treats the Jews as a special and difficult national security problem. I have never seen a shred of evidence to support the belief that the Jews of Russia constitute any kind of security risk. But I am certain that if there has been any weakening of loyalty to the state on the part of the Jews it has been induced by the corrosive terror of their own government.

I know of a case in which a Jewish family was shipped out to Siberia simply because their ten-year-old daughter inquired

in school where Israel was. That was in Stalin's day. But the
memory of this kind of terror does not easily die.

I do not think that Soviet policy toward Soviet Jews reflects
considerations of foreign policy, that it is linked in some way
with Moscow's effort to curry favor with the Arab states and
to oppose Israel in international affairs. The truth is the Soviet
voted for the establishment of Israel as a state and was one
of the first governments to recognize Israel—and, almost at the
same moment, was preparing anti-Semitic measures at home.

Soviet policy toward Israel might play a role in the refusal
to permit emigration to the Jewish state, but I doubt that too.
The Soviet Union, like the Imperial Russian government, has
never liked its citizens to migrate abroad.

The truth is, as far as I could discover, that the anti-Semitic
policy had gravely damaged the Soviet Union both at home and
abroad. It had spread disillusion and discontent among one of
the most gifted and valuable segments of the Soviet population,
the Jews. It had stimulated dangerous and difficult race feelings
in a nation where such problems were dying out. And beyond
the Russian borders the anti-Semitic measures had riven foreign
Communist parties, particularly those where there had been
many Jewish members. This was true in the United States, in
Canada, in England, and in some measure in almost every
Western country. Moreover, it had presented the opponents
of the Soviet Union with a propaganda weapon of deadly effec-
tiveness. I met a bewildered Jewish Communist from the West
last summer. He had come to the Soviet for the first time. In
his homeland he had undergone many sacrifices for his Communist beliefs but had remained firm. Now, for the first time,
he realized that what he had heard about the anti-Semitic terror
was no nightmare. It was real. And he found, too, that anti-
Semitic prejudice and discrimination in Russia was stronger
than in his home country. He was in despair.

"Of all countries!" he said. "To find anti-Semitism here in

Soviet Russia, the first Communist country! This is what is so terrible. Why have they done it? Why? Why?"

I had no answer for him. I had not been able to find any logical, rational, or coherent answer to this terrible enigma myself. All I knew was that the deadly poison had been injected into the Soviet blood stream by Stalin, and there was no evidence that Khrushchev was yet prepared to cope with the results.

VI

The Soviet Shook-Up Generation

ONE SUMMER EVENING, just as twilight was be-
ginning to fall, I found myself turning into Hunter's Row where
the Council of Ministers Building (now devoted to the State
Planning Commission) faces the Moskva Hotel. This is one
of the busiest parts of Moscow. The intersection was torn up
by construction of a pedestrian underpass. Hunter's Row had
become a dead end for traffic, but pedestrians crowded the
sidewalk, strolling slowly under the trees in a perpetual promenade which is so characteristic of Slavic countries.

I was startled to see a woman approaching me who looked
as though she had stepped out of Hogarth's *The Harlot's Progress*. Her cheeks were chalk-white with powder and burning
with rouged-in fever spots. She wore a tight skirt, nipped at the
knees and flared at the hips in such a way that with each step
her body was thrust forward in a kind of lewd gesture. She
slowed as she approached and, turning her death's-head face to
me asked in a hoarse voice: "*Kak vam nravitza* [How do you
like it]?"

I do not know which shocked me most, the bizarre appearance of this woman or the fact that here in the heart of Moscow,
on the doorstep of the principal government building, I had
been solicited by a Soviet prostitute. Never in all my years in
Russia had such a thing happened to me. True, during wartime
many girls frequented the Metropole Hotel, freely offering

81

themselves in return for meals, drinks, a warm bath, and a bar of soap. For years it had been a well-known custom for girls to telephone foreigners at the hotel, engaging them in conversation and trying to arrange a meeting. But all this had come to an end in the icy days of the cold war, when no young Russian woman would have anything to do with a foreigner, no matter what the temptation. And certainly I had never seen open solicitation on the Moscow streets and did not believe anyone else had, at least not since the early 1930's.

I had heard rumors that prostitutes had appeared in Russia with the general relaxation of internal controls. But somehow I had not quite believed it. I knew that in some of the Black Sea resort cities there had been campaigns by the Young Kommunist newspapers against young women of allegedly easy morals—"amateur prostitutes" was the phrase employed. But the significance of this I did not know.

Faced with the evidence of my own eyes I quickly discovered that the Hogarthian woman whom I had met in front of the Council of Ministers Building was not unique. I found that she and her sisters had several favorite places of promenade. One was the lower reaches of Gorky Street. Another was the square block around the Moskva Hotel. The Metropole Hotel area was a favored location, particularly the vicinity of the Metropole Hotel movie houses (three small movie halls are located in the hotel building). There were also two or three cafés where I saw the girls.

One thing puzzled me. Prostitution faces some unusual barriers in Moscow. Not every girl has a centrally located room to which she can take men. Cheap rooms in the heart of the city are not easy to obtain. But where there is a will there is a way. A row of taxicabs was often parked in deep shadow adjacent to the Moskva Hotel. These cabs, I discovered, were a convenient substitute for the cheap hotel room of Paris or New York. And there were said to be a few rooms available in the rabbit warren of buildings which lies in the old Kitai Gorod section of the city just back of the Metropole Hotel.

Later on, in Leningrad, I discovered that prostitution is not an institution peculiar to Moscow. There are girls walking the streets around the Hotel Astoria, too. But, typically, the Leningrad girls dress stylishly, wearing high heels and Western dresses. They often affect a ponytail hair-do.

The reappearance of this ancient evil in a country which long since boasted that it had abolished bourgeois vice is not, as I found, an isolated phenomenon. It is one of the many symptoms of change which I saw in the Moscow streets—evidences of underlying and festering social illness which had long been concealed by the draconian police measures of the Stalin era. In the Stalin days it was claimed that Russia had one of the lowest crime rates in the world. Problems of delinquency and social malfunctioning had disappeared under the beneficent rays of the socialist sun. Such was the story.

Of course, to one like myself who lived in Russia it was obvious that the truth was far different, that behind the façade of police terror there was a witch's caldron of human antagonisms simmering toward a boil.

Today Russia is reaping the harvest of decades of neglect of social needs. I saw a play by Pogodin called *The Aristocrats*. It was written in 1934 and deals with the first great "corrective" labor project—the building of the White Sea Canal. Thousands of aristocrats of the old regime, prostitutes from the Moscow streets, and common criminals were employed on the canal. The play's theme is the rehabilitation of the former countesses and streetwalkers by the healthy influence of ditchdigging. I saw the play only a few days after I had discovered prostitutes on the Moscow streets. How ironic, I thought, that Pogodin's play should be revived just at a moment when life was so dramatically disproving the moral lesson which Pogodin seeks to draw.

In the weeks just before and just after the opening of the American Exposition in Moscow, the Soviet press began to show unusual interest in the seamy side of American life. From a variety of sources articles were published, dealing with American unemployment, bad American housing conditions, the ills of the American schools, the defects of American medical care, and the deterioration of living conditions in America. In the midst of this campaign I found in *Komsomolskaya Pravda* one day a reprint of excerpts from my study of American adolescent delinquency called *The Shook-Up Generation.* I was more interested a fortnight later to find that two chapters of *The Shook-Up Generation* had been published by the Soviet magazine, *New Times,* as a special supplement. Obviously, the difficulties of America's younger generation was a subject which Soviet editors found most newsworthy in view of the opening of an American exposition dedicated to the more attractive features of American life.

The Shook-Up Generation became quite a favorite with the Soviet press. The Russian translation of the title, *Potrasennye Pokalenye,* even became a headline writers' cliché. It is still being used as a caption over photographs of the latest depravity of the jet set in America.

On reading the excerpts which the Russians published of *The Shook-Up Generation* I made an interesting discovery. In my book I compared the horrible conditions I found in some of our public-housing projects with what I had seen in Moscow. The passage dealing with Moscow had been deleted. And a chapter which dealt with delinquency in Russia and other foreign countries was omitted entirely.

The reason for this seemed clear enough. While the Soviet press sometimes wrote about delinquency in Russia, it was not prepared to face up to the problem objectively and realistically.

To admit that a shook-up generation was arising in Russia was to admit that Soviet society today was plagued with deep social ills. This was the hardest of all admissions for a perfectionist society to make.

The fact is that adolescent gangs have appeared in Moscow on a pattern which closely resembles that found in New York City. They have sprung up around the great new Cheremushki housing projects just as they have around the slum-clearance buildings in Brooklyn and lower Manhattan. Why should this be? The new residents of the great Moscow projects blame the trouble on "rough elements" from such slum areas of Moscow as Maryina Roscha. It seemed obvious to me, however, that the Soviet youngsters had been uprooted and sent footloose into a new and shifting environment just as were their American cousins. And they reacted according to pattern. In one project, for instance, a teen-age gang was engaged in robbing apartments. The members called on a colonel's son to help them in breaking into his father's flat. The boy refused. The adolescents pinioned the boy, took a sledge hammer, and broke both his legs.

In another block of buildings two teen-age girls were raped within a week by a gang. In another part of the city two boys were badly wounded by "Finnish" knives in a gang fight. The Finnish knife is a hunting knife with a seven-inch blade. It figures as prominently in Moscow delinquency as does the switchblade in New York City. I could find no evidence that the Moscow shook-ups had invented the zip gun. The American juveniles, it appeared, still held a slender technological edge over the Russian gangs.

The outbreak of terror in the new apartment houses has not yet won the editorial attention of the Soviet press. In fact, a responsible editor of *Komsomolskaya Pravda* who himself is publishing a book on American delinquency assured me that no such thing existed. He and his family live in one of the Cheremushki buildings and he said he had never heard of any of the incidents I described.

However, another resident of the area told me that parents with children were badly upset by the hooliganism. They have formed their own volunteer groups which go out on the streets and into the construction areas which are a favorite hangout for the young gangsters. They are working with them in much the same manner as the street workers of the New York City Youth Board.

The activity of these private citizens is not to be confused with what are called *druzhina*. The druzhina are a kind of voluntary or auxiliary police force organized by the Young Communists. They patrol the streets wearing red arm bands and are supposed to cope with any kind of misconduct wherever it may be found. They resemble the Bands of Hope which used to fight the evils of drink in the sawdust era of American saloons.

The druzhina are said to concentrate particularly on young people who violate social norms of conduct. But, so far as I could learn, they pay little attention to adolescent gang activity. They spend their time making forays into cafés and restaurants where they sometimes catch young people drinking too much. They exhort the drinkers and occasionally drag them off to the police. The police are not greatly impressed by the druzhina and usually take the victims to the official sobering-up stations to sleep it off, releasing them in the morning. Sometimes, however, the druzhina become involved in serious affrays. A Young Communist was stabbed to death in Leningrad not many months ago by a young hooligan. The case received tremendous newspaper attention and was utilized by the Communist propagandists to build up public hatred against youthful offenders in much the same way as noisy "night stick" campaigns are launched by publicity-hungry politicians whenever some particularly shameful adolescent outbreak occurs on the streets of New York.

Drink, however, is the chief target of the Khrushchev regime's moral indignation. In Moscow the sidewalk vodka stands have been closed. So have the *koklayl khals* and the beer parlors. Restaurants are strictly forbidden to serve more than one hundred grams of vodka to a customer. This is known as the "government ration." Two drinking men will sometimes seek a restaurant table at which two nondrinkers are sitting and, with the permission of the teetotalers, will order four rounds of drinks, thus acquiring double the official potion. Brandy and wine are more expensive than vodka and are not rationed. The price is supposed to keep the customer from buying enough to get himself drunk. Liquor stores, however, will freely sell any quantity of drink by the bottle.

Whether these measures cut down alcoholic consumption is questionable. One cynical Russian believes they increase drinking.

"No one has time to go from one restaurant to another for more than one drink," he said. "There are no beer halls any more and no one can afford to drink wine, even if he likes it. So what happens? Instead of drinking one hundred grams or maybe two hundred grams a man goes to a store and buys a five-hundred-gram bottle. He goes around the corner and polishes it off. There is more drinking in Moscow than ever before."

This may be an exaggeration. But a walk through a working-class area of Moscow one evening showed me that the druzhina had made little impact on drinking in that quarter. Even on Gorky Street it was difficult to walk more than a block or so after 10 P.M. without encountering at least one man more than the worse for drink.

Outside of Moscow, regulations on the sale of vodka seemed to be observed in hit-or-miss fashion. In one village I found a restaurant living up to the "government ration." In the next they seemed never to have heard of it. In Siberia vodka continued to be the same staff of life it always had been.

Almost every day I found another change in the street life

of Moscow. Tourists were often approached by shifty young
men who frequented the shadows of the plane trees on Gorky
Street, the area around the Lenin-Stalin Mausoleum, the vicinity
of the GUM department store, and some of the summer cafés.
Sometimes the young men wore pegtop trousers, sideburns,
slim-shouldered jackets. Sometimes they were dressed with conservative care. They looked almost like young Scandinavians
or Englishmen. Sometimes they wore an existentialist or beat-
type fringe beard. Russians, I learned, called them *biznismen*.

I was approached one evening as I was walking to the Central
Telegraph Office.

"Excuse me," said a biznisman in English. "Are you a tourist?"

I said, "No." That brought the conversation to an end. But
two or three minutes later another came up. This time I gave
an equivocal answer and promptly was asked if I would like to
buy some rubles. The black-market men, it appeared, did not
want to deal with diplomats or other permanent residents of
Moscow. But they would give the tourist twenty to one as
compared to the tourist rate of ten to one. (The official rate is
four to one.) If the tourist bargained, he could get thirty or
forty—sometimes even fifty. If the tourist was not interested in
rubles he was offered an "ancient ikon, three hundred years
old." Sometimes the ikon would be genuine and a remarkable
bargain; but usually it turned out to be a cheap modern production.

Some of the biznismen spent the off-season traveling in
Siberia and the more remote Russian provinces. They broke
into churches, pilfered the ikons, and made their getaway.
This has become a fairly large-scale business in the last two
or three years. Soviet law forbids the export of ancient objects
of art, and not a few tourists found their ikons confiscated when
they attempted to take them through customs on their way out
of Russia.

The biznismen also dealt in articles of Western clothing,

particularly sport shirts. There are almost as many Hollywood sport shirts in Moscow as in California. They buy neckties, sport shoes, sport coats, sweaters, jazz records, mechanical pens, lipsticks, cosmetics, nylons, and paperback books, especially mystery stories. A whodunit brings fifty rubles, a sport shirt three hundred. There is not much demand for American cigarettes. Russians are now smoking their own filter-tip brands with cellophane packages which precisely imitate the latest Madison Avenue creations.

What do the biznesmen do with the sport shirts, the records, and the dollars which they buy in such quantity?

There is an active market among young people for almost any Western article. It is the fad in Russia. If it's Western, it's fashionable. The dollars are another matter. Many of them are sold to the thousands of Russians who are now permitted to travel in Western Europe and the United States each year. These Russians ordinarily are allowed to buy only $40 in currency from the State Bank for their Western travels. That does not go very far at Macy's or even in London or Paris. Russians planning to go abroad buy dollars from the speculators at a hundred to one. So do many peasants who like to hoard dollars. There are still a good many blanket-size American banknotes circulating among Russians.

There may have been, I suspect, another outlet for the currency. The black-market activity was going on under the noses of the police. The speculators made little attempt to hide themselves. No plain-clothes man could walk the Moscow streets a day without seeing what was afoot. The conclusion seemed inescapable that the currency dealing had police connivance. Moreover, while speculators occasionally were arrested they quickly appeared again on the streets. My conclusion was that the police themselves had a hand in the activity. Either they were profiting through graft or they were utilizing the speculators as a source of foreign currency for their own purposes.

Possibly, I thought, the secret police have been put on short
dollar rations since the fall of Beria.

The police seemed equally indifferent to other forms of street
speculation. Currency trading made its appearance at the time
of the Moscow Youth Festival in 1957 and has been flourishing
ever since. There is also more private sale and barter than there
ever used to be. The police know of this but they do not interfere. In the streets and alleys back of GUM you could always
find scarce articles for sale. Operators queued up every morning
to get into GUM as soon as the doors were opened. They had
confederates on the GUM staff who tipped them on what scarce
items would be on sale. They rushed straight to the appropriate
counters, made their purchases, and were out of the store almost
before the ordinary customers had made their entrance. Then,
in the back streets they offered their prizes at a 50 to 100 per
cent mark-up.

I knew a carpetbagger who operated in Theater Square in
the old days. He was a salesman of *chorty,* little blown-glass
devils that squirted water in a rather rude way. This man used
to make a hasty appearance in the Square, sell a bag of water
devils at ten rubles apiece, and vanish, keeping a close watch
out for any militiaman who might spot him. He would return a
few weeks later and sell another bagful. Now I found him in
Theater Square almost every day. The little glass devils, produced on state time with state materials at some state factory
near Moscow, had doubled in size but their price had been cut
to five rubles. Obviously production was overfulfilling the norm.
The operator, I reckoned, must be selling fifty times as many
chorty as five years ago.

I did not think that all of these symptoms were to be at-
tributed simply to the negligence or connivance of the police.
They stemmed directly from the general relaxation of controls
inside Russia in the past five years.

It did not seem to me that greater freedom inevitably brought about prostitution, black-marketing, adolescent gangsterism, and currency speculation. The ills, I thought, were certainly not caused by freedom. They arose because Russia no longer was sweeping her problems under the carpet. She was no longer shipping the victims and debris of society out to Siberia. I had been to Siberia and I well knew that if adolescent delinquents were not in the old days to be seen quite so often on the streets of Moscow it was because they had been shipped by the thousand to Siberia.

The relaxation of controls is a tricky business. It produces aberrent reactions. People suddenly want to try out things they never would have thought of before. Take the hula hoop, for example. By the time I reached Moscow the hula hoop was almost forgotten in New York. But it was just arriving in Moscow, smuggled in by way of Poland. Moscow's young people had heard of the hula hoop. They knew what the hoops were because they were used by physical culture societies. But they didn't quite know what people in the West did with them. So they drew the curtains, turned on tape-recorded jazz from the Voice of America, and, couple by couple, two to a hoop, began to experiment. The results would have shocked a New York cop.

One young American was approached by a Russian friend who got him off in a corner and said in a whisper: "Confidentially, tell me. What do Americans do in a hula hoop?"

Another young American visiting Moscow for the first time said, in shocked tones, after meeting some teen-age Russians: "I thought that I would get away from rock 'n' roll in Moscow. But it is just the reverse. These people seem to be attracted to all the worst aspects of American life."

There was, I felt, some truth in this observation. Even out in Siberia you could not escape the sound of rock 'n' roll. Russian students at the universities did not care for Elvis Presley. But they were crazy about rock 'n' roll.

There are not many beatniks among Russian youngsters. But

there will be. This can safely be predicted. As rapidly as they become acquainted with the trend (and this kind of thing seeps in from Germany, Poland, and Hungary) Russian youth will take it up. I saw signs of the beat appearing in a newer generation of what used to be called the *stilyagi* or stylish ones. The stilyagi were famous for Tarzan-style hair bobs, zoot suits with gold watch chains, knee-length jackets, and odd shoes. Now such garb has almost disappeared; but the first fringe beards and sloppy beatnik clothing were showing up. Such names as Jack Kerouac and Allen Ginsberg were known to a few of the *cognoscenti.* But it seemed doubtful if their works would ever be popular either in the original or in translation. I lent a copy of Kerouac's *On the Road* to a member of the Moscow intelligentsia as an experiment. He passed it among his English-speaking friends. Finally, he reported to me with a laugh: "They all want to read it. They keep it a few days and then return it, saying it is very interesting. But when I try to get their opinion of Kerouac they become vague—or, sometimes, admit that they don't quite understand him."

Youngsters at the American Exhibition in Moscow asked to see the comic-book exhibit. They were surprised to learn there wasn't any. They also wanted to "see your books on love and sex, the ones with pictures." They were surprised not to find these either. They complained that "everywhere in the world you can hear American jazz—why not at your exhibition?"

It seemed to me that there was a restlessness about Soviet youngsters that I had not seen before. Of course, it had not affected them all. I ran into many sturdy and dull defenders of the Young Communist faith, but what was new was to find so much dissent in words and conduct—dissent which was reckless of the consequences. Obviously, the youngsters expected no consequences.

This spirit of independence and even of defiance of authority did not exist during Stalin's day, nor for a long time thereafter.

Now a whole generation of youngsters was growing up which did not remember the terror. Some Soviet youngsters challenged an American in one of the sidewalk seminars about his reference to the excesses of the Stalin days. The American defended himself vigorously, and eventually the young Russians went away still unsatisfied.

An older Russian who had been standing by without saying anything came up to the American and said: "You were right to remind them of what happened. Don't give an inch. They do not know what it was like in the old days."

This was true. The young people did not know what it was like to live under Stalin's terror. If you argued with them, they denied that such things ever happened. I knew far more than they did about what life had been like before 1953. Yet, they and their conduct were a testimonial to the basic changes which had flowed from Stalin's death.

The new regime had changed the basis of its power. It had relaxed the use of the police as the primary social force. But it had never really spelled out this change in black and white. And it seemed to me that the same kind of equivocation was to be found in the handling of the social problems which the overthrow of the terror system had presented. When I talked to some of the more responsible officials about these questions they rambled off into wordy disquisitions about the new social approach to such problems—the use of the druzhina and the so-called comradely courts. The comradely courts were bodies of citizens who were supposed to sit in judgment over questions like what to do with a workingman who shows up drunk on the job or a neighbor who commits a public nuisance.

These approaches were described to me as the first stages of the "withering away" of the state which had long been predicted by Marx as the final result of Communism. The new citizens bodies were replacing the formal state apparatus, the police, and the law courts. Lenin's authority was cited for this approach. I found a great many articles about the new methods in the Soviet papers. The subject was a favorite one with *Komsomolskaya Pravda*. And there was much talk, too, of a move to turn over to the Trade Unions the administration of social security and also of a voluntary crusade of workers, launched by a certain Valentina I. Gaganova, who volunteered to help backward workers in a textile plant where she was employed to raise their production efficiency. The crusade sounded to me not much different from the overpublicized and long-since forgotten Stakhonovite drive of the 1930's.

None of these devices seemed to get very close to the real problem. The druzhina hardly had made a scratch on the drinking issue. In a good many nights of walking around Moscow I never laid eyes on a single patrol of the arm-banded comrades. But I saw plenty of drunks. And the comradely courts were much more active on the newspaper pages than in real life.

It was going to take something a good deal more fundamental and realistic, it seemed to me, if Russia was actually going to cope with her rising shook-up generation.

VII

The Angels of Reconciliation

THE APPEARANCE of *Dr. Zhivago* for me was an event long-heralded, like that of a comet whose coming has been foretold for years. I had known of the novel since 1954, had read a selection of the Zhivago poems in the literary journal *Znamya,* and had myself written the first dispatch about the forthcoming work before I left the Soviet Union.

I supposed then, as did everyone in Moscow's literary circles, that *Zhivago* would be published in Russia. Not until the autumn of 1956 did it become apparent that the magazine *Novy Mir* and the State Publishing House had been compelled to reject the manuscript.

The long wait, the beauty of the poems, the controversy over the novel, the genius of the author, all of this heightened my anticipation, so that when, at long last, I finally held the book in my hands I could hardly bear to open it. My reluctance was like that of a child who refuses to look at the Christmas tree for fear he will be disappointed. When, almost by sheer force, I started to read the novel I was swept up by an emotional and literary power more sweeping than any I could remember. I read for hours and hours, not halting until near daylight. I awakened after a brief sleep and finished the book. Then I started at the beginning and read all the way through again, something I had not done since boyhood.

There was nothing in the post-Stalin world more interesting

to me than the struggle of Russia's writers to free themselves from the shackles of Communist didacticism. Here was an area in which the liberalizing tendencies of the Khrushchev government might have greater significance than any other. For it is the writers, and particularly Russian writers, who cut closest to the soul of mankind's problems. Here is where questions of morals and principles and the goal of life itself is the central issue.

There was no one in Russia with whom I would have liked better to discuss these issues than Pasternak. But too many journalists had already beaten a path to his door. I was determined to go to Peredelkino but only as a humble worshiper, paying tribute to a great man.

Easter Sunday struck me as an appropriate day for such a journey because it is the mystery of the resurrection which is central to Pasternak's philosophy, just as it is the imagery of the Orthodox ceremony which colors and transfuses so much of his poetry.

During my years in Russia I had usually gone to the great Troitsa monastery at Zagorsk for the Easter service. Nowhere in the world had I felt the symbiosis of Christian ritual and Christian belief so powerfully and so richly as in the ancient monastery whose thick walls have provided a reliable citadel for the faith for hundreds of years. It would be good, I thought, to visit the shrine of the church before going to see the man whose writing had given a contemporaneity and urgency to Christian belief as profound as Tolstoy's.

Once again on Easter eve I found myself riding out from Moscow on the highway to Zagorsk, past the village churches, each with its long queue of women bringing their Easter *kulich* and *paskha* and their brightly colored Easter eggs to be blessed. The priests had set up great tables outside the little churches. The housewives placed their white-wrapped parcels on the tables and the priest sprinkled them with holy water. The

crowds were big and the village churches looked fat and prosperous. Some had acquired new paint since I last saw them.

The great monastery churches, as always, were filled with
worshipers. I stood for hours in the cathedral amid the believers,
with their slender candles illumining rapt and reverent faces,
listening to the liturgy. Finally came the solemn moment of
midnight, the procession of the ikons, the huge tapers, the
swinging censers, the heavy incense. The chanting priests
forced their way through the mass of believers and outside the
cathedral, making the traditional circle around the church, then
returning to lift the great iron knocker on the cathedral door
as the chimes rang out that most joyous of cries: *"Kristos
Voskres, Kristos Voskres"* (Christ is Arisen. Christ is Arisen.)
And the response of the congregation: *"Voistinu . . . Voistinu
Voskres"* (Truly . . . Truly Arisen).

Then back through the black night the limousine whirled
to Moscow, past little churches where the chanting still went
on, past cottages with lighted windows where Easter feasts were
being eaten, past a sulky militiaman who cried to the chauffeur:
"Drive more quietly." And the chauffeur's angry retort: "I am
driving quietly." Back to a sleeping Moscow; but here, too,
yellow windowpanes dotted the great apartment houses. Easter
feasts were being eaten in Moscow as well as in the peasant
villages.

There was, I thought, as the car sped through the chill of
the night, an eternalness about the Russian Easter which was
fitting to the event. Russian Easter went on and on and on.
Nothing stopped it. Not Revolution. Not Communists. Not war.
I remembered the first Russian Easter I had known—in Odessa
in wartime. A black night. A military curfew. (Odessa had been
retaken only three days earlier from the Germans.) Cavalry
patrols clattering through the empty streets. But we braved the
curfew to see if Easter was being celebrated. It was. The church
was filled with believers who disregarded the curfew at the risk

of being shot. There were Red Army men and Red Army girls in the little church. Believers like the rest.

The belief of the people in Russia was like the people themselves. It flowed like a great river that might be turned aside or dammed but relentlessly moved forward, eventually carrying all obstacles before it.

This was the eternity of Russia, the soul of Russia, the quality of the nation which placed its own Russian imprint upon every institution, philosophy, and belief that fell within its ken. This was what made the Orthodox church in Russia something different from the Christian church of any other nation. This was what had impressed upon the theoretical formulations of Marx a Russian stamp which slowly, year by year, changed the doctrine almost beyond recognition. And this was the Russia which had produced, in its years of greatest repression, Pasternak—a voice so Russian, so indigenous to this soil, this people, this land, that no one could conceive of such a mind or such a person arising anywhere but in Russia.

Easter Sunday was a day half-clouds, half-sunshine. It matched my feelings. I was almost ready to give over the pilgrimage. Something might go wrong. Recently, I had heard, the police had turned several people back who had tried to visit Pasternak. Perhaps he was not even there. Perhaps it would be an embarrassment to him, or even a danger. And what business had I in going to see him? To take him a little gift and thank him and shake his hand. Wasn't I being presumptuous? After all, he was not an old friend. Peredelkino might be a shrine to me, but the Soviet government took a different view. I was on the verge of abandoning the trip, but somehow I managed to conquer my irresolution. I was not going alone. I was going with another worshiper of Pasternak's, a young woman who, like myself, wanted to join in a small tribute to a great man. It would not be right, I told myself, to disappoint her. With inner trepidations we started out.

The ride to Peredelkino takes a little more than twenty minutes by suburban train. The line runs almost due west from Moscow, past the new skyscraper of Moscow State University, the apartment houses that marched across the flat suburban countryside, through a few factory settlements and then into a pleasant country of little pine forests and dacha colonies. Sitting across the aisle in the railroad car was a pleasant-faced middle-aged woman, wearing a gray topcoat with a small gold pin and a neat black hat. She looked to me like a writer, a writer's wife or, possibly, a scientist. Certainly, she was a member of the intelligentsia, and suddenly I felt confident that she, too, was going to Peredelkino. I decided to ask her the directions to Pasternak's dacha, for I was haunted by a feeling that inquiries in the village would bring down the police.

"Pasternak?" she said with a twinkle in her eye. "Of course. You just come along with me. I'm going next door to Fedin's."

Peredelkino has been a writers' colony for thirty years or more. It was once a village belonging to a wealthy nobleman. In the late 1920's or early 1930's it became a settlement for writers. Pasternak has lived there for many years. So has Konstantin Fedin, a distinguished Russian writer, and many, many others.

For a time our path led beside the railroad tracks and then along a village road. Many people were abroad in the spring air. There was a beautiful little Orthodox church with sky-blue domes set back in the pines and a cemetery where people were busy raking their plots, setting out new shrubs and flowers, painting the iron fences, and repairing the ravages of winter. Close by the road was a fresh-dug grave, the earth thrown up in a great mound, wreaths and flowers at hand, and people gathering to lower the coffin to its last resting place.

The woman who was guiding us lagged behind, talking to a friend. Suddenly I felt a cold chill. Beside a small bridge across a little stream I saw a tan Pobeda with a whip aerial parked beside the road and a man lounging in the driver's seat. The machine had the telltale appearance of a tail car. I cast my eye about and noticed a man sauntering slowly about a hundred feet ahead, hands clasped behind him. At intervals he stole a quick glance behind. So, I thought. So. This is the way the pilgrimage to Pasternak is going to end.

In desperation I turned back to the woman who was showing the way. I saw that she was moving off toward a great open field.

"Oh," she said. "There's a shorter path. Just here. Cut across the field. It will bring you straight to Pasternak's, right to his gate."

It was a long walk across the field. I was fearful that when we reached the gate the plain-clothes man would be there before us. But, fortunately, he had been confused by the backtracking and the short cut which had led us out of his sight. I saw him as we entered Pasternak's gate but he was a good two hundred yards away, helpless to intervene—if, indeed, that had been his intention.

We walked up a long driveway, past two college boys who were starting a motorbike, and came up to the rambling old dacha with its brown-stained walls, comfortable windows, and greenish roof—a house that had grown into the background of pines and birches until it was as Russian as its owner. A young woman emerged from the house and watched us carefully as we walked up to the side porch. We said we hoped to see Mr. Pasternak for a moment. There was a long wait while she went inside. A yellow dog emerged from an outbuilding and hobbled toward us. Something was wrong with its hindquarters. The sun shone thinly. The day had not grown warmer. The dog brought a sick and fetid odor to the porch steps where we stood.

At that moment Pasternak appeared. He was both smaller and bigger than I had expected and he was smiling with a sadness which seemed always to have been in his eyes. He took our hands in his and began to make terrible apologies because he could not receive us. Things are going to be better, he said. But we must be very careful now. It is the government's wish. He was so sorry. He had guests inside. It was a holiday. He was so deeply in our debt. Later. Later, he would repay the debt. Forgive him. But for now one must be quiet and content. The warmth flowed from his heart into his hands as he spoke and his eyes became liquid and brown. The dog whimpered as it hobbled in circles more and more narrow. The odor grew stronger. For a moment Pasternak stood there holding our hands silently, then released them slowly, reluctantly, and stood with his face in a golden smile. He thanked us again and again. We tried to say a word, but it was hardly possible to speak; and suddenly we found ourselves retreating down the path toward the gate and the high wooden fence. Pasternak remained on the steps watching us. Then, with a little half gesture of his arm, he turned and entered the house.

We walked back across the field. A family came straggling along, a man, a little drunk, his wife, looking at him good-naturedly and sometimes putting an arm around him. Another family. The father carrying a small boy on his shoulders, singing as they walked along. Down the road in front of an un-painted wooden house with carved fretwork shutters there were three girls dancing a village dance. A boy played the *bayan.* A red-cheeked girl pulled an older woman to her feet, and they whirled about on the hard-packed earth, skirts flying. The driver of the tan Pobeda was slumped down in his seat, fast asleep. In the cemetery the grave had been filled. Men were heaping up the mound and making it neat. People stood silently as they worked. This was Russia. Russian people. One more Russian Easter was nearing its end.

At the station a handsome middle-aged man, wearing a good

but rumpled suit, approached us. He carried a red-paper rose
with green-paper leaves in one hand. His face was covered with
gray stubble.

"Excuse me," he said, in an actor's melodious voice. "This
has been a wonderful holiday. A wonderful holiday. But now I
am without money and, as you can see, I need a shave very
badly. Can you kind people give me a ruble?"

I handed him one. He leaned forward with a prince's gesture
and kissed the hand of my companion. At that moment the
train thundered up to the platform.

Rain was splattering down when we arrived back in Moscow.
At first it looked as though it would be difficult to find a taxi.
But, fortunately, a fat German who said he was a stamp dealer
offered us a ride. He came to Moscow every few months, he
said. Moscow was getting to be quite an important market in
the world of philately.

I did not see Pasternak again during my stay in Moscow. I
made no attempt to see him, because I quickly found that an
effort was being made to liquidate the incredible stupidities of
the Pasternak affair; and in this delicate situation it was better
to stay away from Peredelkino and see if the Russians would not
be able to work the matter out.

The truth, as I discovered, was that Nikita Khrushchev was
taking a personal hand in trying to put matters in order. And,
as I also found, the whole matter was much more complex,
more sinister and, in a sense, dangerous, than most people in
the West had supposed.

Behind the outrageous attack on Pasternak, or so many
persons in Moscow believed, lay a deliberate attempt to turn
the ideological clock back to Stalin. It was, in fact, a plot in
which many people were concerned. Some of them were literary
and literary-political figures. But they had support in higher
quarters—in the Central Committee of the Communist Party
and, almost certainly, within the Presidium itself. Had the

effort succeeded, it was quite possible that it would not have halted merely with the reversion to an old Stalinist doctrine in literature. It very well might have gone forward toward Stalinist doctrines in other fields as well.

But the effort did not succeed; and it did not succeed because Khrushchev got wind of what was up and scotched the conspiracy.

The intrigue had its origin long before the award of the Nobel prize brought the Pasternak case to a crisis. The new literary line had been unveiled in a novel called *The Brothers Yershov,* by Valentin Kochetov, published serially in June and July of 1958. It was designed to draw a distinction between the workers and the intelligentsia. The book set forth the principle that only the workers were reliable defenders of the Revolution. It attacked, either in open or veiled form, practically every literary break with the old Stalinist line and charged that the Soviet intellectuals could not be relied upon to support the Party in time of stress—such as the Hungarian revolution.

The philosophy of *The Brothers Yershov* was the springboard from which the attack on Pasternak was launched, and the men who were the leaders of the attack were the men who had formulated the Yershov doctrine. The Yershov book was a novel only in the most formal sense of the word. Actually, it was a political tract.

Coincident with the assault on Pasternak, Kochetov was named to the editorship of the *Literaturnaya Gazeta,* chief organ of the Writers Union. The denunciation of Mr. Pasternak as a "pig," a "lousy sheep," a "slanderous so-called novelist," and an "internal *émigré*" was carried out by a man named Vladimir Semichastny, then head of the Young Communist League. His demand for the expulsion of Pasternak from the Soviet Union was made at an open mass meeting with Khrushchev sitting on the platform.

The cabal which supported this line was powerful. Among

the literary backers of Kochetov was Alexei Surkov, the secretary of the Writers Union; Anatoly Sofronov, a well-known playwright; the editors of several prominent literary journals; and most of the *aparatchiki*, or bureaucrats, of the Union of Soviet Writers and its newly organized affiliate, the Union of Writers of the Russian Republic. Another supporter, it was said, was the Minister of Culture N. A. Mikhailov. Many believed that the man behind the whole thing was Mikhail A. Suslov, the surviving Stalinist ideologue of the Presidium.

Had the conspiracy achieved its initial objective, Pasternak would have been driven from the Soviet Union. It might well have been victorious. But Pasternak courageously stood his ground. He refused to go abroad on any pretext and declared that he could live only on Russian soil. Exile, he said, would be the equivalent of death.

There was no doubt in the minds of people in Moscow that the cabal had hoped to expel Pasternak from Russia. But Khrushchev refused. It may have been at this point that Khrushchev began to wonder whether there was not more to the affair than appeared on the surface and whether, in actuality, the whole scandal, with its disastrous effects on Soviet prestige abroad, its enormously unfavorable propaganda implications, could not have been avoided. He had not read *Dr. Zhivago* and had relied upon the opinions of the propaganda apparatus. He decided to have his son-in-law, Alexei Adzhubei, read *Dr. Zhivago* and give him an independent judgment. Adzhubei read the book. He reported to his father-in-law that the whole hullabaloo had been unnecessary. *Zhivago*, he said, could have been published in the Soviet Union with the deletion of, perhaps, three hundred words. It was not a book which would bring cheers to good Party liners; its view of the Bolshevik Revolution was negative; but, after all, this was not presented as history but as the viewpoint of a particular character.

Khrushchev hit the ceiling. It was just as he suspected. Once more a literary-political cabal was engaged in an intrigue which had only brought discredit to the Soviet Union. He took steps to bring the affair to an end and, insofar as he had the power, to alleviate the consequences.

A Congress of the Union of Soviet Writers had been scheduled for December, 1958. The conspirators had planned to seal their victory at this meeting. The Congress was now postponed., An armistice was clamped on all parties. Denunciation of Pasternak was halted. The dust was allowed to settle. Then, in May, the Congress was permitted to meet. Instead of harsh Stalinism, a surprisingly liberal note was struck. Adzhubei set the tone with an article in *Pravda* before the Congress opened. But it was Khrushchev who laid down the new line. The essence of it was: No more tearing each other apart. No more plots. No more feuds. Writers were to devote themselves to writing. Reasonable latitude would be allowed to all. Past sins would be forgiven but not forgotten. Let the angels of reconciliation descend upon the battlefield and bind up the wounds.

Quietly, the principals in the attack on Pasternak were dropped overboard. First to go was Semichastny. He was removed from his post in the Komsomol and sent out to the provinces for more seasoning. Kochetov was removed as editor of *Literaturnaya Gazeta*. A long-heralded dramatic version of *The Brothers Yershov* was quietly produced in an obscure theater, but it had been turned into a kind of Russian soap opera with all its political venom extracted. Surkov was replaced as first secretary of the Writers Union by Fedin, Pasternak's next-door neighbor.

Fedin and Pasternak are friends. They respect each other. Fedin had not joined in the denunciation of Pasternak, although he did sign the letter rejecting *Zhivago* for publication. The fact was that no major Soviet writer had joined the denunciation. But in the tumult and the shouting this had been overlooked.

The respected writers of Russia stood beside their comrade. Not that they all agreed with him. Many of them did not like *Zhivago*. Some had never liked Pasternak or his work. But they valued him as a Russian genius.

The way was now cleared for Pasternak to be returned to membership in the Writers Union. This, too, was expected to occur quietly, possibly even without public note.

It was this delicate and complicated arrangement to which Pasternak alluded during my brief visit with him, and it was knowledge of this which kept me from attempting to visit the writer again or to speak with him as a journalist.

But, while the formula seemed to provide for the liquidation of the Pasternak affair, and while a good many persons in Moscow would not be surprised to see the ultimate publication of *Zhivago* in Russia (with minor deletions), it by no means cleared the literary scene of problems.

There was, for example, the Sholokhov problem. Mikhail Sholokhov is the most brilliant literary figure of the Soviet era. His *And Quiet Flows the Don* and *The Virgin Soil Upturned* are known wherever the printed word is known. But it has been twenty years since Sholokhov has published a major literary work. He has spent most of his time down in the Don country, where he was born and where his novels are laid.

For years Sholokhov periodically reported that he had work in progress. But so long as Stalin was alive none of these projects reached completion. Indeed, there were those who thought this was not entirely accidental. No writer in Russia had a higher standing with Stalin. There were those who suggested that the canny Don Cossack knew very well that a new novel might endanger his position and that, therefore, he was very careful never to finish one.

Be that as it may, with Stalin's death Sholokhov's productivity suddenly increased. He had, it turned out, not one but two novels under way. One was a sequel to *The Virgin Soil Up-*

turned. The other was a novel about World War II.

By the summer of 1958 the sequel to *The Virgin Soil Upturned* had been completed. The war novel was virtually finished. Sholokhov turned over the *Virgin Soil* manuscript to the State Publishing House. But horror of horrors! The novel had a pessimistic ending! It deals with a courageous Communist Party worker who is assigned to head a Collective Farm in the troubled days of the early 1930's. He combats intrigue, opposition, plots. His personal life is complicated and troubled. But he finally overcomes his difficulties and the sailing appears clear. Then, in the purges of the '30's, he is arrested and imprisoned. He commits suicide in prison.

Mr. Sholokhov is a fiery man. The Party liners were not eager for a row with him at the very moment when the Pasternak affair was at its height. Nevertheless, the ending was completely unsuitable for a good Communist novel. It violated the first principles of Socialist realism which require Communist Good always to triumph over Bourgeois Evil. The only kind of tragedy which is permitted is the "optimistic tragedy" in which a sacrifice is shown not to have been in vain.

The first approach to Mr. Sholokhov was unsuccessful. He was in an angry mood. He had never been fond of Pasternak, and the news that he had been given the Nobel prize (especially after the judges had contemplated sharing it between Pasternak and Sholokhov) did not make him feel more benign. He intimated to the Party men that if they didn't like his novel, perhaps he, too, might be able to find a foreign publisher.

This hint shook the Party men. A Sholokhov affair on top of a Pasternak affair would be too much. They then proposed that he leave the suicide as it was but carry the story on to some more optimistic situation. To this Sholokhov replied that he planned a third volume of *The Virgin Soil* which would, indeed, end on an upbeat. But he showed no more eagerness to change the end of volume two.

It was decided to see whether a little honey would put the writer in a better mood. He was given a grand tour of Western Europe and returned to Moscow on the eve of the Writers Congress. It was assumed he would speak there in support of the new line of reconciliation. He did not. Instead, he went back to the Don country, there to stay until Khrushchev suddenly appeared in Veshenskaya just before his trip to the United States and invited Sholokhov to accompany him.

Sholokhov was almost the forgotten guest during the Khrushchev expedition. He did comment a couple of times that the reports of difficulties over his novel were "imaginary." He said he would have to hurry and finish the book before someone else started to collect royalties on their version of it. Since his book had been completed a year previously, it sounded to me as though, in the end, he had agreed to make some changes. One report had it that he was sending his hero to Siberian exile instead of permitting him to put a pistol to his head.

On the other hand, Sholokhov had kept Stalin waiting twenty years for a new book. Perhaps he would keep Khrushchev waiting too.

Independence, stubbornness, a willingness to stand alone, individuality of thought and concept—both Pasternak and Sholokhov shared these qualities. Nor were they the only Soviet writers who drew their ideals from high principles. There was a whole school, I knew, of young writers, young poets, novelists, and short story writers whose values had nothing to do with the shabby cant of socialist realism. It was not easy for them. The fight with the bullies of the Communist Agitprop was endless. They had taken lickings. They went two steps forward, one step back. But what was important was not that they sometimes were denounced but that they went on writing.

And there were others among the older writers as well. None, I thought, had charted a course more courageous since the death of Stalin than Ilya Ehrenburg. Ehrenburg is a complex man. He is an artist. Perhaps a genius. He is also an evil-tongued man. A verbal sadist. His relationship with Stalin I had never understood. He seemed to enjoy Stalin's fullest confidence and he seemed to reciprocate it. During World War II he preached blood hatred of the Germans, hatred so violent, so specific, so savage that in the darkest hours of the Red Army's trial Ehrenburg's vitriol was credited with giving the troops the anger and violence that enabled them to withstand trials beyond human endurance.

It may have been this which saved Ehrenburg's life during Stalin's anti-Semitic orgy of 1948-53. It may have been Ehrenburg's audacity, for he was a man who invited Jove to strike. It may have been his outspoken anti-Jewish remarks. With the exception of the late Rabbi Shliffer, Ehrenburg was the only member of the Jewish Anti-Fascist Committee (so far as I know) who was not arrested in that period. He is almost the only survivor of the committee. Why did he survive? Did he attempt to halt the outrages through his influence with Stalin?

I do not know. My impression is that he did not, and I have often wondered how he can live with himself today. Perhaps it is in these complex and hidden circumstances that the answer lies to the remarkable works which he has written in the years since Stalin's death. Most Westerners know only his novel *The Thaw,* which gave the initial post-Stalin epoch its title. But this really is the least of his contributions. He has written what constitutes a testament to the young writers of Russia, a creed of artistic independence and freedom which is universal and eloquent.

In his essays Ehrenburg has spoken his mind with independence which disregards the clichés of the Communist world. The very subjects of his study—modern French painting; the poetry of the brilliant, stricken poetess, Maria Tsvetayeva, who hanged herself after returning to her homeland from White Russian exile in Paris on the eve of World War II; the right of some-

times dissident young poets to their opinions; the "lessons" of
Stendhal; and "on rereading" Chekhov—suggested the boldness
of his thinking.

In these essays Ehrenburg says that a Russian writer must
first of all believe in Russia and have the courage and the willingness to speak frankly about Russia, about the unpleasant
things like race hatred, anti-Semitism, bureaucracy, and in-
justice, as well as about the good things. He must turn his back
on "macaroni" patriotism and realize that in art as in science
there are no national frontiers. And he must not be a spectator.
He must participate in life, and out of this reality fashion his
philosophy and his work.

Ehrenburg's views are not popular in official circles. Sometimes there are long delays before his articles are published. IIis
collection of essays was held up a year by the publishers and
came out only after Khrushchev had proclaimed the new policy
of reconciliation.

I was told that neither Ehrenburg nor Pasternak has a wide
following among the younger Soviet writers. That the Granins,
Dudintsevs, Evtushenkos, Yashins, and Rozhdestvenkis have
their eyes fixed on other horizons, that they are more influenced,
for example, by the young Polish experimenters, by the neo-
realist Italians, and the neo-existentialist French.

This may be true. But history has shown that in Russia it is
the writers who are the bearers of the germ of national spirit.
It was Pushkin, Dostoevski, Tolstoy, Belinsky, Turgenev, and
Chekhov who kept alive and nourished through the long nineteenth century a belief in a Russia in which tyranny and ignorance one day would be overthrown. And, it seemed to me in
1959, that it was men like Pasternak, Ehrenburg, and Sholokhov
—each so different in his way and each in his own way at odds
with the others, but each holding within himself a writer's stubborn necessity for finding and expressing the truth at any cost—
whom the future would record as having kept alight the flame of

Russian spirit during long, dark, and difficult years.

These three men, I believed, would be remembered in a time when the names of the transient rulers of the country had grown vague, forgotten, and dusty. I believed as Pasternak had written in his *Garden of Gethsemane*:

> I will suffer death and on the third day rise
> Again. Like rafts descending on a river,
> Like a caravan of sails, the centuries
> Out of the night will come to my judgment seat.

VIII

The Lonely Artist

Iᴛ ɪs ɴᴀᴛᴜʀᴀʟ, I suppose, in a land where the collective is officially supreme that the theme of individual man, his lonely struggle with fate and the inevitable tragedy of his life, should preoccupy the mind and talent of great artists.

I never thought it accidental that Shostakovich's first symphony after Stalin's death, his sad, inexorable Tenth, was dedicated to this theme. Shostakovich, like every other creative artist in Russia, had spent a lifetime in solitary struggle. There was no more lonely crowd than the artists' collective in the late years of Stalin. Whether a man's talent lay in music, in art, or in poetry, the story was the same. It was natural and inevitable that Pasternak's theme would be identical with that of Shostakovich, for Pasternak's isolation within his own country—and his understanding of that isolation—had been even more profound.

Even so I was not prepared for the spectacle which I encountered on the stage of the Mariinsky Theater in Leningrad. In Czarist days the Mariinsky was the court opera house. In recent years it had been redecorated with a blue-and-gold elegance which nicely contrasted with the red-and-gold elegance of the Bolshoi in Moscow. I suppose there are more beautiful opera houses in the world than the Mariinsky, but not for me.

I had come to the theater that night in a mood of frustration. I had hoped to see the new Leningrad ballet called "Tropoye

Gromo," the Path of Thunder. I did not know much about this ballet, but it had been stirring controversy. It dealt with the race question in South Africa, I had been told. It was the first black-and-white ballet ever to reach the Soviet stage and the Mariinsky production had been described as "very advanced." The filial company of the Bolshoi in Moscow was preparing its own production of "Tropoye Gromo" and planned to sneak it into the program at one of the last performances of the season.

The wonderful classicism of Soviet ballet was rocking under the challenge of creative innovations stemming from its new exposure to the West.

Not that anything could surpass this ballet and the supreme artist of our times, Galina Ulanova. To me no moment in the theater would ever be greater than a night when Ulanova danced. So many times I had sat in the Bolshoi awaiting that moment. Every seat and every cranny of the hall is filled up to the last balcony just under the ceiling. Finally, the curtain rises, and Ulanova appears. The audience, almost seeming to breathe in rhythm, falls under her sorceress spell.

The greatest of Ulanova's ballets is "Giselle," and the supreme moment of her talent comes in the second act when she flies diagonally across the stage. Flight is the only word to describe this miracle.

After seeing Ulanova in "Giselle" for the first time I wrote in my notebook:

How can I put a dream down on paper? How can I make you feel a moonbeam and touch the gossamer wing of a fairy? Where are the words that will make an angel come to life, a star glitter in your hand and a wisp of rainbow in your hair?

It is incredible, fantastic, perfection perfected, the most delicate dream come true, a butterfly brushing your eyelashes, a dress of sheer cobwebs and diamonds, a poem so beautiful it makes your heart ache, a song murmured in your ear.

It is the most thrilling and beautiful thing I have ever seen.

Don't expect this to make sense. I'm still at the Bolshoi last night watching the fairy princess of the whole world and all her assistant princesses float over the stage, toes twinkling like stars and bodies fluttering like hummingbirds' wings.

Foolish people talk about the seven wonders of the world. Foolish, foolish people. This *is* the wonder of the world.

Even so, I knew that when Ulanova and the Bolshoi company returned from New York there would be an explosion of energy which would lead to a new and greater synthesis. Exposure of these wonderful artists to the lean muscularity and bright imaginativeness of American ballet, to Balanchine, to the realism of *West Side Story* and the exhilaration of *My Fair Lady* would, I was certain, set off a chain reaction leading beyond the bounds of imagination.

Already Igor Moiseyev had launched the fight for the new ballet. In an address to the Moscow intelligentsia on his return from America, he had called for new creative frontiers. Russia, he said, must take a new look at American art. It must rid itself of the cliché that America was a land of immature culture. He clearly implied that the ponderous machinery of the Bolshoi company was not the last word. That the Russian dance could learn as well as teach, that it was time to listen to the driving rhythms of American music and look at the soaring dreams of American ballet.

Moiseyev's daring talk had been the opening gun of an artillery engagement. Promptly the heavy batteries of Agitprop, of the dedicated bureaucrats of the Party, the panjandrums of ballet and of socialist realism had laid down a counterbarrage. Moiseyev had been driven to cover. He was warned that talk so uninhibited and enthusiastic was not desirable. True, American culture was worthy of more study. But the watchword was "go slow."

Moiseyev was preparing a new repertoire for his dance group

Excursion boats ply Moskva River past the Kremlin.

Children play beside the Kremlin walls.

Leningrad, Russia's "window on the west," retains its beauty.

Steel goes up for U.S. Exposition in Moscow.

Young Moscow artists debate new trends.

In Moscow's suburbs life is simple.

Fun balloons replace guns in Red Square parade.

Religion holds its own among Russia's women.

Christian Dior styles shown to Moscow audience.

River Ob is harnessed to provide power for Siberia.

Vice President Nixon and Vice Premier Kozlov at Peterhof.

Grandpa Molotov and his two lovely little granddaughters.

Mongolia's grass carpet stretches to the horizon.

Mongol archers compete as in days of Genghis Khan.

Chief Buddhist Lama of Mongolia in ceremonial yurt.

The author carves lamb at feast in yurt.

A wayside point in the vast Mongolian steppe.

Tasha proves his fishing skill.

Mongol girls in ancient ceremonial dress.

China's "blue ants" parade in streets of Ulan Bator.

after their American success. He had spent much time in New York studying American folk art and contemporary ballet. He planned to include several American numbers in his new program. One which was based on rock-'n'-roll themes was the talk of Moscow's artistic circles.

But Moiseyev is an old sparrow. He knows that sometimes in Moscow it pays to make haste slowly. There was already talk that he was becoming "Americanized." Envious remarks were being dropped about his beautiful new Mercedes, gift of Sol Hurok. He cut the American numbers from his new program and presented in their place a collection of banalities—village dances derived from past successes, a Red Army number, a Soviet Youth number, two or three comic sequences. The program was dull and disappointing.

So it was in a mood of frustration that I arrived at the Mariinsky that evening to see, not an exciting experimental ballet, as I had hoped, but a program of miniatures—a program made up of segments from ballets, individual turns, a mishmash of numbers of various genres and, doubtless, of varying talents.

I was happy, of course, to be in the Mariinsky again and to see the new and beautiful curtain, all gold and blue. As the lights dimmed and the conductor raised his baton I relaxed and prepared to enjoy myself. After all it was Leningrad—the Mariinsky—June—white nights.

The curtain rose. Under the white glare of a spotlight on a naked stage stood a lonely man in black tights. From the orchestra swelled up the deep agony of a Rachmaninoff concerto. And the lonely man began to walk down the gray and endless corridor of contemporary time, a small black figure moving slowly, on and on and on like a patient ant in infinity. He was traversing a world in which there was no escape and no hope. It was as though this little man had poked a finger through the cardboard lies which nourish and support us, to show the slippery edge of the waiting abyss. I do not know how long his miming lasted. Perhaps a minute; perhaps five minutes. All I know is that suddenly I saw the curtain fall and listened to the silence as a thousand people held their breaths. Then, with a sob, the applause came like a storm at sea.

I felt the hair rise on the back of my neck. This was not socialist realism. This was pure abstraction, abstraction of movement and abstraction of gesture, such as I had never seen. It was like Marcel Marceau. But this man—Rassadin was the name on the program—began where Marceau left off. Marceau was an entertainer. Rassadin was Despair. Black. Beyond comfort. The only mime whose artistry I thought someday might touch that of Rassadin was that of the young American Paul Curtis. What Rassadin's background might be I did not know. But here was a talent which cut right through to the great void, the nothingness, the edgeless emptiness of the modern world. He had not, I supposed, been in the West. Whether he was familiar with the quasi-philosophy in which the West cloaked its knowledge of this inner vacuity, I did not know. Perhaps Rassadin was unfamiliar with Sartre or Camus. Perhaps he had never heard the music of Hindemith or pondered the logic of Kierkegaard. He might, for all I knew, be ignorant of Kafka and Rilke. Yet, working and living and feeling and thinking and creating here in this greatest of northern cities, this incredible jewel which Peter had set in the Russian diadem, Rassadin had grasped the pathos of our civilization with a surgeon's scalpel which cut clean to the bone.

But it was not only the genius of Rassadin which struck me. It was this Leningrad audience which felt, with sure and certain sophistication, the exact measure of what Rassadin sought to convey and which reacted with an explosive shudder. And this was important. For the artist cannot communicate if the audience does not understand the symbols to which he gives meaning.

For a long time after the program of miniatures I walked

along the lovely canals of Leningrad. The north light stayed in the sky and gave the old bridges, the fine stone buildings, and the dark waters of the Moika and the Fontanka a radiance like cold fire.

In Moscow, I thought, the battle between the new and the old, between originality and cant, between fresh winds and stale air, remains to be fought. The forces of the new would be victorious. They would always be victorious. It might take time. A Nicholas or a Stalin could hold the hands of the clock back by main strength. But the men become old. Eventually they lose their grip. Others may try to stem the tide, but they cannot succeed. In Moscow the battle was yet to be decided. But I had no doubt that Moiseyev, to use but one name, would win.

But here in Leningrad the new had already triumphed. It might be waiting in the wings in Moscow. But here it had taken the center stage and had shown its tragic face under the naked spotlight. And this, in a sense, was the function of Leningrad. Peter designed it, lent it his Saint's name, and used it to displace jealous provincial Moscow. He thought of it as Russia's window on the West, as the port of entry by which Western culture, Western technique, Western art, and Western thought might enter his tortured, backward empire. For two hundred years Russia moved ahead, with St. Petersburg tugging at the bridle like restless horses with a mud-bogged troika.

It was this same city, then called Petrograd, which made the 1917 Revolution—not Moscow. And it was only when Lenin moved his capital to Moscow in the fear that Petrograd might fall to the Germans, that the greedy, peasant ethos which had always characterized the old trading center of central Russia began, at first gradually, but later more and more rapidly, to replace the liberal and radical idealism of the revolution with a cult of cant and reaction.

I did not believe Leningrad was now strong enough to wrest

from Moscow's bureaucrats the creative leadership of the nation. The Party was too possessive. Moscow was too possessive. And too many of Russia's talents had been brought to Moscow. Ballet was, perhaps, an exception. The Mariinsky school had preserved its imperial traditions. It had never lost leadership to the Bolshoi.

But, as I delved deeper into the artistic life of Leningrad it seemed to me that I might be underestimating the vitality of the city. It had suffered grievously during the war. Perhaps a million Leningraders had lost their lives in the siege of 900 days. But I was astonished to see how rapidly the immigrants who filled the vacant places had themselves become Leningraders. The city imposed its ideals, its standards, its sophistication upon the students who arrived from Siberia, the workers from the Ukraine, the young girls from the collective farms of Karelia, and even upon the party hacks who came up from Moscow.

It was not only in ballet. In art, too, perhaps Leningrad was going to show Russia the path out from the whoredom of the Stalin period.

No field of creative activity had been more stultified than art under Stalin. For years Europe's greatest collection of post-impressionist French painting had been kept under lock and key in an attic room of the Hermitage in Leningrad. Stalin forbade its public display.

Now the beautiful Cézannes, Picassos, Van Goghs, Gauguins, Renoirs hung in both the Hermitage and the great Tretyakov gallery in Moscow. The collections, the creation of two remarkable Moscow millionaires, Ivan Morozov and Ivan Shchukin, had been divided. But soon, it was said, they would be brought together again and housed under one roof in a new gallery in Moscow.

The Hermitage had outdone itself in honoring the collection. It had turned over its finest rooms and hung the postimpressionists with spectacular magnificence.

This is the first collection to come out from behind lock and key. There are others which now seem to be knocking so loudly to be let out that at any moment they may win their way to freedom.

Russia possesses another magnificent collection of moderns— Russian moderns. It has almost been forgotten that Russia nourished a brilliant school of abstract painting just before, during, and after World War I. We know of Chagall but we may never have heard of Kandinsky, Tatlin, Malevich, Konchalovsky, and Mashkov. Indeed, they are virtually unknown to the present generation of Russians.

Names such as the "World of Art," the "Jack of Diamonds," the "Donkey's Tail," and the "Target" groups, the Suprematists, the Constructivists are as meaningless to the present generation of Soviet Russians as they are to contemporary Americans. But for twenty-five years, from the mid-nineties to the early 1920's, they lighted up the artistic landscape of Russia like Roman candles.

Today, it seemed to me, those candles were burning again, but this time with delayed fuses. As anyone who knew Russia might guess, the paintings of these revolutionaries of a half-century ago have not been destroyed. They have merely been immured within the walls of the reserve collections of the Tretyakov and the Hermitage galleries. There, in the vast barns where only a few years ago the French paintings lay imprisoned, Russia's nonrepresentational art still is stacked in haphazard fashion, some paintings to the wall, some framed, some identified, others not.

Word was spreading in Leningrad last summer that the banishment was nearing an end. Like the great bell of Uglitch Cathedral which Ivan the Terrible sent to Siberia because it had pealed a tocsin to his enemies, the great Chagalls, Kandinskys, and Maleviches were to be given a reprieve. An exhibition of Russian abstract painting, it was said, was being organized. I could not find out whether the rumor was correct or not. Some Soviet artists thought that it was premature, that it would be another year or two before the general public was permitted to see the paintings.

But the truth was that the banishment already had all but ended. The pictures were not on public view, but any visitor with a good artistic reason might receive permission to inspect the reserve collections. Young women who knew the paintings guided the visitors in their backstairs inspection. So heavy was the traffic to the reserve collections last summer that hardly a day went by without a viewing of the pictures.

This did not mean that all barriers were down and that the defenders of Socialist realism were running up the white flag. But they were beating a retreat. There had been several exhibitions of modern art in Moscow. The first was of French moderns. It came close to starting a riot, so violent were the arguments that raged in the gallery. The present generation of the Soviet public had never seen anything like it. The leap from realistic, sticky sentimentalist story pictures to abstract color and form was too great for a single step. There had also been minor exhibitions of Polish, Yugoslav, and Icelandic art. These, too, aroused violent controversy.

Nevertheless, the Soviet Society for Cultural Relations invited Alfred Barr of the Museum of Modern Art to lecture in Moscow on American art. He was encouraged to make his presentation before an assemblage of museum directors, artists, students, and critics even though they knew that his major emphasis would be on abstract and expressionist art—Alexander Calder, Jackson Pollock, Barnett Newman, Bradley Tomlin, Franz Kline, Andrew Wyeth, and Mark Rothko.

Barr did not convince the bureaucrats. As one said, his exhibition was interesting because it showed the sterility of modern technique. After more than thirty years it had transcribed a full circle. It was in 1913 that Malevich painted his black square on a white ground, seeking, as he said, "from the black square, the barest minimum, to free painting from the ballast of matter." Now, said the Soviet official, after two generations, Americans are back to the black square.

But, as I looked at the faces of those who listened to Barr and looked at his slides of the abstractionist painting and sculpture, those who exclaimed at Calder's "Whale," cried with pleasure at Pollock's compositions, and gasped at Richard Lippold's dazzling golden "Sun," it seemed to me that the younger artists were more inclined to agree with Barr, who said tersely: "Sometimes, it is said that art travels in a circle. But every generation must paint its own. It is not satisfied with the black square which Malevich painted. Each generation must create its own black square."

I thought the same thing when I saw the young artists later in the summer at the American Exposition, where a small collection of American nonrepresentational art was displayed. Every day artists came and copied or photographed the modern paintings. And in the closing hours of the exhibition, even as the paintings were being taken down for crating, a crew of photographers worked to copy each of the pictures in color. For anti-modernistic propaganda? No, indeed. To study, to examine, to try to understand, to try to draw lessons from.

I had no doubt that Russia stood on the threshold of a breakthrough in art. The old Stalinists of the Painters Union had given up their bureaucratic strongholds to respected men of moderate views. Alexander M. Gerasimov, court painter of the Stalin epoch, with his hideous representations of Stalin and his "comrades-at-arms," had stepped down.

And, of course, in their studios the painters for some time had been hard at work on the new art forms. Some had been painting secretly all through the Stalinist years, but only for themselves. There was, I found, a whole body of "cabinet" art, secret nonrepresentational canvases which the artists painted but could not show in public. It had become a fad in the last three or four years to collect these paintings. Many actors, writers, professors, editors, members of the literati and the intelligentsia had their private collections. There was even a somewhat impressionistic artist who had become the "court" painter to the diplomatic colony. There was hardly a diplomat's wife who had not had her portrait done by Glazunov.

The quality of the "cabinet" paintings was not high. The artists had been compelled to work in a void. They were cut off from the vital cross-fertilization of each other's work. There was no one to criticize what they did. They could only guess at the techniques and concepts which were being developed abroad. Their work, for the most part, had a weak, in-bred quality. It lacked the vitality of connection with life which invigorates the nonrepresentational art of the West.

But even with all these defects it was obvious that Russia possessed a hidden stream of modern artistic talent. Some inkling of these talents was given in a public show of work by young Moscow artists which set the newspapers agog with headlines. Soviet *Culture* called it a show that "gladdens and saddens," and Moscow *Pravda* said it represented "questing and mistakes."

On the day I visited the gallery in Kuznetski Most (Blacksmith's Bridge) I found a free-for-all discussion in full swing. Some of the older painters and critics had come to reason with their young colleagues, to point out to them the error of their ways. I could see in some canvases subdued hints of impressionism and abstract thought but nothing revolutionary. But that was not the view of the older painters.

"There are only two routes for the development of art," said a professorial man with pince-nez. "One is that followed in the West, the formalism of France, of England, of America. Unfortunately some of our young painters do not perceive this and the influence of decadent capitalist art is clear in their work."

The young painters stood in a semicircle, quietly listening to their critics. One of them was Sergei Gerasimov, head of the Academy of Art, a fatherly and kind man—not to be confused with the bad old Gerasimov. Gerasimov did not condemn all the work at the exhibition. But there was one piece of sculpture, a bold and ugly head, which Gerasimov placed beyond the pale. "Who would want to look at it?" he asked. I heard two or three young painters murmur, "We would."

I followed the group as it moved slowly about the salon. I noticed that the young painters did not respond to what was said to them. It was as though they listened out of a sense of duty. But they were not really interested. This feeling must have communicated itself to the critics, for presently they started to question the painters, asking them to say what they meant by this painting or that. The young painters shrugged their shoulders hopelessly.

The talk turned to a landscape which showed some fields lying beyond a river. The colors and composition were definitely impressionist. The artist did not want to discuss his work. The older men kept insisting.

"Well, you know," he finally said, twisting his cap in his hands. "You know that stretch of river. Not far from Ples. Well, that's how it appeared to me. At that time. When I was painting there."

The critics pressed him. What was in his mind? Why did he use such colors?

"What can I say," he said, shrugging his shoulders. "This is how I painted it. This is the effect I wanted. See for yourselves."

Heads nodded among the young men. It was as if the gap between the old and the young was too great for communication. The group moved on to another picture and the critics continued to lecture. But the young artists began to drift away. They stood by twos and threes, looking at their works, talking about them in terms which they understood.

Many of these painters were among the practitioners of "cabinet" art. This exposition was as far as they yet had dared to go in public. And even this set the windmills whirling. Rumors flew about Moscow that the Party was disturbed. The exhibition suddenly closed after only a week. So. That's how it is, the Moscow gossips said. The Party is putting its foot down. It was announced that the exhibition was moving to the Central Gorky Park. No one believed it. Or, if it ever did open there, all the "good" works would be eliminated. Controversial pictures like Manukhin's portrait ("a green frog in black water"), Andronov's "Construction Worker" ("depressing colors, formalistic"), and Korzbev's "Lovers" ("crude pornography") would quietly be dropped.

But Moscow gossip was wrong. The show did open in Gorky Park. And every last picture, criticized, uncriticized, good, bad, and indifferent, was shown.

Clearly, the Party was giving ground in the sphere of art more rapidly than people realized. It was even, in its curious way, preparing the public for what was to come. This was the only way in which one could explain the diffident, almost painful but persistent exposure of the Soviet public to art forms which for so many years had been the object of scurrilous attack by *Krokodil* and other organs of Soviet propaganda.

While I was in Leningrad I met a brilliant young poet named Mikhail Dudin, a poet in the Russian tradition, all spirit and fire and energy. Like the other writers whom I met in Leningrad, he could not imagine an artistic world that was divided between East and West. In one of his poems he wrote, "We will build a bridge and on that bridge friendship will stand guard and together we will build a bridge from the earth to the stars, from the earth to the stars."

He told me that there was an exhibit of art that I must not miss. "It is the kind of art which you will like," he said. "We like it, too."

The exhibit was the work of Vyacheslav Pakulin. It was not a large show. Nor were the paintings recent. Pakulin, himself, had been dead since 1951. But here in a gloomy old palace, filled with massive staircases and bric-a-brac, was an extraordinary testimonial to the sinewy and enduring courage of the Russian artist. This was a collection of paintings which Pakulin made in the most grim winter that a city has ever endured, Leningrad in the hunger and ice blockade of 1941-42. In that winter, with paints which must have often frozen, with frostbitten fingers and empty belly, Pakulin had created a series of delicate impressionist images of the city of his heart in the hour of its agony. Here was the snow, the cold, the grim damage and death of war, but somehow transfused by the magic of his brush and given a light and hopeful aura. Even in the worst days Pakulin knew that Leningrad would survive.

During the Stalin years these beautiful paintings could not be shown, for they were examples of that decadent quality of Western art against which the Party had set its leaden face. Now, with their creator eight years dead, the paintings had been taken out of whatever crypt or cubbyhole they had been preserved in and placed on public display.

Once again the lonely artist of Russia had triumphed. I could not but believe that the day would come when this triumph would be universal. For were not the signs of the artistic downfall of Stalinism to be seen on every hand? Had not the grossest expression of the old dictator's clumsy taste—that architectural style which for want of a better epithet I had always called Stalinesque or Gorky Street modern, that incredible combination of geegaws, pillars, balconies, marble, granite, towers, pediments, and gingerbread—fallen, almost at a single blow?

On this, Khrushchev had set down his foot firmly. I did not know whether it was a matter of aesthetics or simple cost accounting. Whatever the motivation, the result could only be good.

The outrageous skyscraper which Stalin had proposed to erect across from Red Square had been nipped in the bud much as had his even earlier outrage, the proposal for a 150-story Palace of Soviets. The Palace of Soviets was not dead. But when I visited the House of Architecture to see the designs submitted in the latest competition I could only smile with amusement. There was not a Kremlin tower in the lot, not an ornamental column, not a single hero-sized statue. Here were cool, clean, crisp, modern designs. Glass and metal and square planes. These architects had been studying the United Nations Building, the new glass palaces of Park Avenue, the light and graceful concepts erected in Caracas and Rio de Janeiro. A new era plainly was at hand in Soviet architecture. Already a few pilot examples had been set up in the All Union Industrial Exposition.

I had no doubt that the forces of the new would conquer those of the old in all the forms—art, literature, music, sculpture. The barriers already had half fallen. There remained battles to be fought. However, there could be but one outcome. The day would arrive when the lonely artists of Russia would be heroes in their own land, and it was not long distant.

IX

At the Literary Bridge

FIRST OF ALL it should be said that there is no such place as the Literary Bridge. That is, there is no bridge and there has not been one for many years. In the middle of the last century, however, there was a bridge which led over a small marshy spot in the Volkhov cemetery on the outskirts of St. Petersburg. It was a remote spot in those times; and when the great liberal critic Belinsky died of tuberculosis in the darkest years of the Nicholas oppression in May, 1848, he was buried just beyond the bridge, because the plot was cheap and Belinsky's widow and his friends could afford no other. To a generation of young Russians the spot became a shrine. When the critic and radical, Dobrolyubov, died of tuberculosis in 1861, he asked to be buried beside Belinsky. Many others followed, and by the 1880's students used to come to demonstrate here against the Czar's tyranny. By this time it was known as the *literaturniye mostik*, the little Literary Bridge.

Today not only literary persons are buried there. Popov, the Russian radio experimenter, is there. So are Pavlov and Mendeleev. And there, too, is Plekhanov, the founder of the Russian social revolutionary movement. And, of course, Turgenev.

Today, as for decades, the Literary Bridge is a favorite spot for Russian students. They go there to sit on the green benches along the quiet walks. It is a place for thought, for study, for communion. When I visited the Literary Mostik on a long and

127

pleasant June afternoon students filled the benches. Not many were reading Turgenev, Dobrolyubov, or Belinsky, however. They were deep in volumes of biochemistry, advanced mathematics, nuclear physics, geology. I had seen the same thing the evening before in the Summer Garden along the Neva—boys and girls, holding hands as they would anywhere, but their heads, close together, buried in texts on cybernetics or ferrometallurgy.

Later I had gone to the Café Sever on the Nevsky Prospekt. I ordered tea and cake and looked around. There was a tired four-piece orchestra, a piano, violin, violin cello and accordion, hacking away at "Auld Lang Syne." The waitresses were as plump and creamy as the ice cream they were serving. There was a splendid old potted palm in one corner.

At the table beyond me a man with horn-rimmed glasses and a green checked sport shirt sat down at a table with a blond student and his blonde best girl. The man smiled at the couple and exchanged a pleasantry or two. Then, he leaned across the table and I heard him say: "Here is an interesting geometric puzzle. How would you construct a right angle to this figure, using only one line?"

The boy and girl studied the geometric figure hastily sketched on a pink paper napkin. The youngsters tried one thing, then another. After ten minutes they gave up. But they promptly took another napkin and sketched a new mathematical puzzle for their neighbor to work out.

There may be other cities in the world where you can see as many signs of intellectual preoccupation as in Leningrad. Moscow certainly comes a close second. And in no Russian city does it seem surprising to see a man in the subway poring over calculus or to hear two girls at a quick-lunch counter discussing a problem in blood chemistry.

But perhaps there is a higher concentration on study and on science in Leningrad than in other Russian cities. Leningrad no longer is the capital of Russia, but it is surely Russia's intellectual center and probably the world's most intellectual city.

If you want to understand the blending of science, education, and technology which has enabled the Soviet Union to break through into the most advanced areas of contemporary technique, the place to come for the answer is Leningrad.

Not that Sputnik was invented in Leningrad, or that the launching platforms for the great rockets were created in the city by the Neva. But a good many of the men who played a major role in these achievements, and much of the stimulus which made them possible, came from this city.

"As fast as we develop brilliant new scientists," an older professor told me, "Moscow takes them away from us. But we immediately develop a new crop. Of course Moscow has fine men, too, but we in Leningrad feel that the real pacemakers are developed here."

Moscow has preempted many of the scientific institutions founded in Leningrad by Peter the Great, Catherine II, and their successors. But Leningrad breeds new scientific facilities faster than guinea pigs reproduce in the laboratories.

American educators and scientists have poured into Russia in the time since Sputnik was launched, seeking the secret of the Soviet achievement. At times the search has resembled a hunt for the philosopher's stone, a search for a specific, recognizable procedure or method in the Soviet system which could be isolated, sterilized, and introduced into the American system to produce the same results.

There is no Soviet educational institution of any consequence which has not been examined in the past two years by at least one probing team of American specialists. They have inspected the Moscow State University from the top of its thirty-seven-story tower to the offices on the ground floor. They have visited the University of Leningrad, the University of Kiev, and almost all the other thirty-nine universities of the Soviet Union. They have consulted the rectors, the pro-rectors, the pedagogical faculties, the middle-school principals, the directors of boarding schools, the mistresses of kindergartens. They have interviewed the Minister of Education and his assistants and the Party specialists in propaganda and agitation as well. They have examined the curriculum and analyzed the entrance requirements and degree qualifications. If any aspect has been left out, you can be certain that another mission financed by the Ford Foundation will be on its way to Moscow next week to look into it.

Not quite so elaborate a study has been made of Soviet scientific facilities. This is not for lack of desire, determination, or foundation funds. It simply springs from the security barriers which the Soviet still imposes upon some institutions. But it is fair to say that in this area, too, never has so much been known by one country about the methods, facilities, procedures, incentives, and objectives of the other.

It is obvious today, as it has been for many years, that Russia has a fine educational system. It is universal, like ours. There are some variations in curriculum and some technical differences in organization. But the similarities between the Soviet general education system and the American system are greater than the dissimilarities.

It is also obvious that the differences are greater in the levels of higher education—that here the Russians concentrate more selectively and more intensively than do we.

It had long seemed to me that some of the Soviet advantage surely lay in the lavish support which the Soviet government gave both to general education and to science. The government was prepared to subsidize completely students at the higher education levels, providing them with tuition-free university careers and giving them grants to cover room, board, and incidentals. This went a long way toward assuring that the country would mobilize all its available intellectual power.

And direction was given to the employment of these powers

by expanding academic facilities in those spheres of knowledge
to which the government had given highest priority and then by
directing the graduates into those kinds of work and those areas
in which the government judged the need to be greatest.

This, of course, contrasted with the emphasis in the American
system upon electives and freedom of choice. Particularly, it
conflicted with the liberty which the American student had in
picking his field of specialization and the kind of employment
he preferred.

Not that the reality of the Soviet system was so authoritarian
as it sounded. I knew very well, for example, that the crack
students of Russia's leading institutions were skimmed off much
as they are in American universities. Competition for able graduates was intense. A good engineer or a good biochemist would
find a choice of attractive offers. And I knew, too, that Soviet
students wangled and pulled wires as much as American students. There was many a way to escape being sent to an unpleasant post in Sakhalin. If worst came to worst and the student actually did wind up in Tannu-Tuva the cause was not
necessarily lost, at least not if the victim was a young lady. For
there was a Soviet law of which advantage could be taken.
Husbands and wives had the right to petition to work in the
same city. So a disconsolate Tamara in Tashkent sometimes
wrote fortunate Feodor in Moscow, proposing marriage but
promising that once she won her transfer to Moscow and got a
job she would promptly divorce him.

Many educators felt they were on the track of the Soviet
secret when they found how great was the emphasis which the
Russian system placed on "hard" knowledge, mathematics,
sciences, languages. The Russian schools, it was discovered, had
little in the way of frills. No courses in driving, no courses in
orientation, nothing to adjust students to "life" problems.

By American standards physical education was practically
ignored. The colleges placed less emphasis on football than

Chicago or Vassar. The great athletes whom Russia was sending
into the Olympics were being trained outside the school system
entirely. Russian schools concentrated on the word and the
book and, of course, on the laboratory in the sciences. But there
were no printing plants, model bakeries, carpentry shops, automobile garages, pottery studios, dressmaking establishments,
or experimental farms in the academic institutions. The line was
sharp between study and practice.

Here again, some of the roving teams felt they had their
finger on the Russian secret only to have it vanish when the
Russians suddenly announced that they were going to turn
their system topsy-turvy in order to get a better integration
between work and theory.

For the last year Russian educators have been feverishly trying to arrange things in a new pattern. An end is to be made of
the *beliye ruki,* the "white-handed ones," the students who do
not know the meaning of physical work. A kind of Antioch College experiment is being introduced. Students will divide their
time between work and study. (In one of the first experiments
toward eliminating the white-handed ones at Leningrad University it was announced that henceforth all students would clean
their own dormitories. Within a week the halls were a mess. The
Party organization forthwith posted a list of "volunteers" for
the cleaning chores, expelled a student or two as an example to
the others, and brought the white-handed condition to a sum-
mary end.)

Some educators have sensed in the Soviet educational innovations a rising anti-intellectualism which would undermine the
notable achievements of the system. The reforms are designed
not only to couple teaching and work much more closely but
also to provide for an interlude of work of two or three years
between high school and college. There will be tightened control over admission to higher education with a bias in favor of

those who have Party sponsorship and who enter through the factory production line.

I talked with a good many Soviet educators about the problems of the new system and found that the accent everywhere was on gradualism and special treatment for the exceptional student. The warnings of the scientists that Russia could not afford to interrupt the training of its most talented young people in precisely those years when their receptivity to knowledge is highest was being heeded.

It seemed to me that behind the façade of the educational reforms the Soviet authorities were seeking to cope with quite another problem—one very deep and very serious. This was the extraordinary weakness in manpower which confronted the country and which would persist for the next few years.

The weakness stems from the tremendous population losses of World War II. The Soviet population in 1959 stood at 208 million. Had it not been for the war it would have been possibly 40 million larger. Russia is now entering the years when the decline has its maximum effect upon labor force and, of course, the military forces. The total school enrollment in the Soviet Union today, with a population about 15 million larger than at the outbreak of the war, is nearly 6 million below what it was in 1940. This means that until 1965 there will be each year a larger shortage of labor.

Nor is this the only problem concealed behind the screen of the Soviet educational changes. A very severe one exists with regard to facilities.

Five years ago the government introduced compulsory ten-year schooling in the cities. Prior to this, as a general rule, most students went to school for seven years. They then found employment in industry or agriculture or transferred to technical schools (roughly equivalent to our vocational schools). Only if they were going on to the university level would they continue through the tenth year of secondary schooling. In other words the last three years of secondary school were linked directly with higher education. The weed-out occurred at the seven-year level. If a student was permitted to go on through ten years he was virtually assured a place in the university.

When ten-year universal schooling was introduced there was no corresponding increase in available facilities for higher education. Youngsters were spewed out of the ten-year school at a rate four or five times as great as there were available places in the universities. Not all of the secondary-school graduates, to be sure, wanted to go on to higher education and not all of them were qualified. But a great many more did want to go than there were places to be filled. Traditionally, the ten-year graduate had always gone to the university. The new ten-year graduates felt entitled to go to college as a matter of course. The authorities had a psychological as well as a practical problem.

The pressure backed up enormously on the universities. Ten-year graduates descended in greater and greater numbers. There was no room for them in the university and, since the course of studies they pursued was a university preparatory course, many were not equipped to go into industry.

What to do? Many of the youngsters could not even find jobs.

One thing to do, of course, and this the government is doing, is to change the basis of the ten-year school so that the youngster who finishes it will be able to get a job. Another is to tighten the requirements all along the line, the requirements to get into each stage of higher education and to stay in school.

It would be possible to expand higher educational facilities. But this would syphon off more of the scarce young manpower so badly needed by industry. Thus, for the time being, it is obvious that this expedient will not be tried.

There are many complex factors in this situation. One is the enormous social pressure which is brought to bear upon the Soviet educational system as a mechanism for improving status.

Education has been the ladder which one generation after another of youngsters has climbed from the father's factory bench or peasant hut to white-collar status and a Moscow apartment. This is why there are scandals of bribery, use of influence, and cheating in exams to get into the universities. With the lack of avenues for social mobility, such as are provided by private enterprise and the diversity of American society, the Soviet educational path has become the prime means of social betterment. Safer than the Party. Easier than the army. More secure than the state.

The emphasis which Khrushchev places on abolition of the distinction between *beliye ruki* and *chornye ruki* is a real one. Russia does not have the shirt-sleeve tradition of America. Russian students do not work in hash houses or take summer jobs with road-building crews in order to finance their education. They do not "work" their way through school as Americans do. The state puts them through.

Moreover, the Russian *intelligent*—and this is the status the college graduate achieves—does not spend his spare time puttering with the car, digging in the garden, painting the house, or scraping the bottom of a boat. Such things are "black labor." They are done by workmen or servants, members of classes in this classless society who are inferior in status. Blue shirt and white collar mean much more in Russia than they do in America because the lines are not blurred. When I had a dacha in Russia with a vegetable garden, it was an endless source of amazement to the villagers that I, a foreigner, should sweat and soil my hands digging with a shovel. I was a "rich" foreigner. I should have someone to do this for me. Besides, planting a garden was women's work.

These, then, are the problems with which the Soviet government is coping, in its typically oblique fashion, with the revision of the educational system now under way. The problems are large. But they are not educational. They are social and economic.

So it is unlikely that much light, one way or another, will be cast upon the Soviet achievements by the tinkering which is now in progress.

The Russians themselves, of course, are far from considering their system perfect. They have been sending delegations over to the United States to inspect our schools and colleges. There are a good many things of ours that they would like to introduce. These apply not only in the field of schooling but also in the field of science.

For example, the same problem of a divorce between theory and practice, which can be found in the Soviet schools, carries over to Soviet science. In our preoccupation with the achievements of Sputnik, we have not paid much heed to the criticism which the Russians have been directing toward their scientific institutions. Much of this criticism sounds a good deal like that which is leveled at the schools. It is contended, and quite accurately, that scientific institutions tend to cluster in Moscow, Leningrad, and a few other principal cities, often far removed from the actual problems with which they contend. Institutes specializing in oil geology, for example, are located not in Baku or Kuibyshev, close to the oil fields, but in Leningrad and Moscow. Steel research is carried on, not in the Donbass or the Urals, but in Moscow.

And here the Russians draw their most fruitful examples from American technology. They don't have the close integration of American research with American industry, the interaction of science and managers, the application of scientific techniques to practical problems which is possible because the laboratory is actually set up as an adjunct to the factory.

The Russians are trying hard to overcome this, but it is not easy. One of the great discoveries of the trip to America by Agriculture Minister Vladimir M. Matskevitch was the agricultural experiment station, the laboratory in the field, attached to the great Midwestern universities, such as Iowa, in which the scientists are out every day in their blue jeans, working with the farmers, seeking to adapt new processes which make for better pigs and better corn, combining the roles of experimenter, propagandist, and friend.

With all its organization and all its science, the Soviet Union had nothing like this. In the five years since he was in Iowa, Matskevitch has been struggling with the Russian agrobiologists, trying to get them out of the ivory tower and into the pigpen where they can work at firsthand on the problems of the farmer.

The tendency of the Russian scientist to shut himself up in the laboratory is not without class connotations. It follows the tradition of European science in general and German science in particular. Herr Professor demonstrates to his students in the laboratory. He does not talk to the peasant in his sabots. I have seen only one great experiment station set up on the American model behind the Iron Curtain. This was in Rumania. The scientists proudly wore blue jeans and red-checkered shirts. They worked in the fields and self-consciously drove the tractors themselves. "They call us Americans," they said proudly.

One reason why the evil genius of Soviet science, the pseudo-geneticist, Trofim Lysenko, has made something of a comeback in recent years has been his willingness to work in the fields. He was toppled from his eminence as the Stalin of Soviet science shortly after Khrushchev's rise. He had been exposed as a nature faker, and a doctorer of experiments. But he went out on the county agent circuit, preaching to the peasants the necessity of fertilizing their fields. He got his feet into the manure and talked the kind of language that made sense to the man with the plow. Then, he came back to Khrushchev with another gimmick, one which sounded attractive to the Party Secretary, engaged as he is in a desperate effort to boost Soviet dairy and meat production. Lysenko said it wasn't necessary to go through the tedious process of breeding pedigreed stock in order to get high-milk-producing cows. Just feed cows well. Give them special care. Their calves will inherit the environmental changes and be big milk producers. This was a re-run in the animal world of his long-since exposed claptrap about conditioned inheritance in the vegetable world.

Khrushchev should know better from his days as a cattle herder. But he seems to have accepted the Lysenko theory because it provides an attractive short cut to the goals he is so anxious to achieve.

Even a cursory glance at Soviet science shows that, brilliant as are its achievements, it suffers from serious drawbacks. The unity of direction which is achieved through government centralized control gives tremendous force to the solution of problems which receive No. 1 priority. But the danger of excessive concentration in a narrow field is acute. The central guidance of the Academy of Sciences cannot match the flexibility of American science.

To supply this kind of stimulation is one of the prime reasons why the government permitted Soviet science to resume its long-broken contacts with the West. It is not enough, the government realized, to give Soviet science the best of all possible access to printed knowledge of the West. This already was being done through one of the most brilliant scientific organizations of our time—the affiliate of the Soviet Academy of Science which is publishing the so-called referatory journals. These are abstracts and indexes of the world's current scientific literature. It is catalogued by specialities and translated from all languages of the world into Russian. There is a monthly journal for each major speciality and an express bulletin to report the most newsworthy developments in each field.

This enormous project bands together 1,800 translators and scientists. It covers every scientific publication in the world.

No other country can match it. So comprehensive and remarkable is this service that it is subscribed to by many foreign scientific organizations (including American) which retranslate it for use of their scientists.

But organizing achievements like this, or creative successes like Sputnik and the elaborate guiding and computing mechanisms which place space objects into orbit, do not communicate any sense of complacency to thoughtful Soviet scientists and educators. They are as busy re-examining their system as we are with ours. Perhaps busier.

One of the most thoughtful of these inquiries is that which is going on in Soviet pedagogical science. This has no direct relationship to the changes being introduced in higher education. Among the stream of American investigators pouring into Moscow last summer were two perceptive students of Soviet pedagogy, Herschel and Edith Alt of the New York Board of Jewish Guardians.

They found that Soviet child specialists were putting the whole Soviet method of child rearing under the microscope.

"For forty years we have been engaged in building an educational system at any cost," one of the pedagogues told the Alts. "Now the main framework of the system has been built. So we now are taking a fresh look at the children, at the system which we use, and at the results which are obtained."

The Alts found a widespread feeling on the part of educators that the loads being placed on youngsters are much too heavy and that children are subjected to excessive pressures. This throws into question the whole Soviet system of utilizing social forces in order to create the type of man which Communist theory has postulated will be the member of Communist society. The fact seems to be that the social pressures tend to break down the child's personality. The results are not always what Soviet theory suggested they should be. Youngsters who are well behaved and adjusted in school turn into terrors at home. The pressure to conform, to do well in school, to pass examinations, to win entrance into the higher stages of education, put so profound a burden on the youngsters that cheating has become a major—some educators say *the* major—problem in the schools. So enormous is the incentive to get all A's that everyone helps the process along.

Now, it was found, Soviet pedagogues were turning for the first time to the kind of Western tools which they had scorned as the implements of bourgeois psychology, testing and measuring and the other sociological and educational techniques which have long since proved their usefulness in analyzing the individual, his problems and his needs.

The more I looked at the perfectionist society of the Soviet —the planning, the direction, the concentration of means, and the simplification of objectives—the more certain I became that the research teams and the surveys were not going to come up with a golden answer as to how Russia put Sputnik into orbit. It did not seem to me that it was something which could be put down on a chart or measured with a measuring technique. Rather, it was the over-all product of a society which, for all its inadequacies and defects, had a direction, a purpose, and a bias which existed outside of any system and which could well be more historic and cultural than ideological.

One of the cafés which I visited in Leningrad is called "The Frog." The university students have given it this name from the hideous green of its walls and plush seats. It is a kind of combination ice-cream and champagne parlor which only exists, I believe, in the Soviet Union. I sat there awhile late one afternoon absorbing the atmosphere of the place and listening to the conversation around me. It was a quiet and cool spot at that time of the day and there were more shoppers from the Nevsky Prospekt than students eating tall glasses of fancy icecream or sipping the fancy *koktayls*.

At a near-by table there was an elderly Russian of the generation which was of University age at the time of the Revolution. Sitting across from him was a young man in a maroon sport shirt whom I took to be a student. Each was sipping pink champagne.

For a long time they sat there, each lost in his own thoughts. Then the old Russian spoke.

"What do you think?" he asked. "Do our Soviet young people today have the same wonderful spirit which made them so exceptional in the nineteenth century? Do the young people today still dream the unlimited dreams which moved the youngsters of the 1860's and the 1880's?"

I wondered what the young man would answer. He pondered and I could not help thinking of the Literary Mostik and how in the 1880's it had been a rallying spot for demonstrations. What was the spirit of the young people who gathered on the green benches today?

Finally, the young man spoke.

"Yes," he said. "Sometimes, people think the younger generation has stopped dreaming. It's not true. We dream of a future just as bright as the generations of the nineteenth century."

Here I thought is where the answer lay, if it lay anywhere. If Russia had a secret weapon, if there was one reason for her achievements, it was not the ideology, not the great institutes which had been set up to utilize the knowledge of her scientists. All this was important, to be sure. But the real secret lay in the spirit of the generations of Russian youth who had not stopped dreaming. God grant, I thought, that they go on dreaming. For in the end, I had no doubt, they would dream their way to a better Russia—better for them and better for the world. The same Russia, free in spirit, to which each generation had dedicated itself at the little Literary Bridge.

X

Herdsman of the "Little Cows"

Mᴀʀxɪsᴛs have a theory that history is made, not by men, but by underlying social and economic forces, by what they call the "dialectic" which shapes and molds the fate of mankind, sweeping it forward with the irresistible power of a river in flood. Conflict arises when mounting social pressure encounters the granite of economic resistance. One who understands these forces and their relative strengths, say the Marxists, holds the key to the "dialectic of history."

I have always thought that this Marxist view profoundly understated the human element and the role which man plays in determining his fate. Man, and especially the leaders of men, in my view, act as the catalytic agents in determining the direction in which a nation or a society moves and, particularly, the pace at which it advances and the goals which it sets for itself.

These thoughts were much in my mind as I returned to Khrushchev's Russia after my long years in Stalin's Russia. I was profoundly convinced that it was Stalin, the individual, who had given the tone of terror and yellow suspicion to the Russia which I had known before. Perhaps any ruler of Russia in those years would have followed the same iron policy of industrialization of Stalin. So the dialectic would assert. But only Stalin and his personal paranoia could have turned Russia into such a chamber of horrors.

142

When I left the Soviet Union in 1954, the country was still being ruled by "collective leadership." Messrs. Malenkov, Khrushchev, Bulganin, Molotov, Kaganovich, and the rest were traveling around in one big Zis limousine and popping out of it like Keystone cops from a tin Lizzie in order to prove their true *kollektivnost*.

Now it was Khrushchev at the top. In America I had sometimes speculated about a possible challenge to his position, but here in Moscow it was easy to see that Khrushchev had it made. No one was going to take it away from him now. He had dealt with his Malenkovs, Bulganins, and Kaganoviches. Marshal Zhukov, who had loomed so big and so imposing, was relegated to a pleasant dacha outside the city where he could, if he wished, work on his memoirs or, if that palled, there were the fishing rods with which he was not very facile. But, said Marshal Malinovsky, he is getting the hang of it better.

I knew something of Khrushchev, of course. He had never been prominent during Stalin's day. When I arrived in Moscow in 1949 he was still down in the Ukraine, running the party there. He came up to Moscow late in 1949, in December I believe, and took over the City Party organization. This was an important post, one of the most important in the country. Zinoviev had held it once.

Living in Moscow in those years I cannot say that I observed any outward change when Khrushchev came to town. He replaced a man named Popov who was an adherent of the late Andrei Zhdanov. All sorts of terrible things were going on behind the scenes about which I knew nothing. Zhdanov had died August 1, 1948, and most of his men were being purged, but I did not know this at the time.

I used to see Khrushchev on the podium at the May Day parades. He stood to one side, neither smiling nor frowning, his snub nose turned up a little, just one more in the line-up of Stalin's faceless functionaries. He was not tall. Stalin didn't like tall men. Khrushchev had not then developed the neat little corporation which his Italian tailors struggle with. He wore a workingman's cap or a shapeless gray Moscow fedora —not the fine black Homburg which he so confidently twirled on his arrival in America in 1959. His suits were rumpled and his trousers flared at the cuffs. He probably had never seen a pair of fine Italian thin-soled pumps such as he wore in Washington. He was a man at one side or in the second rank of the photos published in *Pravda*. His name appeared often in the newspapers, for one of the principal duties of the Moscow Party boss is to attend meetings and make speeches. But Khrushchev's speeches were never published. There would be an account of the proceedings and then the last line: "Comrade Khrushchev also spoke."

In all those Stalin years I do not think more than one or two speeches by Khrushchev were ever published. Once a long article was published under his signature, proposing what he called "agrogorods"—big peasant villages which would consolidate land and facilities (and in the process wipe out the peasants' private land plots). But the next day a brief line appeared, saying that the article represented only Comrade Khrushchev's personal opinion. His ideas were sharply criticized in several articles by other Party figures; and never again, in Stalin's day, were agrogorods mentioned publicly.

Of course, Khrushchev could not have been as obscure a figure as this suggests. Everyone in the Moscow Party organization must have known him well. Yet, in those years I never heard any anecdotes about him. I never heard an ordinary Russian mention his name. The diplomats speculated a little about his appointment and what significance it might have in the behind-the-scenes intrigues of the Politburo. But that was all.

What was really going on during those years? Is it possible that so articulate, so energetic, so quick-witted and intellectually restless a man as Khrushchev was really doing nothing more than walking the gray and narrow path of a Stalin bureaucrat? Did he actually go about the city, year after year, mouthing pious Stalinite platitudes? When the Politburo met, did Khrushchev quietly sit in the corner and speak only when spoken to?

This was hard, indeed, to believe. I remembered the first time I had ever seen Khrushchev at an Embassy affair. He had talked so much and so long that Mikoyan and Kaganovich finally took him by the elbows and propelled him gently but firmly toward the door. Nothing I had seen since indicated that this was not normal behavior for Khrushchev. He is an articulate, persistent man.

No Russian in public life has traveled more widely, spoken more often, talked to more people, and directed his attention into a greater variety of questions, places, and problems than Khrushchev since he came into his own.

How could this vigorous, robust, vocal man have survived those grim Stalin days? He could not have sat silently and cast down his eyes, for this was precisely what made Stalin most suspicious. "Look me in the eye," Stalin would say. "Speak frankly. What are you trying to conceal from me?"

No. Even if Khrushchev had been capable of such conduct it would not have availed him. He could not have survived by that route. Did he, then, bridle his tongue like some of the others and heap encomiums about Stalin's feet like wreaths? This was possible. He had paid his debt more than once to the Stalin "cult" with fulsome articles and orations, larded with the requisite number of references per paragraph to Stalin's genius.

But there must be more to it than this. I studied Khrushchev at every opportunity I had, and there were many in the Moscow of 1959. He was constantly shuttling back and forth—out to Vnukovo Airport, flying off to other countries or his own provinces, coming back, journeying around Moscow to parties, receptions, exhibitions and conferences. I listened to him make his speeches at the "friendship" meetings which he held each time he returned from abroad at the big new Lenin Sports Palace. This, too, was an innovation, and it was Khrushchev's style. Stalin had never traveled, except the short route from the dacha on the Mozhaisk chausee to the Kremlin and back. Stalin hadn't seen a peasant farm for years before he died. He never saw the battlefront during the whole of World War II. He only visited the subway once. He never met the public. But Khrushchev was forever on the go and always with the public.

I watched Khrushchev on informal occasions. I watched him argue with Vice President Nixon in the TV studio of the American Exposition in Moscow. I sat at their feet during the "kitchen" debate and tried to take notes as the words flew back and forth. But it was not until Khrushchev came to America and I observed him through thousands of miles of travel and tramping, of oratory at banquets and fast repartee on the run, in moments of triumph and moments of outrage, that I felt I was beginning to understand not only how Khrushchev had survived during the Stalin years but what was the secret of his leadership today.

There are those who assume that Khrushchev came to the top because he was Stalin's faithful henchman; that he could be relied upon to carry out whatever bloody or infamous business Stalin had on hand; that when Stalin died Khrushchev gained leadership by using the same kind of intrigue and treachery by which Stalin won the Kremlin.

I am sure that Khrushchev was a reliable lieutenant of Stalin's, just as I am sure that he is a reliable supporter of Communism. Were he not both he certainly would not have survived, and he certainly would not have won high Soviet office.

But Khrushchev is not Stalin, and he did not follow the

Stalin path to power. There is a vital difference between the two men and their tactics; and this is at least one great reason—all Marxist dialectic to the contrary—why Khrushchev's Russia and Stalin's Russia turn a different face to the world. Khrushchev's look is not just a false face for the old Stalin treachery.

To understand Khrushchev it is necessary to follow a long path back to the little village of Kalinovka which is situated in the Kursk region not far from the line which divides Russia proper from the Ukraine. Khrushchev was born in this village April 17, 1894, in the mud-and-wattle cottage where his mother and father lived. It was a poor household like most of the peasant households in the neighborhood. Khrushchev had brothers and sisters, but I do not believe he has ever said precisely how large his family was. But it was too large to support on their small plot of land; and Khrushchev's father worked at many jobs, chiefly as a miner in the Donbass coal mines just to the south.

Khrushchev, as he told Spyros Skouras during an argument as to who had started poorest and advanced farthest up the ladder of success, went to work as "soon as I was able to walk." This seems to be almost literally true. Khrushchev's first job was that of a shepherd boy, minding sheep.

"I looked after the 'little cows' as the capitalists called them," he recalled nearly sixty years later. And his first great step forward in life was his promotion from "little cows" to real cows. It was a big event in the life of a Kalinovka shepherd boy, and a note of pride still comes into Khrushchev's voice when he tells about it.

A barefoot cowherd gets a lot of cow dung on his feet. It washes off, of course. But the language of the cowherd has never washed off Nikita Khrushchev's tongue. He talks about the imperialists circling the sheep pen like hungry wolves and he calls capitalism "a worn-out mare." He said of an American

politician with whom he had had words in the course of his
U.S. tour: "He thought he was going to let a fart but he shitted
his pants instead."

Khrushchev was a grown-up man before he ever got any
formal education. But he learned fast in the school of life. As
soon as he was big enough to do a man's job (by Kalinovka
standards, this was when he reached the age of fifteen) his
father took him off to the Donbass. Here the lad from Kalinovka
got acquainted for the first time with capitalism—foreign capitalism, as it turned out. For years he worked in and around
Uzovka (named for Hughes, an English firm with a steel plant
and coal mines). He worked in a factory owned by Germans, he
worked in the Bosse plant which was owned by the French,
and in a chemical works owned by the Belgians.

He had never had a chance to go to school. He was too busy
working as a miner, as a common laborer, a fitter, a plumber, a
mechanic.

Here he got his first impressions of industrialism under the
capitalists. In later years, as he has said, when he came to read
Germinal by Emile Zola he thought the writer was describing
"not France, but the pit in which my father and I had worked."
And when much later he attended his first Party lectures on
political economy and the wage system under capitalism he
felt, he said, "as though Karl Marx had seen the mine my
father and I worked in."

Anyone who wants to understand Khrushchev's views on life
and his attitude toward capitalism, said an American who had
some very frank talks with him, must realize that all of his
initial impressions come from his days in the mines, days when
conditions were incredibly bad—mines seeping with water,
blind pit ponies, black-damp explosions, tuberculosis, starva-
tion wages, idleness.

Capitalists, he said once, "believe in God and rob the people working for them. They throw them out into the streets from plants and factories."

No one who listens to Nikita Sergeyevich long can doubt that he was reared in a good, God-fearing Russian Orthodox household and that whatever his convictions today he went to church as a boy and is thoroughly familiar with the Bible. The parable of Christ and the money-changers is a favorite of his. He says "God grant that you should feel as well as I do" (at the end of his American trip), or "God willing that we should all look as good as they do" (of two buxom Iowa ladies), or "God save you" (if you persist in clinging to capitalism). He speaks respectfully of Orthodox believers, whether at home or in the United States, and bows his head without affectation when grace is said.

Although he emphasizes his own atheism, he sounds, actually, more at home in an atmosphere of orthodox belief than of scientific disbelief. And on more than one occasion he has remonstrated with energetic Communists who wanted to get rough with Church adherents. God, he insisted in Iowa, is on the side of Russian farmers, not American (because He helps the intelligent). He speaks of the Greeks and the Russians as being "brothers in Christ." But he declined to attend church with President Eisenhower because "my people would not understand it."

Khrushchev was twenty-three years old when the Revolution broke out. But he was not a revolutionary or even a member of the Communist Party. He was a Donbass coal miner and he had taken part in workers' meetings, demonstrations, and strikes; but not until 1918 did he join the Russian Social Democratic Labor Party, as the Communists then called themselves. He became a soldier in the Red Army, fighting in the Donbass and, later on, down in the Don country and the Kuban.

I think the young miner, illiterate as he was, began to find himself in those years of fighting with the Red Army on the fast-shifting fronts of the south. Now, for the first time, he was coming into contact constantly with men much better educated than himself and, particularly, with Communists who had an organized and coherent outlook upon the world which up to now he had seen, chiefly, through the eyes of a tough, clever young peasant.

Khrushchev tells a touching story of himself in that period, of a boardinghouse in which he stayed for a time, perhaps in Rostov-on-Don. It was run by a woman whom he describes as "a graduate of a noble ladies educational establishment in St. Petersburg." Khrushchev says, "I suppose I still had coal on my hands when I lived in that house." Most of the others there were intellectuals and members of the bourgeoisie. Probably it was the first time he had ever associated with people so well informed. The people in the house wanted to know what the Bolsheviks proposed to do with the country.

"They started asking me questions," he recalls. "Well, all right, they said. But what do you understand about the ballet? You, a miner? And I must admit that at that time I not only had never seen a ballet, I had never seen a ballerina. So I did not know what it—what sort of a dish it was and what you ate it with. And I said: Wait, it will all come. But if they had asked me what it was that would come I could not have told them."

This was the kind of young man, able, eager, self-confident, gifted with peasant wit and steeped in peasant lore, whom presently the Communist Party undertook to educate, train, and mold as one of the corps of young officials which it was recruiting to provide the framework for the government which was to build the country.

These were difficult years in the Ukraine and the Donbass, where Khrushchev went after being demobilized. Civil war had wrecked the country. There was famine, cold, and disease. He worked again in the mines at Uzovka for a while, now as assistant manager; and then, in 1922, was given a chance by the

Party to enter a workers school, the Rabfak. Here, for the first time in his life, at the age of twenty-six he began his formal education. And here, too, his career was fixed upon the lines which were to determine his future. From this time on he was to be a Communist Party functionary. And much of that time was to be spent in the Ukraine.

It has been contended that Khrushchev took a big part in carrying out Stalin's purges in the Ukraine, but this is not the way I read the record. During most of the purge period Khrushchev was in Moscow, where he had been brought as a protégé of the City boss of that era, Lazar M. Kaganovich. Khrushchev, as was fitting in view of his years of underground experience, had a lot to do with the building of the Moscow subway system. He was in Moscow for nearly ten years, and toward the end of this period obviously came to Stalin's attention. In 1938 the old dictator made him a candidate member of the Politburo and sent him down to run the Party organization in the Ukraine. Naturally, as Khrushchev said to the Central Committee at the time of the critical debate in June, 1957, when Molotov, Malenkov, and the others hoped to oust him, none of the men who worked under Stalin escaped without getting some blood on their hands. But, he added, if I have blood on my hands there is more on those of the others. Khrushchev's job in the Ukraine was not to carry on the purge but to get things in order again after Stalin had eliminated all the previous leaders.

The war was coming on then; and when it struck, no part of Russia was more cruelly wounded than the Ukraine. There has been something of a press build-up in the last two or three years of Khrushchev's wartime role. I think this build-up is firmly grounded. One of Khrushchev's tasks was the organization of the behind-the-lines partisan movement. He flew back of the Nazi lines in little puddle-jumper planes, landing there, setting up guerrilla forces, and then returning to the Russian lines. Recent publicity has centered on his part in the Stalingrad battle. That was real, too. But I think the partisan operations took more daring.

Of Khrushchev's courage and willingness to face any odds there should be no doubt after the victory he achieved in the June, 1957, crisis. The odds against him in the Presidium were probably eight to three. Yet, he won out in the end.

To this day no one knows precisely what went on in the Kremlin in the strange and fateful days when Stalin's life was drawing to an end. Perhaps nothing more dramatic than an old man's circulatory system giving way under an attack of spleen. But if in those last days there was any drawing together of Stalin's comrades-at-arms, any mutual alliance for self-protection against the terrible, mad dictator, Khrushchev's steady nerves and assurance must have gone far toward carrying the day.

Here, I think, we must be coming close to the secret of how Khrushchev survived. No one has talked more than Khrushchev since Stalin's death about what it was like during Stalin's lifetime. Sometimes, he has said, a man did not know, when he received a summons to go to the Kremlin, whether he would emerge alive. He was once asked by a reporter how it was that he, a man who had not been particularly prominent before Stalin's death, had moved up to the top of the pinnacle.

It once happened, he replied, that there were four persons in prison in the Ukraine—a burly anarchist, a clever Social Democrat, a dedicated Communist, and a little Jew whose name was Pinya. They disagreed on many things; for example, on how to divide the food parcels they received. Finally they elected the little Jew to be their chairman and resolve all disputes. They argued about whose turn it was to clean out the cell and the little Jew had to decide that, too. Finally they decided to escape. They dug a tunnel; but when it was done, the question arose of who should go first. The big anarchist, the clever socialist, the Communist—each had some excuse for not going because it seemed certain that the first man out would be shot by the guards.

The little Jew settled the question. I am your leader, he said. You elected me by a democratic process. So I will go first.

The moral of the story, said Khrushchev, is that each man, whoever he may be, finally rises to the level of the responsibility which he is given.

"You know who that little Jew was?" Khrushchev asked. "That little Pinya, that was me."

While he was in America, Khrushchev became indignant when he was asked about a story which had wide circulation in Moscow. The story was that after he had delivered his anti-Stalin speech at the Twentieth Party Congress he was handed a note saying: "What were you doing while Stalin was committing these crimes?" He read the note to the audience and asked the author to rise and give his name. No one rose.

"Well, comrades," said Khrushchev, "now you know what I was doing at that time."

Khrushchev called this story a provocation. But I believe there is truth in it.

Khrushchev is also quoted as having said on another occasion that once, at the Kremlin, Stalin turned to him and said: "*Khokol,* dance the *gopak!*"

"And," said Khrushchev, "I danced the gopak."

The gopak is the leg-thrusting, kicking, Ukrainian national dance. The word khokol is an insult. It is like calling a Frenchman "frog" or a German "heinie." Nothing Stalin could have said could have conveyed more contempt to Khrushchev.

Following Khrushchev around America, watching his extraordinary public presence; his gift for mimicry, for mime, for gesture; his ability to play so many different roles, to suit his mood and style to the occasion, I returned again and again to this story of Stalin's insulting command.

Khrushchev is a sensitive man. There may be some who will

wonder at this remark. But I think I am right. He has the sensitivity of a man who has suffered many, many indignities in life and who has reached a position now where respect comes as his due. But he remembers the times when this was not so. He can himself descend to whatever level he finds himself on. He has traded punches all the way up—and survived. But there was a long, long period in his life when he had to carry out quite a different role in order to survive. And I think the gopak is the secret of that particular period in his life. He was Stalin's talkative Ukrainian (actually he is Russian, not Ukrainian). He could play the fool when Stalin ordered him to. He could make the jokes and salt the conversation with his peasant phrases. He knew how to be comic. He could make himself look a foolish peasant. He knew how to bow in the peasant way, touching the floor with the tip of his fingers. If he had to shovel manure, he knew how to handle the shovel and his nostrils were used to the smell. If Stalin had to have a butt for his rude joke, Khrushchev could serve as that butt. But he never forgot a single indignity, a single rudeness, a single joke.

I do not mean to suggest that Khrushchev survived simply because he was willing to play the jester at Stalin's court. That would be a gross oversimplification. But I think he was shrewd enough to realize that the cap and bells sometimes made a good disguise and that his best defense was not to be taken too seriously. He learned to use his words, his ready verbalization, as a screen and a shield. But underneath it all he was and is a very serious man.

It is quite possible that this served him well with his comrades-at-arms in the slippery atmosphere of the Stalin cabinet. His peasant manner, his child's way of screwing up his face, his way of walking—a little like a village duck—all of this may have come in good stead by causing his associates to underestimate him as a rival or opponent.

Khrushchev reminded me of the Russian peasant and his

traditional way of dealing with his superiors. Always submissive, always presenting himself as an ignorant clodhopper, deferring to superior city wisdom, never understanding what he does not want to understand, always saying yes when you know very well that he means no, never giving the game away and always playing it so that whatever may happen to his master he, Ivan, will survive.

Over the years Russia has had rulers of many kinds—princes, boyars, warriors, chiefs, tyrants, fools, weaklings, madmen, geniuses—but not for centuries had a peasant taken the scepter of power until the rise of Khrushchev.

Today there is a prickly quality about Khrushchev which I think is a heritage of this background. As he says, he never wants to be a debtor in his relations with people. If he is challenged he replies on the spot. When, as he says, someone steps on his favorite corn he reacts—and quickly. He holds a great office and he wields great power. He understands this. He respects the office and its power and expects others to respect it too. He can still play the fool if he wants to. He can make his peasant's bow if he is in the mood for it. He does not dance the gopak but he likes to take a brisk whirl on the dance floor occasionally—often with Yekaterina A. Furtseva as his partner. He loves the back-and-forth of tough argument. He doesn't get as much of it as he used to. When Charles Bohlen was U.S. Ambassador in Moscow, he was Khrushchev's favorite sparring partner. Bohlen's wits are as quick as Khrushchev's and his Russian is not much worse.

But Khrushchev does not get as good arguments from his colleagues as he used to. Mikoyan no longer talks up to him as he did in the past. When Khrushchev twits the Armenian for his fondness for peppery soups Mikoyan does not fire back a remark about Khrushchev and Ukrainian borsht. Not that the meetings of the Presidium now resemble Stalin's one-man rule of the old Politburo. Stalin used to assemble his colleagues only to tell them what he had decided—often in Georgian, leaving it to Beria to interpret his words. Khrushchev likes discussion and he gets it in the Presidium. Questions are brought up, argued, voted upon. It is not like the old days. But it is not the kind of argument that raged when Malenkov, Molotov, and the rest sat around the table.

But if Khrushchev does not get as much cross-talk these days as he would like, he is able to turn to one place where the talk is free, wide-ranging, and vigorous. This is his family. Long before he came to America with his wife, two of his three daughters, his son, and his son-in-law, it was evident to everyone in Moscow that he was pre-eminently a family man. Stalin hid the members of his family away from the prying eyes of the public and imposed a haremlike seclusion upon them. During his days it was not good taste for a Communist leader to mention his family. Only those who were privy to court gossip knew who was married and who was not and who had children. The family never appeared in public. Indeed, to this day it is not known whether the rumors that Stalin took as his third wife Rosa Kaganovich, sister of the old Politburo member, were true or not.

But just as one of the first acts of Khrushchev and the "collective leaders" was to move out of the Kremlin and build for themselves a neat little row of villas on the crest of Sparrow Hills, just below the new university skyscraper and overlooking the great Luzhniki sports layout, so at Khrushchev's prodding have the families of the party leaders and, specifically, his family been moved out of the purdah of the Stalin era.

This is not just a symbolic act, although there is certainly some symbolism connected with it. This is the kind of man Khrushchev is. He was the same down in the Ukraine years ago. He has a big family. Not only are there his four surviving children (his oldest son was a flier who was killed in the war), but he has always had a covey of nieces and nephews around the house, children of his relatives, some of whom lost their parents during the war, who have been raised in his household and brought up as members of the Khrushchev family. This is one reason why there was so much confusion in the United States for a long time about the composition of the Khrushchev family.

Khrushchev's wife, Nina Petrovna, is his second. His first wife died during the famine days in the Ukraine, and he remarried a year or two later while he was studying at the Rabfak. I imagine he and his wife met at the factory school. She, as Americans learned, is a woman of wit and dignity with as lively a curiosity and interest in the world as her husband. It is said in Moscow that no one has more influence upon Khrushchev than his wife. I suspect that this is right. She is a sensible woman and I can imagine her bringing her husband down to earth when, as sometimes happens, his temper takes flight and sends him bouncing toward outer space. But it is not only his wife whose voice is important in the family council. The Khrushchev family is a lively, energetic, Victorian one with diverse interests and personalities. And each member makes a contribution to the family discussions, which range as widely as they ever did around the breakfast table of the New England autocrat. Julia, the oldest, a daughter of the first marriage, is dark and scintillating. She is married to the director of the Kiev Opera, Gonchar, and often is her father's traveling companion as he speeds around the Soviet Union. The second daughter, Rada, is blonde, blue-eyed, and quick-witted. She speaks English, as well as or better than her mother, and is married to Alexei Adzhubei, the *Izvestia* editor, who acts as a second pair of eyes for his father-in-law and who is one of the most gifted members of the Khrushchev inner circle. The younger son, Sergei, an energetics specialist and member of a scientific team which recently won a Lenin prize for secret work, appears shy and diffident. He too speaks English and his father relies on him to explain scientific problems which he does not understand. There is a younger daughter, Elena, who is still at Moscow University. There is a growing number of grandchildren (the eldest are the children of the older son and are themselves married, with great-grandchildren on the way). When Khrushchev talks about his grandchildren it is not just a figure of speech.

Observing this warm and closely knit family, it seemed to me that over the years this may well have been his place of refuge, the one place during the Stalin years where he was able to talk about what he really thought, to drop for an hour or two the mask which he had always to keep over his face in the Kremlin and the guard which he had to put on his tongue.

For all these reasons it is a pleasant and reassuring sight to see Khrushchev and his family together. He is proud of them and they are proud of him.

The greatest of Khrushchev's talents, in my view, is his talent as a politician. I mean a politician in the full sense of the word, a man who derives strength from direct and continuous contact with people. I think that Khrushchev is a little like Antaeus, the Greek god whose strength came from the earth and who faded away when he was lifted off his feet. Without that constant and continuous contact, Khrushchev's strength would wither away.

Even in the Stalin era, Khrushchev risked his position to maintain his connection with the people. He used to go back to Kalinovka to visit his old friends and relatives. Once he carried back to Stalin a report of how bad conditions were in the village—people cutting down their orchards and slaughtering their animals because they could not pay the taxes. Stalin sneered at the report and called Khrushchev a *narodnik* for his concern over the peasants. The narodniks were an idealistic movement in the 1880's noted for their concern over the welfare of the peasants.

There was nothing more natural for Khrushchev to do when
Nixon visited him in Moscow than to take him out on the
Moskva River for a Sunday afternoon, riding around in a cabin
cruiser and visiting the bathing beaches, shaking hands with
Mr. Khrushchev's "slaves." The fact is that if Nixon had not
been in Moscow, Khrushchev would have been doing exactly
the same thing. This is the way he spends his Sunday after-
noons in summer when he is in Moscow. The new dacha which
he occupies (he refuses to use the near-by one where Stalin
lived) was built only about four years ago. It is almost a duplicate of the houses on Sparrow Hills. Instead of living in suspicious isolation, like Stalin, Khrushchev spends his free time
on the river, talking to the boaters and swimmers. Everyone
in Moscow knows this, and on Monday mornings during the
summer people ask each other when they come to work: "Well,
what was Nikita Sergeyevich up to on the river yesterday?"

Khrushchev is not the contemplative man. He told the Union
of Writers that he did not have as much time as he wished
to read their books because he had so many state documents to
pore over, reports of ambassadors, diplomatic notes, and
speeches by the statesmen of other countries. He had to read so
late, he said, that often he had to stick himself with pins to keep
awake. His staff culls many magazines and journals for him,
including some American publications. They know his interests
and bring to his attention things he wants to read about. He
peruses regularly the State Department's propaganda slick-
paper magazine, *Amerika.* So does his wife. His knowledge of
literature is broad but not deep. He quotes from Russian
classics, as does every Russian, but his favorites seem to be
folk sayings or Ukrainian poems and songs he heard as a young
man.

No Russian leader of our times has known his people better
or seen more of them than Khrushchev. He tells his companions:
"Seeing is better than hearing," and "You can't get to know a

country by riding on a public conveyance." And he suits his actions to his words. He is never still. In intervals between conferences and trips abroad he is restlessly winging about the Soviet Union in the new jet aircraft which he loves so well and which enable him to cross Siberia in a few hours. He has poked his nose into the plumbing of Siberian hotels, the vineyards of Moldavia, and the dry-goods stores of Vladivostok. He knows better than any of his colleagues what is going on in the country, what the people want and what they feel. He does not blink at eyesores and shortcomings. He points them out. He sprinkles advice and pithy peasant talk as he goes, and he has a word for everyone—the student who doesn't want to go to the desolate lands of the Far East, the northern farmer who is reluctant to plant corn, the housewife who doesn't cook her husband a good bowl of borsht, and the architect who turns the Palace of Culture into a gingerbread castle.

Someone has called Khrushchev the "peasant czar." He would resent that, and rightly, I think; he does not arrogate a czar's manner and a czar's divine right. But there is a universality about his words and his manner, a paternalistic interest in and attention to every problem from babies' diapers to supersonic aircraft, which makes it sound natural to hear him greeted (as I have heard him) as *batushka*, which means, as nearly as you can get its quality from the Russian, "dear father." It is an affectionate diminutive and peasants used to use it in referring to the Czar.

I was discussing Khrushchev with a Russian newspaperman one day. He said he felt that I and many other Americans had not quite understood what lay behind Khrushchev's rise to top leadership.

"You attribute this to Khrushchev's personal abilities—his success in eliminating his rivals. You make it a personal triumph in which he has won because of his own cleverness," he said. "I think this misses the point entirely. Certainly, Khrushchev is an able man. But so were the others. The reason Khrushchev rose to leadership is that he best epitomizes the mood and aspirations of the Russian people at this time. His program is the program which the people support."

It was the belief of this man that the difference did not lie in superior skill. Malenkov and Molotov, he pointed out, were able, experienced political figures. They were at least as capable at manipulation as Khrushchev. What made the difference was Khrushchev's superior ability at communication with the Russian people, his sense of the people's desires, and his crystallization of these deep strivings in terms of practical programs and action.

"If some other man with some other program had come forward," my friend said, "I don't believe he would have lasted. The people would not have stood for it."

The more I studied the relationship of Khrushchev and the Russian people, the free flow of communication back and forth, the more I tested the actual goals and desires of the people, the more I was convinced that there was validity in the journalist's argument.

Here was a man who was thrust forward by his times, by the course of history, as the Marxists would say. But having been thrust forward, having made the best use of his opportunity, he himself was now giving to this era a specific color and personality which flowed out of his own character.

It was true, it seemed to me, that one could now speak accurately and realistically of a Khrushchev era, just as it had been accurate to speak of a Stalin era.

I began to wonder what kind of a monument Khrushchev wanted to leave behind him. About Stalin there had been no question. He put up his own statue in every village square. He lent his name to great cities and factories. He named mountain peaks for himself. This was not the style of Khrushchev.

Stalin revised the doctrines of Marx and Lenin. He had books written to demonstrate that he was a greater philosopher than any who had come before. This also was not the style of Khrushchev.

In talking about Communism once, Khrushchev said: "It is not bad if in improving the theory of Marx one throws in a piece of bacon and a piece of butter. When you have a hungry belly it is sometimes very difficult to understand the theory of Marxism-Leninism."

This, it seemed to me, came very close to the ambition which Khrushchev had cut out for himself. He was going to try his utmost to put that bacon on the table of the Russian families and that butter on their bread. He wanted this for them and he knew they wanted this for themselves. To achieve this, of course, he must have peace. And if he went about the world preaching peace and pigs, calling for an end to the cold war and more hybrid corn, proposing disarmament and higher milk yields, asking for peaceful competition and better plumbing, I didn't think it bothered him at all to remember the day when Beria used to call him "our potato politician."

If you do away with the devil, Khrushchev sometimes says, the priest is out of a job. As he envisages the Khrushchev era, it is going down in history as the epoch of better feeling in Russia and in the world. He may not achieve his goals. But there can be no doubt that he is moving with the powerful stream of contemporary Russian history.

XI

The Politics of the Presidium

A FEW MONTHS before he died, Stalin mixed up all the political cards in the Communist deck. He reshuffled the pack so thoroughly at the Nineteenth Party Congress that it was impossible to determine whom, if anyone, he had selected as his successor. Khrushchev says today, and I suspect he is right, that Stalin thought he would live forever and consequently never picked any man to take his place. "This made it very difficult when Stalin died," Khrushchev adds with masterly understatement.

Khrushchev has no such inhibitions. He considers himself a mortal man and he has no hesitancy in discussing the question of the succession, even with foreigners. A man already has been picked, he told Governor Harriman. The successor is to be Frol R. Kozlov, the handsome, tall Party leader from Leningrad.

"Isn't that right, Anastas?" Khrushchev said, turning to Anastas Mikoyan.

"Yes, indeed," Mikoyan dutifully replied.

So, if these words are taken at face value, there will be no deadly duel for the succession should Khrushchev suddenly die. Not that anything is likely to happen to Khrushchev. His health seems extraordinarily good for a sixty-five-year-old man who has led a hard life. He complains that a kidney ailment led his doctors to restrict his use of alcohol and he is on a salt-deficient diet, probably because of a tendency to high blood pressure.

But no man who goes at Khrushchev's pace can be considered anything but robust.

The only trouble with Mr. Khrushchev's statement about the Soviet succession is that some skepticism persists that Kozlov really will be Khrushchev's successor. Kozlov is fifty-one years old, a native of Ryazan, not far from Moscow. This is an area noted for its peasant traditions and staunch clinging to the old Russian way of life.

Until recently Kozlov's manners were in the traditionally wooden and pompous style of the big-time provincial Party leader. He used a kind of gruff aggressiveness as a defense against getting involved in discussions of substance. Like so many of the men around Mr. Khrushchev he seemed durable, sturdy, a little heavy on his feet. But his personality has mellowed under the impact of a trip to America and his role as host to Vice President Nixon during part of the Nixon trip to Russia. He dresses with more care, carries himself with a dignity which he did not seem formerly to possess, combs his silvery hair high on his head, chaffs with newspapermen, lets his picture be taken and, all in all, acts like a politician who possesses a good deal of self-confidence. He seems to be sensitive to people, quick-witted, and more gracious than before.

Khrushchev has brought Kozlov forward fairly recently. He had been Party chief in Leningrad, and there was no indication of special closeness between Khrushchev and Kozlov in the past. Unlike most members of the Khrushchev team Kozlov never was in the Ukraine. Kozlov went to Leningrad after the murderous "Leningrad affair" had cleaned out the Party leadership there in 1948-49. He must have had agility to ride out the shifts in political winds since that time.

Despite this evidence of Kozlov's prominence and talent, Moscow is still betting that he has the makings of a Bulganin rather than a Khrushchev. That is, that the job he is more likely to wind up in is that of Premier rather than Party Secretary.

Political soothsaying is particularly hazardous in Moscow, where history has shown that the least likely, the least prominent, the person most seldom in the public eye is apt to wind up with the big prize. This was true with Stalin. It was true with Khrushchev. It may well be true again.

One reason for this, and I have long felt that, perhaps, it was the greatest defect in the Soviet system, is the lack of an established and orderly tradition for the choosing of a Chief of State.

In theory Russia has an elaborate constitutional system, a parliament, a cabinet, a Prime Minister. But the real power does not lie here and, even if an election were to be called upon the death of the leader, it would not be the vote which would determine the succession. It would be the secret political maneuvering which goes on in the highest echelons of the Communist Party. For it is the Party which manipulates the election levers and decides who shall run and who shall win in an election. The Communist Party picks its leader by a vote of the Central Committee. This is a narrow body of 125 to 135 men, and its composition usually is determined by an even narrower body, the Politburo or Presidium of the Party, eleven to fifteen men.

Thus, when a change of leadership occurs it is not through a vote in a national election, it is not through a vote in a parliament, it is not even, as in a hereditary monarchy, the orderly succession of an heir to the throne, known well in advance.

Instead, the leadership must be won by the victor in an intense and bitter conflict within the narrowest circles at the pinnacle of the Party. It becomes, in fact, a contest of will and strength in which the only limit upon weapons and tactics is that imposed by the participants themselves.

Stalin placed no restraint upon himself in the intrigues which led to his seizure of power. Khrushchev, however, imposed a very important restraint—one in which he and his colleagues apparently all agreed. This was not to use the police power or terror against each other.

But, for all his moves to reduce the power of the police, nothing that Khrushchev has done will ensure that it will not be employed again in the next struggle for power. And nothing he has done structurally to the state or to the Party can ensure that there will not be another struggle for power in event of his death. The consequences to the Soviet Union and to the world of such a struggle carried to the limits by ruthless, extraordinarily powerful men could be catastrophic.

This is the reality of the situation. What counts in the succession is not the blessing of "Anastas and myself" but sheer weight of political power and political agility exerted at the fulcrum of the Soviet apparatus. This is why the "politics of the Presidium" is one of the most important questions in the world today. Who is going up? Who is going down? Who is likely to acquire more influence by this policy or that policy?

In Stalin's day a kind of rough chart of political ups and downs was maintained through a device which the old Generalissimo dearly loved. This was a display of the "portraits of the leaders" which occurred twice a year, in November and May. On such occasions Stalin had the portraits of the Politburo hung in order of their supposed importance. If a man dropped from third position to sixth he was going down. If he rose from eight to five he was on the way up. Stalin often manipulated the ups and downs in order to confuse his subordinates and keep them at each other's throats. But the portraits did, at least, offer some kind of a clue to what was going on within the secret-haunted labyrinth of the Kremlin.

The picture game has largely been eliminated from Khrushchev's Russia. The pictures of the leaders are usually hung alphabetically now. Names are listed the same way in the papers. But occasionally deviations occur, and when they do they offer insight on the relative positions of the men around Khrushchev.

For instance, when I was out in the Urals I saw rows of

portraits in two big plants. The display was identical: Lenin, Voroshilov, Khrushchev, Mikoyan, Suslov and Kirichenko. This clearly indicated that the real inner power group in Russia was: Khrushchev, Mikoyan, Suslov, and Kirichenko.

My own guess is that should anything happen to Khrushchev in the near future his immediate successor would be Mikoyan. There is no doubt that the wise, battle-scarred Armenian has been the closest man to Khrushchev in the days since Stalin's death. At each step of Khrushchev's rise you could see Mikoyan striking out ahead, testing the ground, as it were, for Khrushchev to follow. This was true on the occasion of two of Khrushchev's most dramatic actions—his denunciation of Stalin and his trip to America. At the Twentieth Party Congress it was Mikoyan who first openly attacked Stalin—in terms more sharp, in some respects, than used by Khrushchev. And it was Mikoyan who first came to America, measuring the temper of the country and reporting back to Khrushchev what it was like and what he might expect when and if he came over.

Like Khrushchev, Mikoyan is an old sparrow. He is living on time doubly borrowed. He cheerfully admits that he is in the world today because "I have been very lucky." He does not exaggerate. He has been clever, too. Bold when he had to be bold, clever when cleverness was his only protection. He should, of course, have been dead many, many years ago in the infant days of the Revolution. He was a revolutionary in Baku at a time when the city was seized by the White Russians and the British. He and others of the top Communist leadership made their escape on a boat across the Caspian. But they were overhauled and taken prisoner by the British.

The prisoners were brought back to Baku. Their names were compared with two lists of revolutionaries who had been in prison under the White Russians. Twenty-six men were shot; their names were on the lists. Mikoyan was released; his name was not there. The twenty-six "commissars" have gone down in history as martyrs to the Communist cause. "Two or three of those men," Mikoyan says quizzically, "were not even Communists. But they happened to be in jail, so their names were on the lists. I was a leader of the Party. My name was not on the list. I was very lucky."

He was even more lucky in the last epoch of Stalin's life. Mikoyan had been marked for extinction by Stalin. There was no secret about it; Stalin had said as much. He had also said he was going to get rid of all the other old Bolsheviks, Molotov included. But Mikoyan's name headed the list. Perhaps he remembered too much old history about events in the Caucasus, about what really happened down there, about the role of Stalin in the Orzhonikidze affair, the role of Beria in the liquidation of Yenikidze, and many, many other matters.

Whatever the case, Mikoyan was rapidly coming to the end of the road in those last days of February and early March which culminated with Stalin's death on March 5, 1953. It was a timely event for all the older Politburo members. Especially for Mikoyan.

I saw a good deal of Mikoyan during his tour of America. I think I got to know him fairly well. I remember sitting in the parlor car of the Pennsylvania Railroad going back to New York from Washington. Mikoyan had finished his mission and was taking the plane later in the day to return to Moscow. He sat in his chair and looked out over the New Jersey boglands and the industrial slums. The air was dirty with fog and rain. He sat, a little Chaplinesque man with pince-nez glasses, staring with unseeing eyes at the dreary landscape.

In his hands he held, unopened, the battered copy of *Inostrannaya Literatura* which he had carried all over America with him without ever having a chance to read it. It had some translations of American short stories in it.

As I looked at this man who had whirled across the country with an energy equalled only by that of Khrushchev, a man full of zest, lively curiosity, and ready argument, it seemed for a moment as though the public face which he had worn had dropped away and left him there, rather small and alone and old and tired. There were fatigue lines around his mouth and his eyes were far away. Perhaps, I thought, for a moment he is running back in his mind through all the years, the years of struggle, of achievement, of danger, all the battles won and lost, the early dreams and the mounting disillusionment, the comrades who had fallen by the way.

I could not help thinking of the remark he had made to Van Cliburn the night before at the big Soviet Embassy reception. "You know," he had said, "I never wanted to be a revolutionary, really. What I wanted to be was a ballet dancer."

And I thought of the talk we had had on the airplane a day or two earlier and of his remark that he had never gone to a university. "I was a graduate of the school of the Revolution," he smiled, "and a pretty good school it was, too."

"My son," he went on, "of course, has gone through higher education. He is an educated man. They sometimes call me educated. But I am not really. I never went on to higher education. I was thought to be a talented child and that is why I was sent to the seminary. [Like Stalin, Mikoyan was educated for the priesthood.] Our children have the advantages that we did not have. And yet, sometimes I think they are not as strong as we are."

Now Mikoyan was coming to the end of what had been an incredible trip for him, a trip which was to be surpassed only by that of Khrushchev a few months later. He had got things started on the path of better relations between the two countries. Now he would go back to Moscow and report to his chief. Then the next phase of the battle would begin. There was no rest in this eternal struggle of being a Bolshevik. You fought as hard as you could and you hoped that it was good enough to survive another day or week or month. And even now, having

come out into the sunlight after passing through the deep
shadows of Stalin's last days, Mikoyan knew that the battle was
not finally won—that none of the battles were finally won. And
whether the future would take a form anything like the original
aspiration of the Communists he could not know. That depended on the sons—the sons who sometimes appeared more
weak than their fathers.

This is the wise and able man who probably would take the
helm of state if Khrushchev suddenly died. His policies would
differ not a whit from Khrushchev's. But he would not remain
at the pinnacle for long. Mikoyan is sixty-four. He is of the same
age group as Khrushchev, although he has been at the top
longer than anyone now in Moscow. Mikoyan came into the
Politburo in 1926.

Leadership of the Party is bound to flow to a younger generation, the men in their fifties. In a sense this generation already
feels a bit cheated. They had expected to succeed when Stalin
left the stage, and would have, had Georgi Malenkov made it.

Now Malenkov has lost his chance at the prize. There is no
one in Moscow who thinks he has a chance of a comeback. Perhaps he may move up a little from the job of running the power
station at Ust-Kamenogorsk. But he is out of running for the
big posts. This is not for lack of ability. It is conceded that
Malenkov was able. But he has been tarred indelibly with deep
guilt in the Leningrad affair and other outrages. No one in
Moscow seems to doubt that it was Malenkov, hand in glove
with Beria, who carried out this plot with the benign blessing of
Stalin. It wiped out the Zhdanov wing of the Party and with it
the lives of many able and innocent Communist leaders. They
were charged, it is said, with a conspiracy to move the capital
to Leningrad and with conniving to put themselves in touch
with foreign powers. "Malenkov was a clever man. He had
ability and he spoke well," one of his associates said. "But he
lacked principle."

None of the ousted men is given a chance for a comeback. Kaganovich seems to be generally disliked. Shepilov, the erstwhile Foreign Minister, is tagged as an overambitious man who lacked political astuteness. Marshal Zhukov has the sympathy of many high army commanders; but he, too, missed the boat, if he ever had had a chance of catching it. Khrushchev has effectively split the army, and the lines of conflict between the supporters of Marshal Konev and Marshal Zhukov are becoming blurred. The World War marshals are fast approaching retirement (which comes much later in Russia) and a new generation is pushing up. Konev is less active. Malinovsky is very much in the thick of things. But the man in whose cool, determined hands the real army power seems to rest is Marshal Sokolovsky, the Chief of Staff. This is the post he took over quietly, without announcement and under still unexplained circumstances, on the eve of Stalin's fatal illness.

Certainly the army will have something to say about the Khrushchev succession. Nothing that Khrushchev has done has taken the final arbitrating power out of the army's hands, although with the rise of rocketry and nuclear weapons the bases of power within the Soviet Armed Forces are shifting somewhat. The armies are smaller and the technologists and scientists have more voice. But the General Staff still calls the turns.

Of Khrushchev's defeated opponents, the only one who retains general respect and public esteem is Molotov. The feeling of respect for Molotov as an old Bolshevik, as a man of courage and conviction, as an ornament of the regime, and as the only living link with the pre-revolutionary past, extends into the government. Molotov is spoken of in respectful terms by men like Mikoyan and Khrushchev. We respect him, they say, but we disagree with him profoundly. Or, as one of them said: "We would trust Molotov with any diplomatic assignment. But we do not want him to have anything to do with making policy."

In the summer of 1959 there seemed to be genuine embarrassment over Molotov's continuing exile to Ulan Bator and many hints that it would soon end. He was sent there, nominally as ambassador, in 1957. Actually, it was exile. He was not entrusted with the real business of the embassy. The former Soviet ambassador was held on in Ulan Bator to conduct embassy affairs. Molotov was a figurehead.

The source of Moscow's dilemma over Molotov lies in the fact that he retains national respect and he also clings to what are regarded as reactionary Stalinist views on foreign and domestic policy. For example, he not only opposed patching up a peace with Tito, and the virgin lands experiment. He also opposed opening the Kremlin to tourists.

Khrushchev has not driven all of the Stalinists out of the government or out of the Party. There are many men who simply have put their heads down. They remain convinced that the old policies of police terror at home and cold war abroad are the only sound ones for Russia.

These men are not without influence in the government. Khrushchev has removed many of them from the top positions. But others remain, including, without doubt, some who profess to be his strong supporters. There is no real chance for these individuals to overthrow Khrushchev's policies so long as Khrushchev is successful. But in event of a major setback at home or abroad, the question might again become a live one. In such a situation Molotov might be a rallying point for Khrushchev's opponents.

This, I think, is why the government shies away from letting Molotov return to Moscow and retire and write his memoirs. In the capital he would be too visible and too available. At the same time Ulan Bator seems inappropriate. It was thought to get out of the dilemma in the winter of 1959 by naming him Ambassador to The Hague. But news of the project leaked prematurely, got involved in Dutch domestic politics, and had to be abandoned. This makes it difficult or impossible to find another diplomatic post for Molotov in the West, and a satellite post is considered unsuitable.

So Molotov remained in Mongolia under conditions considerably more strict than when as a young man he was exiled by the Czar to Kachug in Siberia, a few hundred miles north of Ulan Bator. Molotov is an old Bolshevik, and you would never know from the dignity and pride of his bearing that he was anything other than the Ambassador Extraordinary and Minister Plenipotentiary of the Union of Soviet Socialist Republics in Ulan Bator.

But the reality of his position is something else again. Early one hot Sunday afternoon in July my son and I were riding along a dirt road that curves up through a narrow valley behind the holy mountain of Bodgo-Khan-Ula, outside of Ulan Bator. I noticed parked along this lonely roadside a green Volga with a chrome whiplash radio antenna, an unusual accessory for this remote spot.

A quarter of a mile away I saw a European wearing a light gray suit, dark glasses against the hot bright sun, and a white handkerchief knotted over his gray hair, trudging alone along the road. As our car sped past, the elderly man glanced up in curiosity, then squared his shoulders and walked on. This was my first glimpse of Molotov in Mongolia.

Another quarter of a mile farther down the road I saw Mr. Molotov's Embassy Zim parked. Beside it was another green Volga security car. Two security cars on a road inhabited by goats, yaks, and yurts seemed to me an excessive concentration.

I saw Mr. Molotov on the same road the next Sunday at just the same hour. He is a man of precise habit. Sunday afternoon is obviously set aside for his weekly constitutional.

I talked with Mr. Molotov a little, just pleasant social conversation. He was busy and rather happy just then because his wife, Paulina Zhemchuzhina, once boss of the Soviet cosmetics industry, later in charge of fisheries, and, just before Stalin's death, sent to exile in Siberia, had just arrived from Moscow, bringing with her the two beautiful Molotov granddaughters, Larissa, nine, and Luba, five, children of the Molotovs' only daughter, Svetlana.

He was playing the role of Grandpa Molotov, when I saw him, and enjoying it. He accepted with pleasure my compliments on the beauty of the little girls and joked with my son as to whether a diplomatic or a journalistic career was preferable.

It has sometimes been suggested that Mr. Molotov utilizes his strategic location, close to the Chinese frontier, for contacts with Mao Tse-tung and Chou En-lai who are supposed to be much closer to his viewpoint than Moscow. I doubt that this is so. I saw no evidence to suggest that Mr. Molotov was playing any kind of a political role in Ulan Bator. This was borne out by diplomats who have talked with him. Their feeling was that Molotov was exercising the greatest care not to give grounds for any accusation of contact with opponents of the regime— or, indeed, contacts of any kind except those which his government approved. Everyone who visited Molotov found that he had great interest in what was going on in the world. He questioned his guests in lively fashion but offered no opinions of his own. In no case was he alone with a guest for more than a moment or two. Either at his own initiative or that of someone else, another official invariably joined the conversation after a minute or two.

There was a general feeling in Ulan Bator that Molotov's exile was drawing to a close, that one way or another Moscow would find another spot for him. At sixty-nine he obviously was not going to make another challenge for Soviet leadership. And even his strongest political opponents would like to see him spend his remaining years under circumstances a little more pleasant than being confined to one of the most remote diplomatic missions in the world.

The figure most often mentioned in discussion of any movement back toward a Stalinist line is Mikhail Suslov. He is the most enigmatic member of the leadership group. He has little to do with foreigners, except for leaders of foreign Communist parties. Unlike most of Khrushchev's associates he rarely attends diplomatic receptions and seldom is seen around Moscow.

In contrast to Khrushchev's other associates who are, in the main, like himself gregarious extrovert politicians, Mr. Suslov appears like a shadow of the past. Alone among the new Presidium members, Suslov still wears in summer an old Russian visored cap. His colleagues follow Khrushchev's style and sport bright new panamas.

By all the rules of logic and political inclination, Suslov should have supported Molotov and Malenkov in their ill-fated cabal against Khrushchev. He did not, and thereby proved that he had a political acumen greater than theirs. Since then his role has been anomalous, seldom to the fore but never long in obscurity.

It seems likely to me that the presence of a conservative Stalinist in the ruling group is useful for Khrushchev. It provides a magnet to polarize the support of the Stalinists who survived Molotov's ouster. And Suslov is very useful in dealing with certain foreign Communist parties where the Stalinist influence is strong, particularly the French Party. And it may be that Suslov gets on better with the Chinese than Khrushchev. About this there is much speculation.

Suslov has some very important lieutenants in the Khrushchev organization—at least their lines of patronage seem to lead to Suslov. Suslov is a former editor of *Pravda*. His adherents are mostly *Pravda* men. They include Pyotr N. Pospelov, a former *Pravda* editor and old Stalinist ideologue. There is also Leonid F. Ilyichev, a former *Pravda* editor, former chief of the Foreign Office Press section, and now head of the Agitprop, the Central Committee's agitation-propaganda section, and Pavel

Satyukov, the present editor of *Pravda*. The widely despised Minister of Culture, N. A. Mikhailov, is another Suslov protégé.

This is a formidable team, with considerable access to Khrushchev and probably a certain influence with him. It is their task to protect Khrushchev's ideological flanks. They thrash about with great vigor. Ilyichev specializes in sarcasm and nasty little stories which usually do the Soviet Union a good deal of propaganda harm. This is so obvious that some suspect that Ilyichev is deliberately trying to poison the atmosphere and sabotage the main line of Khrushchev's policy. This would serve the hidden opponents of Khrushchev, since the basic opposition to Khrushchev's line comes from men who are convinced that it is not possible under any circumstances to get on with the West. Thus, the nastiness and ill-will created by Suslov's underlings support the long-range political objectives of the Stalinist group.

However, despite his strong and able lieutenants, his connections with former Stalinists, and his allies among the former Communist parties, not many in Moscow think Suslov has a serious chance of succeeding Khrushchev. Such a chance could only arise in the event of catastrophic misadventure or disaster which would throw the whole Khrushchev line into question. Such a development hardly seems likely.

When all is said and done, the succession in Moscow really is determined by the Party and by the person who can command the greatest support within the Party. This is the reason why political observers in Moscow thought that Khrushchev might be succeeded by Alexei I. Kirichenko.

Kirichenko is even less known to foreigners than Suslov. But among Khrushchev's lieutenants he has been one who carried heavy burdens. Mikoyan said in 1959 that Kirichenko should see foreigners more often, and Khrushchev added that foreigners would find Kirichenko a lot harder to deal with than himself.

Who is he? Well, he is a fifty-one-year-old Ukrainian who has been associated with Khrushchev ever since Khrushchev went down to Kiev in 1938 to take over the Party apparatus. When Khrushchev moved up to Moscow in 1949 Kirichenko stayed behind as second secretary of the Party organization. The most important step in his career occurred on June 13, 1953, when he became Communist Party boss of the Ukraine. He took over the job from a man named Leonid G. Melnikov. At the time everyone supposed Melnikov was Khrushchev's man and that he had been ousted through machinations by Beria. This, so I thought then, was the tip-off move which led to the arrest and ouster of Beria two weeks later.

History shows that probably just the opposite occurred. Probably Melnikov and Beria had been dickering; Khrushchev discovered it, ousted Melnikov, put the reliable Kirichenko in his place, and then with his colleagues moved forward to deal with Beria. From then until early January, 1960, Kirichenko's career followed Khrushchev's step by step up the ladder. Melnikov got a diplomatic assignment to Bucharest and then dropped out of the picture.

Kirichenko is a tough, big-framed man with bushy eyebrows and an eagle's stare. His specialty is heavy industry and Party organization. His presence in the layout of pictures in the Urals factories was testimony to his inner importance in the Party structure.

Someone suggested to Khrushchev in 1959 that Kirichenko "runs the Party for you." Khrushchev drew himself up with hauteur.

"I am a very jealous man," he said. "A very jealous man about the Party. Nobody runs the Party for me."

Nevertheless, insofar as Khrushchev delegated the job to anyone, it was to Kirichenko that he delegated it. And there was no doubt in Moscow that the big men of the Party, the ham-fisted provincial secretaries, the big bosses of the Urals plants

and the Donbass, the big city managers—these men would go
down the line for Kirichenko. When a very important meeting
of the Soviet security chiefs was held in the spring of 1959 to
lay down the Party line on the role of the police in the newly
relaxed internal situation, the man who spelled it out was
Kirichenko. This indicated that the police also fell within
his special area of supervision.

Speculation over Kirichenko's role was set back in January,
1960, when he was sent down to Rostov to take over a regional
Party assignment. This was clearly a troubleshooting assignment. But it removed Kirichenko from his strategic position
near the Moscow levers of control.

There are other men in the wings or moving onto the stage
who may play a role in the succession. Two of the ablest are
Averky B. Aristov, a serious, darkly handsome man on whom
Khrushchev relies to get jobs done. I have seen him in and out
of his seat on the Presidium of the Supreme Soviet half a dozen
times in an hour, carrying out orders relayed to him by Khrushchev. Aristov is the man who announced Kirichenko's assignment to Rostov, and he may have inherited some of Kirichenko's
Party power. Another man of genuine ability is Alexei N. Kosygin. He was the only one of Zhdanov's Leningrad protegés to survive. In the worst of the Stalin days his life hung by a thread.
He has moved slowly and painstakingly upward in recent years.
Today, mature, quiet-spoken, keenly aware, Kosygin at fifty-
five directs more and more of Soviet industry as head of the
economic planning agency.

"I like to talk to Kosygin," a diplomat said to me. "There is
no nonsense about him. He is intelligent. He knows what he is
talking about and he speaks to the point."

The man whom Moscow has picked to succeed the ailing
Marshal Kliment Y. Voroshilov as President is Nikolai G. Igna-
tov, a reliable and colorless man who already has taken over a
good many of Voroshilov's functions.

Behind this group stands a varying company of men close to Khrushchev whose influence waxes and wanes. Some of them are very able, men like V. V. Matskevich, for example, the Minister of Agriculture, an old Khrushchev hand from the Ukraine and one of the shrewdest and most competent men in the Khrushchev cabinet. Another is Mikhail Menshikov, Khrushchev's Ambassador to the United States. He played an important role in the opening up of a new relationship between Russia and the United States. A third is Georgi A. Zhukov, the former *Pravda* foreign editor, who has demonstrated his vigor and ability as a Soviet bureaucrat in the exchange program between the United States and Russia.

But in the long run the influence of these men may not be so great as that of the young Turks. These men are the most interesting group that Khrushchev has around him. The most prominent and able is Alexei Adzhubei. A whole generation of active young Soviet officials, journalists, and others look to Adzhubei and his policies. One Soviet journalist whom I know has bet a dozen bottles of champagne that Adzhubei will be editor of *Pravda* within three years. This may come true. In the meantime, for the first time since Bukharin, *Izvestia* has a real editor who is making the dust fly. Adzhubei doubled the circulation of the youth paper, *Komsomolskaya Pravda*, in his five years of editorship. Moscow expects him to do at least as well on *Izvestia*, which currently has less than one-third the circulation of *Pravda* (1,300,000 against over 5,000,000).

Adzhubei is thirty-four years old, blond, blue-eyed. He talks hard and straight and his handclasp is warm and vigorous. It is time for young men to shoulder greater responsibility, in his opinion, and he is doing it. He is a graduate of the Moscow University journalism school, the first journalism graduate to reach a high post in the Soviet Union. He was only twenty-nine when he became editor of *Komsomolskaya Pravda*. He likes to work with young editors and young reporters and he likes new ideas and new techniques. He is a great believer in eyewitness reporting and contends that a story is best told in human and exact terms. He is a good, lively, and thoughtful writer and correspondent himself.

Another man in this younger group is Alexander N. Shelepin, the forty-one-year-old Communist Youth secretary whom Khrushchev picked to run the State Security organization. Shelepin and Adzhubei are friends and were closely associated in the Young Communist movement.

To me it seemed plain that Khrushchev was trying to strengthen the influence of the young Turks, drawing upon men from the youth organization in order to leaven and freshen the stodgy cadres of the Party hacks who comprise the backbone of his organization. For the moment the younger men are more gadflies than rivals of their elders. But their day is coming.

Khrushchev should not be confronted with any real challenge to control over Soviet affairs unless or until age impairs his ability to handle the manifold business of the state. Should his health hold good, the relative influence and position of the age groups will gradually change. The influence of the men of the sixties will wane and the vigorous young forty-year-olds will press forward more and more vigorously. These are the men, regardless of the difference in age, who seem today to be closest to Khrushchev in spirit and policy.

XII

Siberia Is Russia's Future

THE FIRST TIME I saw Siberia it was wartime and I was accompanying Eric Johnston, then head of the U.S. Chamber of Commerce, on a trip into the interior. Our host was Mike Kulagin, the boss of western Siberia, the toughest, cockiest Communist I have ever met. He rode with Budënny's cavalry during the Civil War and delighted in demonstrating with gestures how he cut down white Cossack officers with a single saber stroke "right to the ass." I have seen only one man who could drink more vodka than Kulagin and this man, an American correspondent, to Kulagin's amazement, drank him right under the table. Kulagin boasted that "all the riches of Siberia are at my disposal." He tried to give a whole casket of jewels to Johnston as a token of Siberian friendship. Johnston managed to refuse the embarrassing treasure trove only by convincing Kulagin that "party discipline" would not permit him to accept the riches. The "discipline" was that of the Republican party and the ingenious argument sprang from the brain of Johnston's traveling companion, William L. White, who correctly deduced that "party discipline" was the only thing which Kulagin would understand and respect. Kulagin sadly promised to keep the jewels for Johnston. "I will keep them here," he said. "And they will grow. Perhaps the next time you come to Siberia the Party line will have changed and you can accept them."

Last summer I went back to Novosibirsk for the first time

in fifteen years to see again the raw and bustling city on the
banks of the River Ob which was Kulagin's joy and pride.
Again, I was traveling with a distinguished visitor. This time
it was Vice President Nixon.

History repeats itself even in Siberia. Mr. Nixon was taken
to the same villa on the high pine-covered bluff above the River
Ob where we had stayed with Mr. Johnston and where, a few
days earlier in 1944, the first American Vice President to visit
Novosibirsk, Henry Wallace, was accommodated. Mr. Nixon
was given the same bedroom and the same bed that Mr. Wallace
slept in fifteen years earlier.

I found Novosibirsk as hearty, enthusiastic, and rough-and-
ready as it had been fifteen years ago. Once again I was reminded of the American West in the pioneer days—the rush
of construction, the bragging, the grandiose plans for the future.
I went again to the Novosibirsk Opera House, which was Kulagin's supreme glory. It was and is the biggest opera house in
Russia, and Kulagin was as proud of it as Sam Insull was of the
Civic Opera House he built on the banks of the Chicago River.
I saw again the fantastic ninety-ton fire curtain, made of solid
concrete and the only one of its kind in the world. So Kulagin
assured us, and I accepted his statement without question. I
never understood why this remarkably cumbersome device had
been constructed. Possibly there was a shortage of asbestos.
In any event the Opera House was still safe from fire. I doubted
whether even an atomic bomb would penetrate Kulagin's
curtain.

In 1944 the house had not yet been used for opera—indeed,
it was not quite finished. But this time we saw a performance
of "Swan Lake" which was lovely and graceful. The ballerina
was the equal of the younger stars of the Bolshoi and the corps
de ballet was better than any in America.

In 1944 every one of the apartment houses and office buildings along Krassny Prospekt, the principal street of Novosibirsk, seemed to have been turned into a hospital for the war wounded. The convalescents sat in the windows or stood on the balconies, sunning themselves in the strong July sunshine. And they moved down the sidewalks, an endless stream of the limbless, the halt, the blind, the bandaged, and the scarred. If you wanted to see the human toll of war, Novosibirsk was the place to go in those days. Now the human wrecks have been widely dispersed. I saw no more men on crutches or little roller-skate platforms in Novosibirsk than I would find in any Russian provincial town.

No longer did the hot, dry summer winds of Siberia whip clouds of dust in my face as I walked in the center of town. Most of the streets had been paved or asphalted.

This time we did not visit the great Chkalov aircraft factory, which in wartime was one of the principal producers of Yak fighters for the Red Air Force, or the huge optical works which had been evacuated from Moscow. But the plants we did see were hustling, busy shops. They were the same kind that Kulagin showed us in 1944, where, sometimes stopping to chuck a teen-age crane operator under the chin or putting a friendly arm around snub-nosed blonde Natasha, busy at her shell-turning lathe, he seemed to know almost every worker by his first name.

But not all of Novosibirsk was familiar. There were acres of new industrial establishments which had proliferated on the outskirts of the city, new industrial housing sections to replace the old wooden labor barracks with their barbed wire and guards, a new jet airport to accommodate the Trans-Siberian flow of TU-104's and TU-114's.

And when we visited the River Ob, we did not go for a romantic moonlight ride on a paddle-wheel steamer, laden with mountains of caviar, champagne, and sturgeon-in-jelly, with the wild heel-kicking dancers of the Red Army ensemble and the artists of the Leningrad Philharmonic playing Tchaikovsky while Kulagin fired salutes high over the Siberian birches with his Very pistol.

No. The visit to the River Ob this time was to see the mighty Novosibirsk hydroelectric plant and the great dam which has been thrown like a giant's sandbox across this turbulent north-flowing watercourse.

The Novosibirsk I saw in 1944 was a wartime city, a city of evacuated industry, evacuated workers, hospitalized troops, refugees, deportees, forced labor. It was the hub of the western Siberian war effort, a city of less than half a million suddenly swollen to more than a million. The enormous Novosibirsk railroad station, the biggest on the Trans-Siberian, with waiting rooms almost as vast as those of the Grand Central, was a bottleneck through which daily tens of thousands of people were transshipped. The floor of the station was packed with sleeping refugees, resting troops, families going east, families going west. The scene at night reminded me of Doré's illustrations for Dante's Inferno, a maze and jumble of people—some sleeping, others merely sitting, children whimpering, mothers nursing babies, blind wounded helping each other, nurses pouring tea from tin buckets, old women stupefied with weariness.

Today Novosibirsk is a city of about one million permanent residents. It is the hub of a new effort which is going forward with much of the drive and energy of a wartime campaign. Novosibirsk is to be the core of the great new industrialized Siberia which Russia proposes to construct in the next fifteen or twenty years.

So rapid has been the growth that each of the institutions shown to Mr. Nixon was new since my wartime visit. Construction of the great Yefremov heavy-machine-tool plant, which turns out hydraulic presses not only for Soviet use but for China, Hungary, and other Communist states, had been under way when I first saw Novosibirsk, but only after the war did it go into production. It has expanded since that time. Now it is one of the largest and most modern of Russia's heavy-machine plants. Russia's machine-tool industry already has exceeded that of the United States in volume and, in some specified fields, in quality. Half of the Yefremov plant's production is now going for export.

These are the "machines that make machines," and it is this rapidly increasing Soviet capacity for production of machine tools which I have always felt should concern most deeply any serious student of the comparative industrial systems of the United States and Russia. The machines that make machines are the ones which Khrushchev counts on to put the Soviet ahead in the peaceful competition of the two systems about which he talks so much. The task of the Yefremov works, together with other new Siberian tool-making plants, will be to tool up the new industries of this vast land which now stands on the threshold of development.

The big gray-columned buildings of the Yefremov works are impressive, but not so impressive as the sight of the River Ob. The Ob at Novosibirsk is a broad river, flowing between bluffs on which birch and pine forests sprawl out in all directions for hundred of miles.

When I first saw it in Mike Kulagin's company we walked down a wooden staircase at the government dacha to a landing stage, boarded a beautiful white river steamer, and cruised for hours in the Siberian midsummer twilight between islands and along the dark and mysteriously forested shores. The evening sky was touched with colors like a painter's palette. Long after midnight the hues of rose and yellow and purple glowed softly in the northern clouds. This, I thought, was Siberia, the vast and endless land of forest and river and sky which generations of Russians had penetrated and crossed and recrossed without leaving more than a few faint traces on its eternal spaces.

But even the Ob has changed under the hammer blows of Russia's new rulers.

This time we approached the river along broad construction roads, piled with the debris of building. Here were great earth-moving machines, bulldozers, heavy trucks, and all the gear of the mechanical age. Long before we reached the river we could see the mountainous earth wings, a hundred feet high, which build up to the concrete grandeur of the new hydroelectric plant. The dam is three miles long, and it has backed the river up for more than 130 miles to form an enormous lake which has submerged villages, parts of railroads, and farming fields.

Big as this dam is (capacity 420,000 kilowatts, seven turbines, a twelve-story powerhouse), it is only a medium-sized installation by the titan's standard of the new Soviet. Even though Russian planners have turned their back on Stalin's giganto-mania and his enormously costly program for power development of the Volga River, in Siberia they have in full swing the world's greatest hydro program. The resources which lie available to the Soviet engineers beggar the imagination.

I saw on the Angara River outside Irkutsk in eastern Siberia the twin to the Novosibirsk plant, a twin which is half again as large, a 660,000-kilowatt installation. This is the first of a series of eight or ten dams on the Angara. The biggest of these, at Bratsk, will produce an estimated 4,500,000 kilowatts of firm power. The total hydro potentiality of the Angara is estimated at 10,000,000 kilowatts. That of the Yenisei at more than 18,000,000, the Lena at 18, the Amur at 6.5, and the Ob at 5.7. By comparison, the total resources of the Volga are placed at 6.2. Grand Coulee, America's biggest, is less than half the size of the Bratsk plant whose turbines are expected to begin turning in 1961.

The Soviet planners propose to tie the enormous spaces of Siberia together with a network of high-voltage transmission lines. Already they are using 400,000-volt transmission lines and they are planning 500,000-volt lines. This is greater voltage than any in America.

The Russians, like the Americans, do not plan to put their chief reliance on hydro power. In fact, because steam generation is demonstrably cheaper in most instances (except for some of the extraordinarily low-cost Siberian developments like that on the Angara) the Russians are investing the lion's share of their effort in steam plants.

Cheap power is one fundament of the new Siberia. The other is science. I do not know whether the steamboat which took the Nixon party down the River Ob was the same which Kulagin used fifteen years before. My impression is that it was not. The Nixon steamboat seemed smaller, more compact and efficient. There was no luxurious afterdeck, no Cossack dancers, no choirs.

Nor was the river the same. It has become Lake Ob, dammed up behind the concrete breastworks of the hydroelectric plant. While the steamboat carried us across the blue waters, Chairman V. T. Zabulayaev, the heavy-set director of the Novosibirsk economic region, outlined the plans for transforming Novosibirsk into one of Russia's greatest industrial centers, a new rival to the Pittsburghs of the Urals and the Donbass. More than eighty big new plants will be thrown up within the next six or seven years. Assembly-line construction techniques will be used, prefabricated factory units, standardized machine processes.

After an hour's ride across Lake Ob, we arrived at the installation which Admiral Rickover felt was the most important of all those which Mr. Nixon was being shown. This was the new science city of Novosibirsk, the brain center for the whole development of Siberia. In the summer of 1959 the science city was largely a raw construction site, hewn out of the red earth and green pine. For a mile or two along a curving section of the shoreline the bulldozers have cleared the land. The sky is crisscrossed with the tall cranes which the Russians use for their building. Steam shovels are at work and trucks are carting away soil and bringing in fill.

Only one building was actually completed at the time of Mr. Nixon's visit, an administrative center. But in 1960 the first scientific units will be established. Before the end of the year, more than 1,000 of Russia's top scientists will be installed in new quarters set down in the Siberian wilderness. When the city is complete, there will be a self-contained community of 35,000 scientists and their assistants and between 1,500 and 3,000 students with 4,000 teachers in a new graduate university. Next to Moscow and Leningrad this will be the greatest scientific center in the Soviet Union.

The role of the center will be to coordinate all scientific work in Siberia. It will direct the program to transform Siberia into the most productive region of the Soviet Union. Here will be devised the strategy for unlocking the untold mineral resources of the great continent. And here will be devised plans for exploiting these riches most economically and efficiently. The emphasis will be on welding raw materials to the power which the new dams and thermal and nuclear plants make available.

Never before has a master scientific plan for the exploitation of the wealth of an entire continent been attempted. It is this grandiose concept which lies behind the Novosibirsk center which caused Admiral Rickover to stress its importance.

The Novosibirsk center will not be a solitary lighthouse casting a single beam of light across the Siberian depths. There will be satellite science centers. I saw the most important of these at Irkutsk. It is rising along the Angara River in close conjunction with the new Angara dam, just as the Novosibirsk center is adjacent to the new Ob dam.

The Irkutsk center is a precise duplicate of the Novosibirsk center, only smaller. It will provide a cadre for the expansion of the Irkutsk state university and it will specialize in problems of the eastern area and the Siberian north. Irkutsk is a wonderful old Russian city, three hundred years old. It is a provincial city, with linden trees and many parks. Slowly walking blonde Siberian girls promenade at night in air heavy with the fragrance of phlox and tobacco plants. The city is steeped in the romantic traditions of Lake Baikal (the deepest and largest fresh-water body in the world) and the revolutionary idealism of the Decembrists, many of whom were exiled to this area 125 years ago after the failure of their attempt to bring about reforms in St. Petersburg. "It is good that you came to see us this summer," an Irkutsk woman said. "You are seeing the last of the old Irkutsk. Next time you come you will find a big new city. We will be the Moscow of the Far East."

The new centers will provide the scientists and teaching personnel with living and working facilities at least the equal of, and in many cases better than, those that they might command in Moscow or Leningrad. Special inducements of pay and rapid advancement are being offered. The slogan is "Go East, Young Scientist." Many are heeding it.

The isolation of Siberia is crumbling under the impact of the new Soviet jet transport system. Omsk is only three hours from Moscow. Novosibirsk is another hour. Irkutsk is six hours from the capital. The Transsiberian still requires twelve days to go from Moscow to Vladivostok—ten hours by jet. The journey from Moscow to Irkutsk took six months at the time the elder George Kennan made his famous inquiry into the Siberian penal system.

Nor is the jet a rare and occasional service for the privileged. On the tarmac of every airport across Siberia I saw TU-104's parked in clusters of ten or a dozen. In a city like Novosibirsk or Omsk or Irkutsk, never more than a few minutes go by without hearing the roar of the jet planes. The jets have chopped Siberia into two-hour bites and made it as convenient to live on the banks of the Ob or the Irtysh as the Dnieper or the Dniester.

The Soviet leadership is trying a new combination—a combination of science, education, electrical power, and better living conditions—instead of the traditional exile and penal labor. New Siberia is to be a land of comfortable living. Not comfortable living on the American scale, of course—nowhere in Russia do you get that—but living which is comfortable enough to erase that big and traditional difference between what the Russians call the "center" and the "periphery."

This is not going to be accomplished for everyone and not overnight. For key figures in the new plan, the members of the science teams, however, comfort and convenience will be provided from the start.

The Soviet government does not enter this scheme with any illusions that it will be easy. It knows that you can go only so far on enthusiasm and propaganda. The great virgin lands gamble—Khrushchev's plan which has put 90,000,000 acres of Siberian and Kazakh soil under the plow—was launched as a youth crusade. In the first year and half, some 300,000 young people, mostly from the cities, were conned and cajoled into migrating to the remote steppe country to help sow the wheat. At least half of them had no qualifications for farmwork. At least half of them went, not because of real desire, but because of pressure; the Komsomol ordered them to "volunteer." Many went because they were unhappy or dissatisfied with life and were looking for any new alternative to the boredom of here and now. Five years after I saw the first "volunteers" being processed at Barnaul, it was estimated that not more than two out of every five remain. Bad living conditions, barracks life, lack of recreational facilities, inability to adjust to work on the farms, sent two-thirds of the youngsters limping back to the cities.

This disturbed the government. At the Twenty-first Party Congress in February, 1959, only two speeches are known to have been censored out of the stenographic report of the session. Both dealt with the unrest of the youngsters in the virgin lands, the failure to provide decent living conditions, bad working conditions, the breakdown of local facilities, the numbers who have deserted for European Russia.

For the new wave of Siberian development, the government hopes to establish a positive psychology, one that breaks the pattern of the past. It wants to create the kind of living and working conditions that will prove attractive to people, will induce and inspire them to go to Siberia, to settle there, to build their lives there while building the economic framework of a new country.

For centuries Siberia has been identified with prison, police, persecution, exile, with sorrow and suffering, with cold and compulsion.

It is no accident today that when you go to Sverdlovsk, the Urals gateway to Siberia, you get no help from the officials in searching out the once-famous house of Ipatiyev. Ipatiyev was an obscure Siberian merchant, and his plaster-covered brick house in Sverdlovsk is located on what is now Karl Liebknecht Street not far from the city cathedral.

There is only one reason for remembering the House of Ipatiyev. This is the house in what was then dusty, provincial Ekaterinburg where Czar Nicholas II and his family were confined for some months in the dangerous and unsettled year of 1918. And in the basement of this small, obscure building, the Czar and his family died, in July, 1918, shot at the orders of a jittery commissar who feared that they might be liberated by a rapidly advancing White Russian army.

There is no mark on the House of Ipatiyev today to show that the Czar was ever confined there. No plaque to mark the site of his execution. No mention of his imprisonment in the local guidebook. Tourist officials fall into vague confusion when you ask about the execution and where it took place.

It was not always thus. The last time I was in Sverdlovsk, fifteen years ago, the House of Ipatiyev was a museum. The Czar's effects had been carefully preserved. The clothes he wore on the last day were in glass cases together with other morbid mementoes. The guides took you into the basement and pointed to the bullet marks and bloodstains on the walls and floor. There was a plaque on the house which told in detail what had happened.

Not a trace of this remains. It is possible to find the House of Ipatiyev without too much trouble. Passers-by will show you the way. But now it is occupied by the archives department of the local Party. Admission to the building is only by permission of the Party secretary. The basement where the executions occurred is a storage place for old documents. The signs have been taken down. The Czar's artifacts have been removed to the State Museum. But there they are not exhibited. They are tucked away somewhere in storage. There is, it is said, no interest now in showing such things.

This careful sponging of the Sverdlovsk slate is not accidental. It is part of a deliberate effort to close the book on all the crimes that have made the very word *Siberia* a synonym for terror around the world.

Control of the development of the subcontinent has been wrested out of the hands of the secret police and vested in the hands of Soviet scientists. The concentration camps have been torn down. The prisoners have been freed. Many have gone back to where they came from, but many chose to stay on as free workers. The new program hopes to make Siberia as much a synonym for opportunity and free advancement as was the American West in the nineteenth century.

No one can yet say whether this experiment will succeed.

But like almost all Americans who visited Siberia in 1959, I felt that I had much in common with the Siberian people. To listen to them talk was to be transported back to the days when the covered-wagon trains were beating their way across the Great Plains.

"I'm a free Siberian citizen," one young man told me. "I live in Siberia because I like to think for myself. My opinions are my own opinions, not the government's opinions. Here I can build my life with other free-thinking men and women."

This young man had settled in Siberia by choice. He was an educated man, graduate of an institute. He had a good government job. He loved to camp, to hunt, to fish. In the summers he spent his vacations on the great Siberian rivers, the Lena and the Yenisei, camping and prospecting.

"We like Americans in Siberia," he said. "In the old days many Americans traveled across Siberia. We hope to see many of them come again. Siberia and America have much in common. We are big countries, free countries."

The young man's emphasis on "freedom" in Siberia may sound unusual. But I thought I understood what he meant. Siberia is a long, long way from Moscow. Over the last two centuries it has absorbed thousands and thousands of nonconformists sent to its desolate wastes first by the Czar and then by the Bolsheviks. It has developed its own tradition of free thinking and of independent opinion. After all, as a Siberian once told me during the Stalin days, why shouldn't we Siberians think as we please—we are already in Siberia.

It seemed to me that if the Soviet could harness this free and independent spirit of Siberia to the new program of science and education and power, it would create a force which would give the whole of Russia a new vitality the equal of many, many Sputniks.

I wished that Mike Kulagin had lived to see his Siberia standing on the verge of breakthrough into the new era. This was

what Kulagin had dedicated his life to. He was not a native
of Siberia. I think he came from the Don country or somewhere
in the lower Volga. But no greater enthusiast for Siberia ever
existed. He had thrown his incredible energy and all the force
of his peppery and exuberant personality into the cause of
Siberia. In the few days we spent with him in 1944, he talked
almost continuously of what Siberia would be like once the war
was over. He was going to do his best to keep in Siberia not
only the great industrial establishments which had been evacuated from Moscow and Leningrad ("They can develop new
ones—we need these here"). He wanted to keep the orchestras
and choruses and theaters which had been sent to the safer
rear as well.

"This is the country which is Russia's future," he said. "Sure,
life is hard here. We need culture as well as industry. The day
is going to come when people will fight for a chance to come to
Siberia. Siberia is Russia's future."

I could imagine the early Siberian explorers, the Stroganovs,
the Orlovs and the rest coming back to Moscow and talking
the same kind of language. Siberia is Russia's future. It well
may be. And I hoped that the new generation of Russia, the
brilliant young scientists, the devoted young Party people, the
students, the technicians, the workers, and all the rest who
went East in search of that future, would not meet the bitter
fate and disillusion which so often has overcome those who have
dedicated themselves to the cause of Siberia in the past.

I hoped they would not fall victims to the fate which befell
Kulagin. He did not live to welcome Vice President Nixon to
Novosibirsk, nor to lend his enthusiasm and his spirit to this
new Siberian crusade. He had died a few years ago. His
obituary took only a few lines in *Pravda*. Cause of the death was
not mentioned. I thought I knew, however. I was pretty certain
that Mike Kulagin died of a broken heart, like a whole generation of Communist leaders. For he had not stayed on in

Novosibirsk many years after I saw him in wartime. If Eric Johnston had ever gone back to Novosibirsk to see whether those jewels were still there, Kulagin would not have been on hand to welcome him. For one reason or another, and no reason, of course, was necessary in such times, Kulagin fell from favor in the late forties. He spent some years in exile. It was only with Stalin's death that he was restored to good standing, but by then it was too late. He died within the year, one more victim in the endless series which Siberia has claimed. It was time, I thought, for Russia's Siberian future to start coming true, time for the spread and growth of a new spirit of freedom in this eastern land which had seen such great tragedy.

XIII

To the Heartland of Asia

THE ALTIMETER of the TU-104B held steady at 30,000 feet and on the horizon I could see the rim of the Siberian taiga, marked with a red line like a fevered vein. We had left Omsk and the Irtysh and, racing east through the dusk that lasts no more than two hours in June, were meeting the rising sun again just east of the Ob. Our destination, incredible as it seemed, was Mongolia, the heartland of Asia, the homeland of the World Conqueror, the Scourge of God whose Empire once spanned half the globe.

I sat by the window of the TU-104B looking out at the Siberian dawn and tried to remember when I first had read of Marco Polo, of Kara Korum, of the Golden Horde, of the horsemen who appeared out of nowhere and thundered across history's pages all the way to the gates of Vienna. When, in 1944, I had visited Samarkand and Tashkent—the oasis cities of the hidden deserts of middle Asia—when I had made my pilgrimage to the tomb of Tamerlane, the onyx slab beneath which the great lame prince of Mongols has lain these hundreds of years—I dreamed that one day I might follow the trail deeper and deeper into the very heart of the Asian continent, to the secret land where Kara Korum, the lost capital of the Great Conqueror, still lay hidden.

Now it was difficult to realize, as I sat in the great jet aircraft racing across the Siberian wilderness at a steady 500 miles an hour, that within a few hours my son Michael and I would actually arrive on Mongol soil. I was excited for another reason. Mongolia had never been an easy land to enter. It was difficult in the day of Marco Polo, Carpini and Rubruck. It was still difficult today. Few travelers wanted to go and fewer obtained visas. It was not only the mystery of the past that was drawing me East. It was the mystery of the present. Mongolia lay at the frontier of Russia and China. It did not seem likely that I would manage to make my way to Peking this year. But surely in this borderland which for 1,500 miles separated the two great Communist empires I might find some clues to the Chinese puzzle, some answer to what lay behind the silken veil of secrecy with which China and Russia cloaked their relations.

Of course, we were not there yet. We had to change planes at Irkutsk. But last-minute obstacles hardly seemed likely. I had cabled Premier Tsedenbal asking permission to come to Mongolia with my son, and his reply was favorable. Everything should be all right. I looked at my watch. It showed 11:30 P.M. —Moscow time. But outside the sun was rising huge and red over the endless forests. At midnight by my watch the sun stood shoulder high to the north, shining from a cloudless blue sky, and in another half hour we stepped from the plane at Irkutsk— six hours out of Moscow.

The green-capped Russian border-patrol captain was friendly and courteous. "Are you going to Mongolia as tourist or by invitation?" he asked. "At the invitation of the Premier," I said. He smiled and waved us through. Not so with the Mongolian passengers. They were ushered into another room. Their luggage was inspected with care, every bag and every box. Some even had to turn their pockets out. Why? Already there were mysteries.

Not until we started up the ramp of the plane for Ulan Bator did I realize that the aircraft was Chinese, not Mongolian—a Russian-built DC-3 carrying the stars of Communist China. The cabin attendant was a solemn Chinese who wore a light tan summer suit with brass uniform buttons. He looked grimly at Michael and myself and turned away. The plane, I thought, was as close as I was going to get to the Chinese Communists. Perhaps it was just as well.

We climbed quickly and in twenty minutes were high over Lake Baikal, steel blue and very deep against the sharp gray cliffs and green pine forest.

The great lake vanished and there appeared red-brown mountains, spreading across the landscape as far as the eye could see, a tangle of peaks, devoid of trees, devoid of cities, devoid of roads or trails, as empty as the mountains of the moon. This was Mongolia. The plane pitched and tossed in the upward-rising air currents from the jagged surface of the earth. Never had I seen a landscape more forbidding. Gradually, the high peaks flattened out and deserts, yellow and barren, emerged. This was not the Gobi—that, I knew, lay to the south. But how man could survive in such a land it was not possible to imagine. I had been prepared for grimness, but not for the outer region of purgatory.

The rusty desert and the brown mountains lightened imperceptibly. Now I could see shades of gray, blending into green. The plane dropped, and suddenly we were flying down a fertile green valley which formed an oblong bowl within the high mountains. Huddled at one end of the valley was a disorderly jumble of buildings. This, I thought, must be Urga or Ulan Bator, the City of the Red Warrior, as it now is called. There was no time for further observation. With a hard bump the plane landed on the grass strip and we stepped out into a pleasant sunny June day with scattered clouds.

Mongol women in purple silk gowns with golden cords around the waist and Mongol men with brown silk gowns and yellow sashes were waiting—friends and relatives of the Mongol passengers. There was running and squealing and embracing. A good-looking young man in gray European suit came up to me. "I am Lotchin from the journalists' association. Will you have a glass of tea?"

This was Mongolia. It had taken a long time to get here. I wondered whether any traces of Genghis Khan might remain after seven hundred years, plus forty more of Communist rule.

We got into a taxi. It was a pastel green Russian Volga, driven by a black-haired Mongol woman who might have been thirty years old or fifty. She wore a black beret, tiny earrings of gold with small diamonds, a green silk gown patterned with large roses, green pantaloons, and between her yellow teeth she clamped a cigarette like a Paris apache. The taxi was brand new; but the door handles were missing, the doors themselves were badly sprung, and the speedometer needle spun wildly as we jolted over the road.

This was Mongolia—the land, as I sometimes thought of it, of yurts, yaks, and yogurt. Almost immediately I saw the yurts, the conical white-canvas tents in which the Mongols live. The canvas is stretched over a light wooden fretwork. In winter it is lined with felt. Mongols, Mr. Lotchin told me, do not call them yurts. They call them *ger*. "Did you ever see those animals before?" he asked, pointing to a shaggy herd grazing beside the road. They looked like cows which had been crossed with Afghan wolfhounds. No, I said. Those, Mr. Lotchin said, are yaks. But the Mongols do not call them yaks. They call them *sarlaks*.

Yurts, yaks, and yogurt. I wondered. If yurts were ger and yaks were sarlaks, what about yogurt? Yes, said Mr. Lotchin, we have yogurt. But we call it *tarig*. *Yak*, *yurt*, and *yogurt*, Mr. Lotchin explained, were Russian words. He did not, I found, like Russian words very well. In fact he disliked the word *yurt* so much that he never let it pass his lips. In his vocabulary they were "conical Mongolian national tents." Actually, Mr. Lotchin did not like yurts by any name. Even when they dotted the landscape, nestling white and pleasant against the green hills, Mr. Lotchin preferred not to see them. They were to him—and to many other educated young Mongols— a symbol of backwardness, of the nomad life which they hoped soon would be left far behind as Mongolian Communism marched forward to a new and, as they thought, happier and more advanced society. Camels, I found, also depressed Mr. Lotchin. He pointed to a mangy caravan slogging slowly across the hills.

"In the old days," he said, "when foreigners came to our country they always wanted to take pictures of camels. Now it is no longer interesting for them."

I thought I got his point and my hopes sank. Mr. Lotchin seemed to shut the door on the past and look only toward a grim and still unrealized future. Did this mean that I would spend my days in Mongolia visiting children's crèches, inspecting collective cowsheds, and talking to members of the state planning commission about the three-year plan? Not that I did not want to learn about Mongolia's present. But it was the tapestry of Mongol history, the heritage of the horsemen whose hooves had cut an indelible mark on the annals of almost every nation of Europe and Asia, which had drawn me to the East. Was it really possible that I had flown halfway around the world to be pumped full of statistics and propaganda? The thought chilled me.

We were housed in a Russian-built guest house. We were the only guests. It was located far outside town in a lonely valley, spotted with yurts, herds of sheep, horses, and occasional yaks. Our hosts were genial but touchy. They did not want me to get close to ordinary Mongols and their life.

True, we went in to Ulan Bator each day. We visited the great Gandan Monastery and drank five-elements *tzi*—water, milk, salt, butter, and tea—with the old Chief Lama Erdenpel Gavge. At seventy-two he had been chief of the Mongol Buddhists for fifteen years. We sat in his beautiful yurt, piled high with inlaid chests and Oriental carpets, sipping the rich tea, nibbling at mounds of sweetmeats, and skirting lightly over the question of Tibet. Among the "yellow priests" of Buddhism, the Lama of the Mongols ranks next to the Dalai and Panchen Lamas of Tibet. The Mongols took their Buddhism from Tibet, as well as much of their ancient culture.

The Lama was proud of his great monastery, one of four in Ulan Bator. True, no longer was every third Mongol in the city a priest. But there were still ten thousand priests, attendants, and assistants in the great Buddhist establishments. And if Mongolia was no longer a Buddhist theocracy, at least the Buddhist faith was recognized by the Communist rulers. Indeed, as the Lama pictured it (and subsequent investigation seemed to prove that he was right), Buddhism was for all practical purposes the established church. A good many Buddhist temples had been closed, but antireligious propaganda did not exist in this Communist land.

What, I asked, of relations with Buddhists elsewhere? Were pilgrimages allowed to holy places? Yes, said the Lama. There were frequent exchanges between the Buddhists of Inner Mongolia (in China) and those of Buryat-Mongolia (in the Soviet Union). I mentioned Tibet. I knew that, since time immemorial, caravans had plied the Gobi and the high passes that guard Tibet and on down to Lhasa. I knew that, until very recently, pilgrimages were exchanged at least twice a year between Ulan Bator and Lhasa. Were the caravans still plying the ancient route? The Buddha's face of the Chief Lama hardened almost imperceptibly. No. There were no pilgrims from Lhasa. Nor were there any from Ulan Bator to Tibet. He spoke firmly and asked a monk to pour more tea, to pass again the sweetmeats. Tibet was a closed subject.

One day we visited the National Library and there stumbled upon a treasure trove of the Mongol past, a treasure worth an emperor's ransom. Here we found the world's greatest collection of Mongol documents, most of them taken from the great Buddhist monasteries. Here was the epic Danjur, translated from Tibetan into Mongolian, in 225 volumes, illuminated in gold and silver and written in ink made of powdered rubies and emeralds. And the 108 volumes of the Kanjur. Together the collection weighed well over six tons. There were dozens of variant editions, each volume swathed in silk. There was even a precious papyrus on which was enscribed, or so it was said, the personal script of Buddha himself.

As the great volumes were carefully unwrapped, and I examined the ancient writings in ink so black it seemed carved of basalt, I thought of the thousands of monks in their great lamaseries, laboring year after year to copy out the commentaries. The odor of the thousand-year past was so strong I seemed to feel it in my nostrils.

But what of the present? Would we get a chance to journey out of Ulan Bator? Would we be permitted to travel some of the old caravan routes into the Mongol past? I had told the authorities that there were two things I wanted to see in Mongolia: the Gobi desert and Kara Korum. It was impossible to determine from the pleasant but laconic comments of Mr. Lotchin whether my hopes would be satisfied. We were going to go on a trip to the interior, he said. But where or when or for how long he did not seem to know.

One Sunday morning a jeep appeared at the villa and we started out. Our destination was the interior. We were going to see something of the country, some collective farms, some historical relics, perhaps one of the ancient capitals—Mongolia has had eight in the past, I was told. More than this Mr. Lotchin would not say. It was a little baffling, but at least we were on our way. The jeep was laden with extra tins of gasoline and water. There was even a great box of cheese, hard-boiled eggs, bread, and Russian canned meat.

Through the night it had been raining and the gravel road was packed down hard. Overhead great Asian buzzards circled slowly, floating on the air currents which carried them from one valley to another, wings outstretched like sailplanes.

Each time I saw the ugly brown birds and the shadow of their wings falling across the green valley, I was filled with sudden anger. So, I found, was Michael.

"I wish I had my gun," he said. "I'd kill every buzzard I saw."

I felt the same way. Our feeling, I found, had been shared by the great Russian explorer of the nineteenth century, Nikolay Przhevalski. Never in his life, he wrote, had he seen anything so insolent as these birds of prey. It was beyond belief. During the whole of his journeys in Mongolia they followed his caravan. They would light on the back of a camel and peck at the camel's hump, literally eating the animal alive.

I wondered whether the birds still acted as scavengers of human flesh. Przhevalski told how starving beggars lay in the streets of Urga, covered with rags and crawling parasites. Around them circled the pariah dogs and overhead waited the buzzards. The patience of the dogs and the birds was extraordinary. Not until the last breath of life had departed did they close in, fighting each other for the remains. The Mongols, he said, did not bury their dead. They took them to a stony field beside the city. There the dogs and carrion birds did the rest.

In a matter of minutes the city was behind us and we were heading westward in the wide valley—at first on a tarred road, which soon changed to gravel and then vanished. Half an hour later we were riding over the open grass road, the ancient yellowed trail of the Golden Horde, the track across the endless pasturelands which horsemen and caravans and herds of animals had followed for a thousand years and more.

For hours we pushed westward. The country was open, rolling and green. Nowhere were there signs or arrows. Nowhere a road. Nowhere a city or a village. As Carpini wrote

seven centuries before: "Here are no towns or cities. This land
is nearly destitute of trees although well adapted for the pasturage of cattle. Even the emperor and princes and all others
warm themselves and cook their victuals with fires of horse and
cow dung."

And so it was today. Suddenly I realized that we had left the
twentieth century behind. We had journeyed backward into a
time and place where the horse again was king and man was
only his companion in a world of endless grass. And it occurred
to me: the answer to the question which so long had baffled me.
From whence had Genghis Khan and his horsemen come? I
had always imagined Mongolia in terms of the burning Gobi,
bronzed by sun, a land bereft of water and life. But like so
many of my impressions this was founded on ignorance. I had
not realized before that, like a jewel in the lotus, Mongolia was
a hidden world of the greenest pasture man had ever known.
Here in the secret recesses of the Asian continent was the succulent turf that had bred and nourished the greatest horse
armies in history.

And nothing had changed. This was the same emerald uni-
verse in which the Mongol warrior had lived. Today, as a thousand years ago, this was a land of grass reaching to the blue
infinity of the heavens. You could travel from the Tien Shan
Mountains to the China frontier and never see a city, never see
a road, never leave the carpet of grass.

How much longer might it remain so? Not very long, I
thought, because most of Mongolia's contemporary problems
of economy, society, and politics sprang from the enduring
nature of this pasture and the curiously complex and interknit
nomad life the Mongols had built upon it.

Today we could still follow the trail of the caravans across
the virgin meadows, free of bulldozed roads or plowed fields.
Nowhere else on the Eurasian continent could we see grazing
lands so endless, dotted only here and there with white tents

where the herdsmen pitched camp beside their horses and sheep.

We drove 140 kilometers before we came to the first village. We stopped at a whitewashed *guanz,* not an inn and not a restaurant, but a primitive teahouse with clean plank tables where you could spread your food and a kitchen which provided the traveler with five-elements tea or soup. (Sometimes there was so much mutton fat in the tea it was hard to tell it from soup.) Two women ran the guanz. One was dark and pretty, wearing gold earrings and a little lipstick. She had a wide gold band on her finger and a cheap blue-and-red glass bracelet. The men paid little attention to us. They puffed their slender silver-bowled pipes with expressionless faces. But the girls ogled and stared.

On we drove. Two or three times we passed a truck laden high with wool on the way to market, for it was shearing time in the high valleys. Once we passed a caravan of six camels, plodding patiently across the steppe. They were laden with lattice and canvas for two yurts and with great crimson and black chests and boxes, like a picture out of the Arabian Nights.

Darkness fell, and we jolted onward through the velvet darkness. We crossed a wooden bridge over a shallow river, and the jeep ground to a halt. Tasha, our cheerful moon-faced jeep driver, said something to Mr. Lotchin.

"A wonderful place to fish," Mr. Lotchin explained. Tasha was a sportsman. He pulled on a pair of hip boots, snapped together his collapsible rod, and was off to a reedy bank thicker with mosquitoes than New Jersey. Tasha patiently cast and cast again. Fish were rising to feed, but his luck was poor. Presently he gave up and we started again.

For a time we followed a solitary telegraph line. Tasha peered out to catch a glimpse of the poles as they marched across the dark countryside like matchstick men. Then they vanished. We raced onward across the roadless space. Tasha

looked up at the star-spotted sky and navigated as did the
helmsmen at sea before the days of the compass.

Sometimes in the far distance we would see a light, possibly
the glow of a fire beside a lonely yurt. But we rushed through
the night without halting. This, I thought, is how the Mongol
cavalry moved at night across this uncharted land, following a
westward star, swiftly and surely. It had been their destiny,
and the world had shaken before them. But now the great flood
had ebbed and ebbed until only in these fortress valleys where
it all started did the Mongol still hold sway—an anachronism
in history that would not much longer endure.

Finally, at 2 a.m., with Michael and me dead-tired and long
since confident that Tasha surely must have lost his way, lights
suddenly flared up ahead. We had reached our destination—
Tsetserlig, an ancient caravansary in central Mongolia.

Now our introduction to Mongol hospitality began. The next
day we visited a shepherd's community in a high mountain
valley north of Tsetserlig. Here for the first time we feasted
in a yurt. Hardly had we been seated on the low chests which
rimmed the tent when great foaming bowls of *kumiss* were
presented to us. Kumiss is the national beverage of Mongolia,
lightly fermented mare's milk. It tastes a little like thin sour
buttermilk. The Mongols keep it in great Chinese jars, sometimes as big as those in which Sinbad hid his sailors.

A moment later a dozen other dishes appeared: soft fresh
yogurt; a kind of cottage cheese called *beslik;* brown curds,
hung on a string beside the tent wall until they were hard as
stone; steaming bowls of tzi.

The *pièce de résistance* was a metal basin of lamb, what the
Mongols call *ootz.* It was placed before me and I was handed a
beautiful knife of inlaid silver and enamel, an *utga.* My duty
was to carve and serve the lamb on the point of the knife. For
the children there were tender lamb hoofs to gnaw on, for the
adults delicate morsels of lamb jaw and cheeks.

The host's wife appeared with a jar of fresh colorless liquid. Spring water, I thought. Wonderful! I took a bowl and drained it back. Fire! Liquid fire! The "spring water" was *irik*, a harmless milk product, lightly fermented, the host said. Actually, it was *raki*, high-potency alcohol flavored with anise, common to all the Turk and Arab lands from Morocco to the borders of China.

"There is nothing better than lamb," said one of the wrinkled Mongols, squatting on his heels.

"True," said another, leisurely drawing out his ebony and silver pipe and putting into its narrow bowl some dry fragrant morsels which he called tobacco but which would never be recognized in North Carolina.

"What more can a man want," said the first. "Good lamb to eat and good horses to ride."

"Ah, yes," said the other. "Our animals are good this summer. So our life is good. After all we live for our animals and our animals live for us."

This was life in the Mongolian heartland as it was being lived in this pleasant summer of 1959. Below the surface, as I well knew, changes were coming fast. But no one in the yurt seemed aware of them as he chewed his lamb bones and washed down the meat with bowls of irik and kumiss.

There was, I supposed, some plan for our travels. But Mr. Lotchin did not divulge it and I did not really care. We were living in a world whose like existed no other place—a world of man and animals and plants such as Frémont found when first he rode west across the great American plain. We traversed carpets of flowers that perfumed the valleys. Here were yellow primroses and golden buttercups splashed against the thick grass; violet canterbury bells; wild larkspur, tall and spiked; white and gold milkweed; acres of wild mustard; and great beds of nodding purple aster.

The air was pungent with *aiga*, an herblike fennel so strong that it perfumes the flesh of the lamb. And after the rain our nostrils were puckered by the scent of *halga,* a fragrant burning nettle.

Some fields as we rode through them looked like an artist's smock, splotched with tiny scarlet lilies, Indian paint, creeping lavender, bluebells, columbine, and great white mushrooms.

This was no empty vegetative world. I watched one day beside the surging falls of the Ulan (Red) River as a great carnivorous hawk, big as an eagle, circled ready to dive. Suddenly from a clump of bushes whirled upward two brown thrushes, crying piteously and fluttering in widening circles. The hawk closed in on one thrush. Then the other feinted nearer and drew him away. For ten minutes the pair maneuvered the great predator farther and farther from their theatened nest. Finally the birds vanished in the distance, apparently successful.

Below the Ulan waterfalls, in the turbulent rain-muddied water, Tasha went fishing. This time his luck was good. He pulled out three fat *tsooherbur,* a kind of rough pike.

"Ours is a wonderful country," a young Mongol doctor said as we sat beside the carved gorge of the Orkhon River. "We have very few people. Only a million or so. And our land is very wide. So our rivers are filled with fish. And our fields and forests are filled with animals. There is always good sport."

Certainly, I thought, few countries are richer in wild life— mountain goats and snow panthers in the high peaks, bears and wolves at lower elevations, and antelopes, *hulans* (wild donkeys), *habtagais* (wild camels), and *tahis* (the wild horse first observed by Przhevalski) on the plains and deserts.

Near every water course we saw flocks of handsome Indian geese, orange and brown and white. They sturdily stared at the approaching jeep but took quickly to the air every time Tasha halted to put them under the sights of his single-shot .25-calibre rifle with its half-inch solid barrel and hand-carved shoulder rest.

We saw wild turkeys, scrawny and bony as those our fore-fathers first saw in New England, and statuesque gray and black cranes that seemed to have stepped out of a Japanese print.

Tasha's eyes roved the countryside as he drove the jeep. He paid little heed to the great brown hares and the countless *surum* or Mongolian prairie dogs. But when he spotted a dab of alien color on a butte he slowed the jeep to a halt, reached for his gun, and then slowly started the machine up the steep incline. As the jeep bucked forward he pulled back the string of his cotton cartridge bag with his teeth and fingered out a bullet, slipping it deftly into the chamber of his gun.

Suddenly the jeep nosed over a narrow ledge. A hundred feet higher, its forelegs sprawled like a lazy dog, sat a great grayish-red fox, big as a wolf. Tasha swung the jeep broadside and pulled his trigger. Click! The cartridge (like half of the ones he used) was defective. He ejected the shell and dropped in a fresh one. But just as the shell rammed forward, the fox whisked about and disappeared to the higher ledges.

The next day Mr. Lotchin announced that we were going to visit an old Mongol capital. The name of it was Erdeni Dzu. One of the eight capitals, he pointed out. I swallowed my disappointment. Obviously we were not going to get to Kara Korum. We pushed across the valley, over mountain passes and lonely heights. Here and there in the high divides, on the crests of foothills or jagged peaks, we saw cairns of stones. Sometimes a sheep's skull or the skeleton of a mountain goat adorned the pile. These were landmarks to aid the horseman in his solitary course.

Finally we descended into a wide valley, the valley of the Orkhon River, rich with grass and rich with sheep. It was raining slightly. We picked up a local official who would show us the old capital. Again we jolted over the fields and saw in the

distance a great dun-colored wall, decorated with curious turrets, 108 of them, as I later learned.

A rose-silk-robed old Mongol greeted us. This was Erdeni
Dzu, he said. It was named to honor Buddha. Erdeni Dzu was
the Mongol name for Buddha. The capital was built in 1586 at
the orders of Abdai San Han. It was a great and luxurious city.
Here once fifteen hundred Buddhist priests lived. Here was the
special shrine to Buddha, still standing. Here the massive tombs
of Abdai and of his son, Gombor-doj. Here the stone foundations of the great royal yurt, as big as a Barnum and Bailey tent.

Now only the temples still stood. But once it was the glory of
the East. Of course, not such a capital as Hor Horeen. Hor
Horeen was the wonder of the world. It was the capital of
Genghis Khan, planned by him, ordered built by him, but
never seen by him—for he died in 1227 before it was finished.
Only in 1235 under his able third son, Ugedi, was it completed.

The old man rambled on. Erdeni Dzu was built on the site of
Hor Horeen. But it was only a quarter as big. At the four great
gates of Hor Horeen had been four great markets. At the east
gate, a market for grain. At the west gate, sheep and goats. At
the south gate, cattle. And at the north gate, horses. All trace
of Hor Horeen had vanished. For centuries man did not know
where it had been located. Then the Russian Geographic Society sent an expedition down the Orkhon River. In 1889 they
found traces of the capital.

We went into the temples. Here was the Temple of Buddha
as a young man. Here the one to Buddha as a man of middle
age. Here that to Buddha as an old man. Rooks flew about the
roofs. But the shrines were in perfect order. There were the
offerings of grain, the thousands of images of Buddha, the great
horns and drums. All that was lacking were the priests.

For more than twenty years the shrines had been a state
museum, the old man said. Services were no longer held. I
noticed that the odor of incense was heavy in the air, as strong

as it had been in the temples of Ulan Bator. I wondered what this might mean.

The old man droned on. Here, over in the corner on a shelf, were some of the articles they found in excavating Hor Horeen. A few old coins . . . buckles . . . some stone dice . . . a plowshare. . . .

Hor Horeen . . . a curious name, I thought. I had not heard it before and yet the story of its discovery seemed strangely familiar. Hor Horeen . . . Hor Horeen. . . . Suddenly I gasped. Hor Horeen—why this was Kara Korum. This was the City of Black Sand. The Capital of the Golden Horde. This was it. This was what I had come thousands upon thousands of miles to see. We were walking on the very spot where the towers of Kara Korum once stood. The old man was telling the history of Kara Korum. But I had not recognized it in the different pronunciation.

How strange, I thought. And yet, somehow, how typical that this young Mongol Communist should bring us here to see Kara Korum in this casual, almost grudging fashion, to see what remained of the city which once had been the greatest capital in the world. He had never really told us what the place was. It was as though, in a way, he did not want to recognize the tradition of the Golden Horde, the powerful sway which it still held over the imagination of men, the fact that the memory of Genghis and the memory of Kara Korum still burned more brightly in the minds of his countrymen (and the world) than any vision of Marx or Engels.

Indeed, it was a very stubborn image which persisted here in Mongolia. I did not think that it would be possible to progress very rapidly to the cult of materialist technology until the hammer and the sickle could be superimposed more strongly upon the *yarlik* of the Golden Horde.

The empire of the Horde had crumbled. When Kara Korum was built, the armies of the Great Khan held sway from the pleasure palaces of Peking to the besieged castles of the Danube. Now all this had vanished and a Communist state stood in its place.

The wheels of fate spin out a curious pattern.

The rain was spattering harder as we turned our backs on the ruins of Kara Korum and headed once more for our jeep. The rooks cawed after us in the crumbling green porticoes. And I kept wondering who was still burning incense at the shrine of Buddha in holy Erdeni Dzu.

XIV

The Plowed Fields

Nothing remains today of the ancient capital of Kara Korum from which the heirs of Genghis Khan ruled the known world. Not one stone upon the other. You will not find it on any map.

But a few miles away the name, at least, of Kara Korum is preserved in the designation of a great state farm which has more than 500,000 acres at its disposal.

Here a rare sight may be seen—a rare sight for Mongolia: plowed land. For twenty miles along the Tarany River a two-mile swath has been slashed in the virgin grasslands by tractor-driven gang plows.

And here, I thought, as I saw the lush wheat standing firm and rich on the black soil, here is Mongolia's fate. Here is the revolution which is being made in this ancient land. Today it is only here and there that you can see such a spectacle. We drove two hundred miles across the grasslands and saw only three small strips of plowed land, experimental plots.

There had been a cloudburst a few hours before our jeep passed through. The water had cut across the plowed earth like a hot knife in ice cream. Never had I seen land ravaged so swiftly. It did not merely wash away the soil; it carved it out, two yards at a time.

What, I wondered, would happen to this wonderful green world when the gang plows tore off the natural cover of all

213

these valleys? For the plow was coming; of that I was certain. The officials said that it was, and here at the Kara Korum state farm the pattern of what lay ahead was outlined as clearly as if it had already happened.

You could not call Shulen Bator an educated man or one who knew much about agriculture. But the Communist Party had assigned him to do a job and he was doing it. This job was to make a revolution. Perhaps Shulen Bator did not quite understand that this was his job. But a revolution it was, more or less.

Shulen Bator was the chairman of the Kara Korum state farm. Its task was to raise grain. Before 1956 the land had belonged to the local people. It was grazing land, like all the land of central Mongolia. Some of the people belonged to collectives; more of them did not. They grazed their horses and sheep in the succulent valleys. They lived in their yurts. It was a good life. It was the life they knew by heritage and tradition. It was a simple life; it was lived by a simple formula. If the rains were good, the grass was good. If the grass was good, the sheep were fat and the horses abundant. If the animals fared well, the people fared well. So it had been in the time of Kara Korum. So it was today.

But not for much longer. It made no difference if the Kara Korum farm was only getting started, if in its third year it had only 37,000 acres in wheat and another 25,000 acres of virgin soil plowed for the first time this year. It made no difference that the farm still was really a livestock establishment with 3,000 horses, 2,000 cattle, and 15,000 sheep. Nor that Shulen Bator knew so little about wheat that when I asked him what variety he had planted he answered, "Pshenitza," which is merely the Russian word for wheat.

None of this really made any difference. What made a difference was that the herdsmen who had always lived in these valleys no longer were free to range the land. The land had been taken from them and given to the state farm. The machinery for the great change had been set into motion.

What happened to the people? I asked Shulen Bator. They had a choice, he said. They could go to work for the state farm, or they could go elsewhere. I guessed that most of them had stayed; although, if some had relatives or tribesmen living in more distant valleys, perhaps they had been able to pack their possessions, load them on camels or mules, and drive their flocks over the mountains. Not too many, I suspected, had been able to do that.

Land cultivation, the plow, the tractor, irrigation—all this was new to Mongolia. It cut across not only the economy but the whole way of Mongol life. For a thousand years Mongols had lived by their animals. A man reckoned his wealth by his horses and his sheep—particularly, by his horses. Cattle counted for less. None but barbarians tilled the soil.

And this was Mongol life. You could travel from one end of Mongolia to another and never pay for food, lodging, or transport. Anyone, so Mr. Lotchin told me with pride, would lend you a horse to the next encampment of yurts. Everyone had horses. And any traveler was welcome to share the *ooga* and the comfort of the yurt for the night. Money? No Mongol needed money. Mr. Lotchin was proud of this. He was proud, too, of the changes which were coming to his country. He was impatient, however; he thought the pace was much too slow. He had not yet perceived that you cannot have both plowed fields and the traditional hospitality of the nomad.

But Premier Yumshglin Tsedenbal understood what it all meant. "Radical changes," as he said to me, sitting in his big government office looking out on the quiet night in Sukhe Bator Square. "Radical changes are coming." Indeed they were, and they were further advanced than most Mongols realized.

What was happening in Mongolia, as gradually dawned on me, was simply this: Premier Tsedenbal and the nation's Communist rulers had embarked on a program which was designed to catapult the country from the eleventh to the twentieth century in a term of not more than ten years.

As recently as four years ago, 90 per cent of the livestock of Outer Mongolia was owned by individual herdsmen. Collective enterprises and state farms split the remaining 10 per cent.

Now, Mr. Tsedenbal assured me, Outer Mongolia had been 100 per cent collectivized, largely within the last twelve months. This might be so. Traveling over the countryside I had some reason to doubt the comprehensiveness of the process. I thought a good bit of it was "paper" collectivization. After all, it has been traditional for Mongol herdsmen to live together in large families or tribes. They herd their cattle jointly. They live together and work together (most of the work, actually, being done by the women).

It is not too difficult to "collectivize" a tribe by simply giving it a name and a number and designating the tribal elder as the chairman of the new collective. I had seen this done often enough in the mountains of the Caucasus or in the remote areas of Soviet Asia. It makes the statistics look good and it is painless —until the government begins to move in on the new collective.

No doubt much of the Mongol collectivization was of this nature. But the government was deadly serious with its over-all intention of shifting the country away from its traditional patterns. It was determined to impose an economy based on tillage, grain production, fodder production, cattle feeding, and dairying rather than on meat raising on natural grass.

To introduce tillage meant an end to the nomadic life of the people. It meant an end to the traditional ties of tribe and family. It meant an end to the horse. It meant an end to the Mongol life as it had been lived since the time of Genghis and as it was still being lived.

This was not going to be easy. It was already producing a sense of unease and social discomfort in the land. It was bound to cause more. People do not give up their ancient ways with any lightness—not if they are a proud and stubborn people like

the Mongols, a people accustomed to living in independence
and isolation, a people long sustained by national tradition and
tribal dignity.

The Kara Korum state farm was actually the skirmish line of
a war that eventually would embrace the whole country. If
general headquarters of this battle was the government building on Sukhe Bator Square, the war college certainly was the
new State Agriculture Institute headed by a smiling young
man named Zhamianzhav who graduated only ten years ago
from the Ulan Bator State University.

It is the task of the Institute to train the personnel who will
lead Mongolia away from the life of the yurt to the discipline of
the farm barracks. The Institute, the director said, is turning
out two hundred trained agricultural specialists a year; but he
conceded that the number of livestock and veterinarian specialists outnumbered those who study land cultivation by three
to one.

I asked him whether they were planning to introduce the
cultivation of corn, whether by any chance they had been
influenced by the great campaign in behalf of corn carried on
by Nikita Khrushchev. Corn, I pointed out, was regarded as the
best all-around crop for livestock feeding as well as grain. He
smiled but seemed little interested. I caught a look of cold
disapproval on Mr. Lotchin's face.

Mongolia, the director told me, had 20,000,000 head of livestock. Of this number 2,000,000 are horses, 2,000,000 are cattle.
The rest are sheep and goats. The country has a population
roughly estimated at 1,000,000.

Why, I asked, are there so many horses? Would it not be
more economic to reduce the herds of horses and devote the
pasture to cattle?

Mr. Zhamianzhav was shocked. So were his associates.

"In Mongolia," he said with dignity, "we respect the horse.
The horse is our national tradition."

As we left the director's office, I paused a moment to look at the courtyard of the school. Work was going on. There was a wooden platform in the center of the square. Students were bustling about.

"What are they doing?" I asked.

"They are busy putting up a monument to the horse," the director explained.

As we drove away from the Institute, Mr. Lotchin seemed deep in thought. "Maybe it would be better if you were in charge of our agricultural program," he finally said.

If Mongolia is to turn from its history and give up the horse for the plow, she will have to rely on imports or simultaneously develop the paraphernalia of industrial civilization—factories, cities, transportation networks, skilled labor.

This, of course, Mr. Tsedenbal and his colleagues are fully aware of. And they are hard at work laying the foundations for the industrial component of the new Mongolia.

Ulan Bator is the battlefield of this struggle. The capital city even looked like a battlefield. The streets were trenched and barricaded. Earthworks surrounded the central plazas. But they were not military field fortifications; they were the symptoms of social change. Simultaneously, the central city was being provided with water mains, sewer mains, and conduits for central heating.

Blocks of new buildings—apartment houses, factories, new social and educational institutions—were going up on all sides. However, the city was still a great encampment of yurts. Mayor Bata estimated the population at 160,000 today and said it would rise to 230,000 in the next twelve or thirteen years. He probably overestimated a bit. But certainly 125,000 of the city's residents still live in yurts behind drab little fences which hold their livestock. The yurt is excellent housing for a nomadic horseman. But it is hardly fit for modern city life, especially a city where the temperature drops to fifty below zero in winter,

with a cutting wind that whips the dust off the snowless un-
paved streets.

The battle against disease and squalor is far from over. No
longer does venereal disease affect 60 to 70 per cent of the
population, but there are other problems. A start has been
made at reducing the dreadful toll of tuberculosis (kumiss is
believed to be a sovereign remedy for the white death). Typhus,
cholera, and smallpox have been cut back and no longer reach
epidemic proportions. But what the doctors call "the winter
sickness" still takes a heavy toll. "Winter sickness" is a euphemism for pulmonary and bronchial illnesses which stem
from the cold, drafty life in the yurts. It strikes hard at infants,
young children, and aged persons.

I got into a little argument with Mayor Bata about child
mortality figures. There was an obvious discrepancy in one of
the figures he gave me. Mayor Bata is a tough executive who is
Premier Tsedenbal's right-hand man. I dropped the question
when I saw that it was, for some reason, a sensitive one.

The next day I was taken to see the Deputy Minister of
Public Health, Mr. Radnadorj. I found him so nervous he could
hardly light a cigarette. We talked about various health problems, and gradually he gained a measure of composure. He gave
me a series of figures on the birth rate and the death rate. It
became apparent that his nervousness was connected in some
way with my discussion of the day before. The birth rate as
recently as 1952, according to the Deputy Minister, was 13.4
per thousand and the death rate was 6.0 per thousand. In 1958
he said the birth rate had jumped to 40.3 per thousand. The
death rate had risen slightly, to 10 per thousand. The population was now increasing at a rate of 30.3 per thousand. He gave
me an infant mortality figure of 8.0 per thousand in 1952 and
5.6 per thousand in 1958.

I did not challenge these remarkable figures. I put them down
in my notebook. I did not believe them, but at the time I at-

tributed the exaggeration to pride or overenthusiasm.

A more realistic picture of the problem of child health was given me by the pleasant director of the Ulan Bator Children's Hospital, Dr. Lubsandagva. The hospital is an imposing one, housed in a building which until three years ago was a big military establishment.

Dr. Lubsandagva said frankly that there was no hope of eliminating the winter sickness until the yurt had been done away with. Next to winter sickness, he said, the great problem was diseases of the stomach. These stem from dietary deficiencies which result from the fact that the Mongol diet contains practically no greens, vegetables, or fruit. It is 99 per cent meat and milk products.

Shock troops for the coming Mongol revolution will be provided by the small but growing Ulan Bator State University and a few other institutions of higher learning. The University, I discovered, had 2,500 students, 700 in medicine and the others in languages, liberal arts, and natural sciences. When founded in 1942 it had only 90 students.

The Rector, Dr. Tsevegmid, was a lively little man, as proud as any midwestern state college president of the rapid growth of his school. Someday he hoped he would be able to visit America and inspect our universities. "People are always asking to take my picture, but they never send me one," he complained as I was snapping his portrait. As we left the college he took me outside to see the college mascot—a friendly and lazy deer which the students had raised from a fawn after finding it wandering about the college grounds.

Dr. Tsevegmid thought there were 100,000 persons in Mongolian schools of one sort and another. I thought this was quite an exaggeration. There are two other higher educational institutions, the agricultural institute and a teachers college which has 500 students.

The pace of industrialization in Mongolia would not take

your breath away. But, on the other hand, when you start from zero you can come a long distance quite rapidly. And zero is where Mongolia started from, as recently as 1952. I could find virtually no industries which dated back earlier than that year except for a small meat-packing plant (which I believe worked largely on orders for the Red Army), a small leather plant, a vodka mill, and a few local dairies. And this despite the fact that Communism came into power some thirty years earlier.

Now Mongolia is getting the framework of a small colonial industrial establishment. The biggest plant under construction —and it will be the biggest in the country—is a textile and leather factory. It expects to be processing 1,300,000 sheepskins a year, beginning in 1960. It will turn out 1,200,000 pairs of shoes. Its woolen textile layout will be as modern as any in the world.

Another big and expanding enterprise is the Nalaikha coal combine forty miles outside Ulan Bator. This is a fine, high-level mine. I found the shafts and tunnels as clean and dry as any mine in Russia. It turns out almost 500,000 tons of coal a year, enough to meet the requirements of Ulan Bator. The coal seams lie close to the surface, and the mine will soon be transformed into an open-cut operation.

The managers of the mine proudly told me they had a herd of 5,000 horses to provide the miners with kumiss and 25,000 sheep and cattle to provide them with meat.

I saw most of the larger industries of Ulan Bator: a fine modern dairy, a glass factory (whose principal products seemed to be milk bottles, blue-glass cake dishes, and big mugs for kumiss), a candy factory, a flour mill, a macaroni plant. The wages in these plants ranged from 300 to 600 tugriks a month, with higher pay for higher production. For reasons which I could not fathom, the pay on state farms—at least according to what I was told—averaged somewhat higher. State farm workers were said to get 600 to 700 tugriks a month, plus the privilege of pasturing flocks of up to thirty animals on the state pastures.

In any event, it proved quite impossible to discover what a tugrik was worth. The State Bank changed dollars into tugriks at the rate of four to one. This is the same as the official ruble rate of four to the dollar. In Moscow the ruble and the tugrik were said to be at par with each other. But in Ulan Bator the exchange rate was given as 2.4 rubles to the tugrik.

The dollar rate, of course, was nominal. Not more than a few thousand dollars a year could possibly enter the Mongol treasury. It seemed likely to me that the ruble rate had been adjusted to favor the tugrik to provide a kind of indirect subsidy to the Mongol economy.

I could find no rational basis for Mongol prices. A man's short leather jacket cost from 156 to 190 tugriks. A long leather coat cost 306 and a woman's nutria coat cost 15,000 tugriks. Lamb sold at 5 tugriks a kilo or 100 tugriks a whole lamb. Camels sold for only 200 tugriks, and horses for 300 or 400. Bread cost 2 tugriks a kilo but few Mongols ate bread. Cigarettes cost 1.5 to 3 tugriks. A postcard cost one tugrik, and a steel knife with a little bonework and engraving 88. An elaborate knife and case cost 1,800. Suits cost 500, shoes 90, a shirt 80 and a woman's rayon dress 179. A wool rug cost 3,480, and vodka 40 to 50 tugriks a bottle. Meals cost 40 to 50 tugriks, and hotel rooms 100. But rent in the few state apartment buildings was only 6 or 7 tugriks.

The truth was that, in a nomad economy, money was not important. Mongols have been much more accustomed to valuing goods in terms of lambs or horses than in terms of coinage. They have been more used to weaving their own garments of wool and tanning their own leather than in buying cloth and shoes off the shelves of a store. Their trading place has always been the passing caravan or the bazaar of the East.

And they have not yet given up their nomad ways or their

national habits of dress and custom. They still preferred the *dal*, the traditional long robe with its high collar and long sleeves that extend beyond the hands. The sleeves can be used as a kind of primitive gauntlet for protection against winter cold and snow. The dal enfolds the body from left to right. It is held around the waist by a sash. In winter it is padded with sheepskin. In summer it is usually silk in dazzling colors of electric blue, shocking pink, shimmering yellow, royal purple. Men and women wear the same colors.

Today, as in the days of Genghis Khan, men and women wear knee-high soft leather boots, often with a Turkish turned-up decorated toepiece. Hats are often conical. In winter they are rimmed with sable or beaver.

Only now are Mongols beginning to learn the Western custom of shaking hands. Their great personal holiday is New Year's— not the New Year's of the Christian calendar, but the New Year's of the ancient Mongol calendar which usually falls in February. They exchange gifts and greet each other by stretching out their arms slightly and bowing gently.

These, I thought, seemed small matters. And yet they were strands woven into the social and economic life of the country —a coherent and integrated life, a stubborn way against which the Communist shock troops must prevail if they are to achieve the radical transformation of society which they propose.

Could it be done? I did not know. Surely it would take force. Surely it would produce violence. It would be a struggle more deep and ruthless, in the end, I suspected, than the great Russian drive to collectivize the farms.

My conviction of this grew deeper as I watched the national holiday unfold, a holiday the like of which exists nowhere but in Mongolia. This is *Naadam*. In literal translation it means "play." In the days of Genghis, Naadam lasted a month. Then, as now, it occurred in July, traditionally a month of relaxation for a nomad people. By July their herds were safely in the high mountain pastures. The shearing of the wool was well behind them. The foaling and the lambing were over. It was the season of plenty. A time for relaxation and preparation for the campaigns of fall and the trials of winter.

In the month of play the Mongols dedicated themselves to what were called, then and now, the "three games of men"— horse racing, archery, and Mongol wrestling.

By the time the Communist regime came into being, Naadam had been reduced to a week. Now it lasts three days. And today, as seven hundred years ago, it is basically the same three games of men.

True, the Communist regime has added a full program of modern track and field sports. There are parades and pageants and the same kind of physical-culture societies and exercises I had seen so often in Moscow. This, it was clear, was the Communist line—a line of oblique attack, designed to shift attention away from the ancient games to the modern approved sports of the Communist world.

They had not halted there. A new sports stadium with 15,000 seats had been built in Ulan Bator, that spectators might sit on the concrete benches and watch Naadam instead of squatting on the green lawns in front of the ceremonial tents as in days of yore.

But none of the modern innovations had materially altered the character of Naadam. In the week before the festival the horsemen began to descend on Ulan Bator from the four corners of Mongolia. They came as families and as tribes. They rode their horses and they packed their yurts on wooden-wheeled carts or camel back. Encampments sprang up on the grass fields around the city like mushrooms after rain.

When the great holiday finally dawned—sweltering hot, although there were occasional showers—it was not the ballet of the gymnasts which drew the spectators. It was not the high hurdles or the broad jump. It was the *mergens*, the archers, some

of them men of seventy, some of them boys of seventeen. They
competed to the keening chant of old men. I listened to the
chant rise and fall. It rose when an arrow toppled the target
of earthen pots. It fell when the winged shaft fell short. So it
had been in the time of the Great Khan.

And in the stadium it was not the relay races or the gyrations
of the sports clubs which held the breathless attention of the
crowds. It was the Mongol wrestlers, who strutted before the
audience with arms flapping in a strange pirouette which I was
told had been modeled on the walk of the eagle. Then the
wrestlers crouched and struggled in the ancient conventional
formula. If elbow or knee touched the ground, the contestant
lost. I watched with the crowd as Damdin, a twenty-nine-year-
old, four-time champion, won over opponents who bore the
titles of "The Elephant," "The Eagle," "Great Mongol," "Titan."
Damdin was called "The Lion." For a fifth year he triumphed as
the crowd roared. So it had been in the time of the Great Khan.

And then, as the shafts of late afternoon sunshine cut ver-
tically through the foothills, I watched the greatest competition
of all, that of the horsemen. I watched the big race of the year,
that for boys and girls, six to fourteen. There were 440 youngsters
in the race, each wearing the strange Crusader's helmet of cloth
which Mongol horsemen have worn for centuries. Less than a
handful failed to finish the course. They came galloping over
the wide range, raising dust like a herd of cattle. It was not a
sprint. This was a 45-kilometer gallop over cattle trails. The
youngsters whipped their horses past the finish line, shouting
shrilly, boys and girls together, stirrup to stirrup, hell for
leather. So, too, it had been in the days of the Great Khan.

I watched the old horsemen as they marshaled the youngsters
at the finish line and rode off with them across the darkening
hills to the campfires where the white tents were pitched.

I wondered what were the thoughts in the minds of Mr.
Tsedenbal and the others as they watched too. No one who

witnessed this sight, no one who saw the passion and the iron determination carved into the muscles of these youngsters and the quiet, calm, and careful comradeship of the elder brothers of the horse could possibly underestimate the task which the Communist rulers had undertaken in attempting to shift the whole basis of Mongol society onto new foundations.

I thought of the ancient Mongol legend—the legend of the dragons' eggs of the Gobi. Who disturbs those eggs hidden for centuries under the hot sands of the desert will loose upon the earth once more the dragons that ruled the world before man started on the path to civilization.

Not a few of the dragons' eggs have been dug from their ancient hiding places by the scientists of the Communist state. They have been brought to Ulan Bator and placed there on exhibit in the museum. The eggs, say the scientists, are those of dinosaurs. Talk of dragons is nothing but primitive superstition.

To which, of course, the older Mongols gravely shake their heads. Time will tell, they believe, the fate of those who fly in the face of ancient tradition in this land where the race of man is said to have had its birth.

XV

The Blue Ants

WHEN I LOOKED OUT the window of the guest
house in which we stayed outside Ulan Bator I often saw a
sturdy young man in blue cap, blue-denim coat, and blue-denim
trousers working in the garden. He was setting out petunias to
form red stars in two whitewashed rock circles.

On the highway that led from the airport to the city there was
a large crew of sturdy young men in blue caps, blue-denim
coats, and blue-denim trousers laying asphalt on the cobble-
stones. A few miles further on, a larger force of sturdy young
men similarly garbed were working with trucks and bulldozers.
They were preparing the approach to a new bridge over the
Tola River. Another group of blue-uniformed young men was
setting into place the steel girders of the bridge.

Across the river and along the flatlands near the city, eight or
ten four-story apartment houses were being built. In the windows of the completed buildings I often saw the blue-denim
workers. They were living in the apartments while finishing the
other buildings.

On the main square of Ulan Bator and on all the approaches
to it there were teams of workers in their dress of blue. They
were digging ditches, laying sidewalks, setting out trees, putting
in curbstones, erecting buildings.

Indeed, wherever I went I saw the men in blue. These were
not Mongols. They were blue ants. Chinese laborers. The gift, I

learned, of the generous Communist Chinese Government. It
not only was providing the labor. It was also paying the wages
of the labor crews, taking care of their shelter and food, providing the supplies and equipment. So far as I could learn, all
the Mongol government had to do was to tell the Chinese what
they wanted built.

These were not spindly, beaten slaves. They were fine, husky,
muscular young men. They carried their heads high and their
shoulders squared. I saw them in the early morning drizzle doing
calisthenics on the sandy banks of the Tola. I saw them working
under their great straw hats in blazing sun while the Mongols
slept in the shade of buildings or the thickets of willows along
the river. I watched them pedaling briskly on their bicycles
across the Tola River bridge at the end of the day.

It was not only in Ulan Bator that the blue ants were busy.
We found them training the Mongols to run a glass factory they
had built for them, and they were erecting an addition to it.
We found them working under arc lights far in the interior to
build a new bridge to replace one which floods had swept away.
We found them digging irrigation works on new collective farm
tracts.

They were installing the machinery in the fine new textile
plant in Ulan Bator. They also were putting in the looms and
the spindles—and every bit of the equipment had been purchased through the Chinese National Sales Corporation. There
was nothing but the finest and newest English machinery from
Platts, William Whiteley & Sons, Prince, Smith and Steels, and
Metropolitan Vickers.

Even the repairs to the great Gandan monastery were being
made by Chinese workmen.

How many of them were there? I could not find out precisely.
Mr. Lotchin said he thought there were ten thousand. Premier
Tsedenbal said twenty thousand. My own guess was that the
number was substantially greater. Almost every construction

project in the country was dependent upon Chinese labor. Russian technicians were helping on some factories. But the labor was Chinese. The blue ants were the first and possibly the most dramatic evidence that struck my eye of the struggle between the giants of the world of Communism, Russia and China, over which was to control the future of Mongolia.

I had traveled almost a quarter of the way around the globe because I thought that here in Mongolia I might find tangible clues to the reality of relations between Moscow and Peking. And I was not disappointed.

The truth was, as I quickly discovered, that Mongolia was locked in a complex power struggle. Not only were Russia and China nakedly competing on sphere-of-influence terms. The Mongols themselves had their own deep involvement. Some leaned to Russia, some to China. And some, it was quite apparent, hoped that out of the great power rivalry might emerge a new and greater Mongolia.

It was much too early to forecast how this complicated situation might evolve. But there was every sign that the Russians were losing ground to the Chinese.

I hardly expected any of the Mongols whom I met to tell me their secret political sympathies; but it was not difficult to guess the attitudes of many.

The top leaders, the men like Premier Tsedenbal, President Sambu and Mayor Bata of Ulan Bator, were Russian-trained, Russian-oriented—and undoubtedly Russian-selected. For, in point of fact, Mongolia had been a Russian protectorate since a Communist regime was established in the country, with the aid of the Red Army, in 1921.

I found Tsedenbal an able, alert, attractive young executive. He was only forty-two but appeared even younger. He knew a little English. He had been in the United States in 1946, remembered his visit clearly, and hoped that he might come again some day. He had been educated in Moscow, however, and his

sympathies lay with the Soviet Union. He it was who had embarked his country on the revolutionary course of putting the
plow to the virgin pasture—a policy which had its inception
in Moscow. He was under no illusions as to the difficulties that
lay ahead. Already there had been deep repercussions and a
split in the Mongolian Communist Party. Only a few months
before I arrived in Ulan Bator, Tsedenbal had ousted his opponents, who wanted to go slow and retain the Mongol tradition of nomad pasturage.

But Moscow had decreed that the *selina,* the virgin soil, be
plowed—just as it had been in Kazakhstan and southwest Siberia. Moscow held that only thus could Mongolia be put on a
rational economic basis and only thus could a foundation be
laid for a political and social structure which might survive
independently.

A radical step, admittedly. And it brought into the inner
councils of the Communist Party a split which, I was fairly
certain, reflected quite clearly the division of sentiment in the
country—pro-Russian, pro-Chinese, and Mongol independent.

In a sense, of course, the Russians were right, although it
seemed clear that the sources of the current Mongolian crisis
really lay in Moscow and not in Ulan Bator.

What had happened was that from 1921 onward Mongolia
was the forgotten stepchild of the Communist world. I could see
no evidence that the Communists had made any effort to start
the country down the path toward any kind of modern economy. At first, they did not even change the theocratic basis of
the country. Until the death of Bogdo Gegen, in 1926, the nation
continued to be a religious monarchy with the Communists
ruling in the name of the king-god. Only after his death was it
formally changed into a republic.

For years thereafter, Mongolia was left to its own devices.
The Russians seemed interested in the country only as a re-
mount source for the Red Army cavalry. Meat was purchased

for the Red Banner Far Eastern Army. Mongolia was a convenient shield against the Japanese Kwantung Army in Manchuria but too exposed to Japanese attack to make investment worth while.

Even after World War II had removed the threat of Japanese attack, Mongolia slumbered on. Only when the Chinese Communist regime had established itself did Moscow suddenly become interested in improving the situation in Mongolia. In fact, most Russian projects—dated from 1952 or later—and they still were very small. This was a time coincident with two deaths; those of the Mongol leader, Choibalsan, and of Stalin. Whether there was a connection I was not prepared to say.

Not that Russia had not made a mark on Mongolia. Russian was the second language of most educated Mongols. English, rather than Chinese, was the usual third language. The Mongol Army wore uniforms hardly to be distinguished from those of the Soviet Army. Mongol militiamen were uniformed like Russian militiamen; they used the same system of hand signals for traffic control.

A visit to the Mongolian Foreign Office was like a visit to a branch of the Soviet Foreign Office in Moscow—procedures, décor, and even language were little different. Those Mongols who had abandoned the beautiful national dress of silk gowns had adopted drab Russian clothing. They did not wear the Cromwellian blue uniforms and blue caps of the Chinese.

The repertoire of the Ulan Bator drama and opera theaters resembled that of Soviet provincial theaters, not Chinese. Ulan Bator was trying to build a ballet, not a new Peking Opera. And the vast and windy acreage of Sukhe Bator Square, in the center of the capital, with its red stone mausoleum housing the remains of Sukhe Bator and Choibalsan, derived its inspiration from the Red Square and the Lenin-Stalin Mausoleum.

Such contemporary art as Mongolia possessed stemmed straight from crude Russian socialist realism. The architecture of the new government buildings and apartments being erected in Ulan Bator was Gorky Street style, second class.

But this was a superficial imprint; and it seemed to me that the new Soviet economic and social program had come too late.

It was true that the Mongols had welcomed the intervention of the Russians in 1921. Then the Russians were regarded as liberators after the centuries of Chinese and Manchurian oppression. But now nearly forty years had passed in which the roles were reversed. Too many young Mongols seemed to think of the Russians as colonial rulers. There was an undercurrent of bitterness, deep and dangerous, which only occasionally appeared on the surface.

I caught a reflection of it one day in the Mongolian State Museum. The guide was pointing to the portraits of the leaders of the Mongol revolution, Sukhe Bator and Choibalsan.

"That is our great revolutionary leader, Sukhe Bator," the guide said. "He died in 1923, of poison administered by our enemies. And that is Choibalsan. He died in 1952—after an operation by the Kremlin doctors."

The Kremlin doctors! A curious phrase, indeed.

Whatever the inference, it was clear each day I spent in Mongolia that close to the surface there were conflicts and tensions and suspicions. Many of these obviously stemmed from the deep split in the country. I could not guess at the source of others. Some, perhaps, came from the centuries of isolation of Mongolia. Nothing breeds suspicion like isolation, and mountain people the world over are noted for their hospitality—and suspicion—toward strangers.

I had noticed the care with which Soviet border guards checked Mongol passengers. I found the Mongol border precautions equally rigorous. Planes were not permitted to take off from Irkutsk for Ulan Bator except at hours which permitted them to cross the Mongol frontier by daylight. Presumably any plane crossing after dark is automatically fired upon.

I have never been submitted to a customs examination so thorough as that which I received on leaving Ulan Bator. Every item in my suitcases was examined, every piece of paper was looked at, each book thumbed through and shaken. Even the shaving soap was punched. A half-dozen small Mongol coins were seized (export of currency is not permitted). Another foreign visitor lost a twenty-five-cent ball-point pen because he had not declared it on entry. Only after an hour's argument and a threat to appeal to Premier Tsedenbal was my film permitted to pass.

An Italian correspondent who was invited to Ulan Bator for the national holiday was summarily expelled after making some bitter remarks because his escorting official refused to let him visit the single, shamefully shoddy bookstore that the capital boasts.

I found it impossible to take a step in the country unaccompanied by Mr. Lotchin or some other Mongol escort. They refused to permit me to visit the bazaar. ("It has been torn down." "We don't have a bazaar such as you have in Western countries.") They would not let me go for a walk in the center of the capital by myself. It took days of arguing before I was permitted to visit the Soviet Embassy. A trip to the post office was a major undertaking, and an effort to take a pair of glasses to a repairman almost resulted in physical violence.

Some of these incidents, of course, stemmed from the hypersensitivity of young Mongol intellectuals who were anguished that I might get the impression that Mongolia was a backward country. Their naïveté would have been touching had it not been so irritating. It was impossible to drive down a street in Ulan Bator without seeing at a glance that this was a country far more backward than the most remote Asiatic provinces of the Soviet Union.

But not all the restrictions stemmed from fearful pride. Many of them, it was obvious, arose because conditions in Mongolia are unsettled. There are unquestionably many Mongol citizens who resent and hate the efforts of the government to change their way of life. There are open although not excessive controls on the movements of people. Police check all wheeled vehicles going in and out of Ulan Bator. They are particularly careful after dark. Uniformed police are no more numerous than in most Communist countries. But I noticed that they were often equipped with walkie-talkies. I saw no labor battalions or prison labor in rural areas. Not far from the Soviet Embassy, however, I saw two large prison compounds, surrounded by barbed-wire barricades, guarded by security police, and protected by wooden watchtowers.

Premier Tsedenbal seemed to move around without excessive security. He had only one security car with his limousine, and he walked through crowds several times with only a small plainclothes detachment.

Nor was the army very conspicuous. The parade of military at the national holiday was a good deal bigger than Moscow's but not impressive as to quality or equipment. There were several large barracks in the foothills back of Ulan Bator, but I saw hardly any troops as I traveled about the country.

And almost every Mongol official commented on the relaxation of the great burden on the economy made possible by the demobilization of troops and cutback in military expense. This was, they said, because now Mongolia was no longer surrounded by enemies.

It seemed likely to me that these statements were correct and that the large army maintained for protection against Japanese aggression had been dissolved. But it did not seem to have helped the country much with its labor problem. The men presumably had gone back to their nomadic life. Most were unfamiliar with such implements as hammers and shovels anyway; neither are used by men who live in yurts and tend cattle all their lives.

This, of course, was what lay behind the Chinese move to inject large numbers of skilled laborers into Mongolia. Even with capital, machinery, and technical advice Mongolia still lacked the skills to build roads, construct buildings, or set up factories. Peking had stepped into the breach. She was, I was told, constantly urging the Mongols to take more labor—free. It was an offer that was most difficult to resist.

Yet, if the steady influx of skilled, able, aggressive Chinese continued, it was apparent that they would acquire an influence far out of proportion to their numbers; for they were culturally, technologically, and even physically far more advanced than the descendants of Genghis Khan's horse cavalry. And, by agreement with the Mongol government, the Chinese had the right to opt for Mongol citizenship and stay permanently in the country—a Trojan horse of formidable size.

Nor was this the only string to Peking's bow. The Chinese obviously did not expect to win over the faithful among Moscow's trained top leaders. But they were concentrating on the second level: the young Mongols who would be the leaders of the next generation—the young men who had graduated in the last few years from the Ulan Bator State University, the young doctors and teachers, the engineers just back from courses in Prague and Budapest.

This level of the Mongol intelligentsia, small in numbers but strong in leadership potential, was being taken to China on excursions, trips, and study courses. They were being shown the way of the China revolution—how an Asian land was advancing with giant strides to world power, lifting itself by its own bootstraps. For the China slogan was: "Do It Alone. Do not rely on the West." And "West" in Ulan Bator means Russia, not America. Indeed, I even had the curious experience a time or two of hearing young Mongols referring to "Western countries like Russia and America."

These young people came back from China with glowing

eyes. The Chinese way was *The Way* for Mongolia. Not the way of the Russian oppressors, the conservative and backward West. Mongolia must look East.

When I had heard some of these young men talk I thought I could understand a bit more clearly the hearty reception I got when I visited the Soviet Embassy. "Ah, an American. How good to see you!" There was something of a comradeship of the West in Ulan Bator.

And I thought I understood what lay behind the remarks of a Russian official who had spent many years in Mongolia when he raised his glass of vodka to me at a Ulan Bator reception and said: "Really, now, standing here in Mongolia tonight, can you think of any reason why we Russians and you Americans should fight? Is there anyone here to whom you feel more close?"

And, truth to tell, he was right.

"To peace," I said, raising my glass.

"To peace—and the closest friendship of Russia and America," he replied. "That is what we both need and what we are going to have."

Intimately aware as they are of the grinding collision of interests between the two great Communist empires which lie to the north and the south, the Mongol leaders would like very much to move out a little further onto the world stage and try, if possible, to attain a little leverage against these enormous pressures. This is the classic device of the weak state which lives in the shadow of great neighbors. The fact that Mongolia is Communist and that her leaders are Russian-oriented does not change the *Realpolitik*.

What Tsedenbal would like is American recognition and a seat in the United Nations. As he frankly says, it is only American opposition which keeps Mongolia out of the UN. This would then enable Mongolia to broaden its diplomatic relations, obtain contacts with European nations, trade more widely, and break out of the shell of isolation in which it has long lived.

It now has diplomatic relations with about fifteen countries—the nations of the Communist bloc plus some Asian and neutral states.

Mongolia wants to play the time-honored role of the small, weak country, balancing one big power against the other and calling, in case of need, upon uncommitted third powers. This is the game which Iran played before World War II when she brought Germany in as a makeweight against Russia and England.

Thus far, with monumental nonchalance, American policy-makers have neglected this remarkable opportunity at Communism's back door. We have never had diplomatic relations with Mongolia, and the State Department's position today is based on the astounding fiction that no such country even exists.

In their tentative push for big power recognition the Mongols have been trying to broaden their contacts with the West. They have permitted three or four journalists to come in. In September, 1959, they entertained representatives of fifteen or twenty countries at a great congress of specialists on Mongology. Unfortunately, even these tiny steps aroused almost paranoid suspicions among the long-isolated officials. Visitors at the September conference found Ulan Bator tense and uneasy, their Mongol hosts strained and sometimes distant. It is not an easy task to emerge from a shell.

But there is another and perhaps even deeper current moving in this troubled land. Here, too, only signs are seen drifting to the surface. But they are not without significance. This is a movement toward a greater Mongolia. How deep and how broad this sentiment may be I could not determine. But I felt certain that the concept of Greater Mongolia was shared by all Mongols, those in Russia and China as well. And it was not difficult to see that it was a factor which both Russian and Chinese policy is taking into account.

The 1,000,000 Mongols, more or less, in Outer Mongolia add

up to a relatively small country. I think this figure is not un-connected with the curious sensitivity which I discovered in Mayor Bata and the Deputy Minister of Health concerning Mongolia's birth rate. I think these officials wish to do every-thing possible to convince the outside world—and particularly China and Russia—that Mongolia's population is increasing at the greatest possible rate. If Mongolia is to retain its independ-ence and preserve its great empty lands against the population pressure from the south, the Mongols are going to have to in-crease very rapidly—much more rapidly than is possible even with the fantastic number of births which they claimed were occurring.

They had next door an example of real population pressure. There are, in theory, about 1,500,000 Mongols in China's Inner Mongolia. But Chinese are pouring into the area. They now outnumber the Mongols better than seven to one (in part be-cause of administrative changes incorporating large Chinese populations into Inner Mongolia).

To the north lie the lands of Buryat-Mongolia in the Soviet Union with a population of just under 700,000, about half of whom are Mongols.

While it does not seem realistic to suppose that the Mongols will ever again manage to unite these broken populations under one state, the two great powers are aware that they face bur-geoning Mongol nationalism. The Russians, characteristically, have reacted by dropping the word "Mongol" from the title of their Buryat-Mongolian autonomous republic. That this seman-tic change will convince the Mongols that they are now Buryats seems dubious.

The Chinese are trying to play the game both ways. They are trying to attract the Outer Mongolians toward Inner Mon-golia. But at the same time they are submerging the Inner Mon-golians in a sea of Chinese immigration which has provoked protests and resentment on the part of the Inner Mongolians.

The frontier between Inner and Outer Mongolia is closed—at least theoretically. It seemed to me that this was due to a desire by the Chinese to prevent the carrying on of Mongolian national propaganda.

However, the advantage clearly lies with the Chinese in any use for their own ends of the Greater Mongolia concept. They have far more Mongols in their country, and the traditional ties between Inner and Outer Mongolia are old and intimate.

One of the nationalistic measures imposed on Mongolia by the Russians was the substitution of a modified Cyrillic alphabet for the traditional Mongol vertical script, a modification of Sanskrit and Tibetan. The change was imposed in 1946, at about the same time that Moscow decided to impose similar scripts on the Soviet Asiatic republics.

Thus, since 1946, Cyrillic has been Mongolia's official script. It is taught in the schools; and the official newspaper, *Unen* (which means "Truth" just as does *Pravda*), is printed in Cyrillic. But in all the time I was in Mongolia I saw only one Mongol official who employed Cyrillic to write notes or memoranda. All the others used the old Mongol script.

The Chinese have not suppressed the Mongol script in Inner Mongolia. Their newspaper is still printed in it—which is one reason why the paper is so popular in Ulan Bator. Nor have the Chinese suppressed the cult of Genghis Khan. His temple and his supposed remains have been set up again, and pilgrimages of Mongols (including Mongols from Outer Mongolia) are encouraged to visit the sacred relics.

Although for centuries Mongols hated the Chinese and particularly the Manchus for their overlordship, these memories are dim today. Russia is the recent overlord.

"The momentum of the Chinese initiative is so great, the attractive force of Chinese dynamism is so overpowering," an Asian diplomat observed, "that it is hard to see how, over the long run, Russia can maintain her position here. She is still the first power in Mongolia. But five years from now this may well no longer be true."

To me this made good sense. The ideological and practical ability of Russia to counter the Chinese offensive effectively seemed limited. And the demographic ability of the Mongol state to resist indefinitely the huge and growing pressures from the south and east seemed equally limited.

I was asking a young Mongol one day about the different alphabets which Mongols had used over the centuries. There had been eight different alphabets, he said. "Every great conqueror wants to perpetuate his memory by changing our alphabet," he said. "Mongolia has not always been a fortunate state in her neighbors."

My feeling as I left Ulan Bator was that the time might not be far distant when there would be another change of the alphabet.

XVI

The Coming Conflict

I FLEW BACK from Mongolia convinced that my long suspicions that deep conflict existed between Russia and China were correct. I did not know what form the conflict would take in the future nor how long it would be in maturing. But the outlines of it were there, open and unconcealed, to be seen by anyone who managed to penetrate the Mongolian fastness.

Nor did I believe this conflict was of recent origin. There were many reputable diplomats who had insisted for years that conflict between the two great Communist Empires was inconceivable and impossible. They felt that Moscow and Peking followed a policy of close co-ordination. Some even insisted that it was a single policy, dictated by Moscow and faithfully carried out by Chinese puppets.

In the long years that I spent in Moscow I had come to believe that behind the façade of formal friendship and the exchanges of communiqués and delegations there lay deep and ugly rifts.

But only recently had enough evidence become available to make it possible to piece together a hypothesis that would explain many curious mysteries.

It seemed entirely possible to me, for example, that the motivations behind the Korean War were entirely different from those which we in America supposed. We had assumed that

241

this was a blow directed at the United States, a Communist move to undermine our position in the Far East. Instead, I had a strong suspicion that it had been intended as a blow by Stalin at Mao Tse-tung.

It is still not possible to prove this theory. But there has been a striking accumulation of evidence pointing in this direction.

It should be recalled that after the 1927 debacle of the Canton Revolution (when Chiang Kai-shek broke with the Communists) Stalin turned his back on China. Canton was a striking failure for the policy of international Communism. From this time on, Stalin more and more devoted himself to the policy of building Communism in one country. Moscow wrote off China.

Mao and Chou En-lai were left to their own resources. Even after the success of the Long March and the gradual build-up of Chinese Communist power Stalin gave little sign of interest. He told Patrick Hurley and others during World War II that the Chinese were "margarine Communists"—not real Communists.

In later years it was suggested that Stalin was cleverly misleading us, that actually he was supporting Mao while ostensibly disparaging him. This does not seem to fit the real evidence. During these years Stalin was dealing with the Chiang Kai-shek government. He wrecked the industry of North China and Manchuria in 1945, carting away industrial establishments instead of leaving them for his supposed Chinese Communist friends to take over. He clung to diplomatic relations with Chiang until the last possible moment. Not until Chiang left the mainland did Moscow switch allegiance to Mao.

If you examine *Pravda* for the year 1948, the year in which the Chinese Communists were coming to power, you will see a strange and curious thing. Although Communism was triumphing on a scale of undreamed-of breadth, *Pravda* hardly saw fit to mention it. Only the most laconic and occasional reports were published of the Chinese Communist successes.

The year 1948 was a critical year in Moscow—a year of deep suspicion and dark plots in the Soviet capital, of the break with Tito, of the start of the offensive against the Jews, of the still obscure but terrible "Leningrad affair" in which many leading Communists lost their lives.

In January of 1949 Stalin arrested Mikhail Borodin, Anna Louise Strong, and a number of Borodin's associates. Police closed down the Moscow *Daily News* which Borodin edited. Borodin was the man who masterminded the Canton Revolution for Russia. Miss Strong, an American, was one of his oldest associates. Both were deeply interested in China and the Chinese Communists. Miss Strong was a close personal friend of Mao and Chou. She had been in Belgrade, and she had come to Moscow on her way to China.

There has never been a satisfactory explanation for the arrests (Miss Strong was finally "rehabilitated" in 1958 and since then has taken up residence in Peking).

But if Stalin was disturbed by the rise of Mao, if in fact there was deep conflict between Mao and Stalin, an explanation of these strange events becomes possible. It was hinted in Moscow in 1949 that Miss Strong was suspected of being a go-between from Tito to Mao. Stalin may have felt that his enemies in the Communist world were coming together and that Borodin and Miss Strong represented a link, potential or actual, between Tito and Mao.

Mr. Khrushchev (who seems to have no reason for fabricating history on this point) has said that, in fact, there was a serious split between Stalin and Mao at this time. He has told foreign Communists that relations between Stalin and Mao were so strained that had it not been for the international situation and pressure by the United States there might have been an open break. Stalin, he said, insisted on treating Mao as a dependent. He wanted to exploit China as a colony. Stalin was overbearing.

Blithely unaware of any rift, the Truman administration was carrying on a discussion as to the desirability of recognizing Red China. It was finally decided late in 1949 to delay for a while "to let the dust settle" in China. Thus, perhaps one of the greatest diplomatic opportunities of the century slipped through our fingers.

The situation between Russia and China, Khrushchev contends, remained critical until Mao finally came to Moscow in December, 1949. Mao stayed for two months and left on February 13, 1950, after signing the draft of the Sino-Russian alliance, agreeing to terms for a small Soviet loan (since repaid) and permitting Russia to maintain her strategic bases in the Far East (Port Arthur, Dairen, and the Changchun railway) until a Japanese peace treaty was signed. Joint Sino-Russian exploitation companies were set up to develop Chinese resources.

The negotiations between Stalin and Mao were arduous. I was in Moscow at the time, and I recall the curious press treatment, the absence of references to Mao for days and even weeks at a time (until we began to wonder whether he had not secretly returned to China). This was in bewildering contrast to the usual custom of giving great publicity to such a distinguished guest.

The economic terms of the treaty were so niggardly as to arouse comment. It seemed significant that Russia was maintaining her military position at full strength despite the victory of the Chinese Communists.

From what we know of the personalities of Stalin and of Mao it seems certain that the negotiations were difficult and acrimonious. At almost this exact time Secretary of State Acheson made the famous address in which he failed to specify Korea as a point in the American defensive chain in the Pacific.

In her drive from the islands to the China mainland Japan had moved by stages, first to Korea, then, after defeating Russia, into North China. Finally she seized Manchuria and set it up as a puppet state.

In the spring of 1950 the Russian position was not unlike that which the Japanese had held. Russia had her treaty ports and the railroad. She held North Korea as a Russian province and as such beyond the influence of the Red Chinese. Her troops were on the Amur River north of Manchuria. She lacked South Korea and Manchuria. If she held both of them she could, of course, put Mao into a nutcracker and force him to agree to what she wanted. If Stalin preferred, he could detach Manchuria; it already had been given quasi-autonomous status in the Chinese regime.

There is reason to believe that Stalin may already have made further arrangements in Manchuria but he lacked the Korean piece on the chessboard. If by a lightning stroke Russia's puppet army in North Korea could seize South Korea (and in Moscow the only possible reading of Acheson's statement was that this would encounter no armed resistance by the U.S.A.) then Stalin would be in a position to dictate to the upstart Mao.

Of course, the whole plan fell apart when the United States and the United Nations opposed the rape of South Korea. Instead of a quick clever trick that would put his Chinese ally at his mercy, Stalin found himself involved in a long, bloody war which almost became a world conflict. Eventually the Chinese Communists entered the war, and gradually the power basis in the Far East began to shift away from Russia and toward China.

Stalin's motivation in ordering the attack in Korea is still unproved hypothesis. But one more missing piece has since fallen into place. In 1956 the subscribers to the Soviet Bolshoi Encyclopedia received a special notice from the publishers. They were instructed to slit out the page containing the biography of a Chinese Communist official named Kao Kang and paste in a page containing no reference to him. The only other occasion on which this had been done was after the execution of Beria, when subscribers were asked to rip out his biography and insert an article on the Bering Sea.

Thus, the inference was clear that the case of Kao Kang was of the same magnitude as Beria's. Or that, perhaps, they might be in some way connected. And who was Kao Kang? He was the boss of Manchuria, the special administrator of the quasi-autonomous region. Little was ever published by the Chinese press about him—except to call him a traitor.

What was the nature of his treachery? I believe he was Beria's man or Stalin's man or Russia's man—call him what you will. If this is true Stalin had the whole chessboard set up. There was to be no escape for Mao after Korea. But Stalin misjudged the United States, and the whole game failed.

There may have been even more to it. There have been hints and rumors in the Far East of a plot to assassinate Mao in 1949 or 1950. But this would not really have been necessary. Had Stalin possessed Manchuria, Korea, the northern railroads and naval bases, Mao could not have stood up to him a day. Stalin could have dictated his own terms.

I do not think you would have to look very far in Moscow today to find Russians who wished that Stalin had succeeded in his plot to subjugate Mao.

If, as I strongly suspect, the inner history of Soviet-Chinese relations followed a pattern so Machiavellian, it was hardly accidental. The roots of Russian-Chinese conflict in the Far East go deep. The fact that both countries now fly the Communist flag no more resolves their basic power conflicts than the fact that England and Germany were both capitalist powers enabled them to liquidate their dangerous rivalry in 1914. In the case of Russia there is a long history of popular fear of Eastern peoples, stemming from the days of the Mongol conquest. Russians had never felt secure in alliance with China.

The feeling appeared to be mutual. It was easiest to observe among Russian and Chinese students in Moscow.

A Russian said: "Last summer I was in Sochi. It was a very hot day. A bunch of Chinese students, boys and girls, came out on the beach and did calisthenics in the sun. They exercised for an hour in dark blue sweatshirts. Then they made a circle on the beach, took out their textbooks, and started to study Marxism-Leninism. It was a frightening thing to watch."

Or take the case of a Chinese student at Moscow University. The boy decided to save money from his state stipend of 300 rubles a month. He wanted to buy a Soviet 35-millimeter camera. By going without lunches he managed to put aside enough money to buy the camera. But his Chinese comrades found out what he was doing, and he was summoned before a "comradely court."

"You deprived your body and your brain of the food calories needed to study at your highest capability," the comradely prosecutor charged.

"Or," said another, "if you are able to work at full capacity on less food you should have given the extra money back to the state."

The student agreed to sell his camera, give the money back to the state, nourish his mind and body fully in the future, and work harder than ever to deserve the solicitude that the state was showing.

"Imagine!" said a Russian. "What can you do with people like that! They are not human."

The Chinese students stick closely together in Russia. They have few outside friends. American students at Moscow and Leningrad universities found them hostile. North Korean students introduced themselves to Americans with the words: "We are Koreans, not Chinese. We would like to be your friends."

These attitudes could be dismissed as reflecting cultural differences of two diverse peoples. What counts, of course, is the attitude of the people at the top. Here, it seemed to me, cold demogogic, economic, and power factors played a decisive role.

Khrushchev paid his first visit to Peking in the autumn of 1954. He went East with a mission that included Bulganin, Madame Furtseva, and several others. In Peking he negotiated a revision of the unequal treaty of 1950. Russia relinquished its special rights, special bases, special privileges. It was the first time that the two nations had ever dealt as equals. On his way back Khrushchev stopped over in eastern Siberia. He inspected the lands north of the Amur. He visited Khabarovsk (until that time the Far Eastern capital of the police empire). He stopped off at Birobidzhan, the semiabandoned Jewish settlement area. He had a look at the vast open spaces of Siberia and Kazakhstan. Malenkov was still Premier, but Khrushchev's power was rising rapidly.

A few weeks later Khrushchev made what history may record as the most significant speech of his career. He called in the young Russians of the Communist Youth League and launched a crusade to send them to Siberia to open up the virgin lands. This was the start of his great gamble to put the plow to the selina. He called on the young people to go east, to fill up those vacant spaces that lay across the frontier from China (he put it almost but not quite that openly). He asked that they go to Eastern Siberia, settle down, raise families. Russia needed people on those vacant lands. "If about a hundred million people were added to our two hundred million even that would not be enough," he said.

Several hundred thousand young people have gone to Siberia since Khrushchev's call. But most of them have settled in western Siberia and Kazakhstan. The Amur reaches are still vast wildernesses. Of the 250,000,000 acres of arable land in Khabarovsk Krai, for instance, only about 500,000 are under cultivation. Population movement has been only a trickle despite enormous inducements to rural settlers. (They have been offered free transportation for themselves and families, livestock, household goods, plus special bonuses including tax exemption, food, grants and loans for building houses and purchasing livestock.)

But on the other side of the frontier the population pressure increases inexorably. In three years 1,380,000 Chinese settlers moved into Inner Mongolia, the northeast and northwest provinces—those regions adjacent to Russia's eastern provinces and Mongolia.

And this is only the gentle lapping of the first waves of China's population tide. Chinese statistics may not be entirely reliable, but the figures which Russians cited to me were a current population in the neighborhood of 650,000,000,* with a growth factor possibly as high as 25,000,000 a year. The Soviet population is 208,000,000 and the growth factor is about midway between 3,000,000 and 4,000,000 a year.

Even without the steady northward movement of the Chinese, these are the kind of figures which must cause any prudent Soviet leader to examine closely his plans for the future. For it is perfectly apparent to anyone who reads the statistics that not only are there going to be heavy and continuous population pressures on those great vacant lands of Russia's to the East (lands, incidentally, which in most cases were at one time the property of China), but also there is going to be a steady tilting of the power axis away from Moscow and toward Peking.

China is not just growing in numbers. She is growing in economic weight. And no one knows this more intimately than the Russians who are assisting this growth. Russians who have been recent visitors to China speak with awe and concern about the pace of Chinese industrial development.

"You cannot believe it," one highly placed Russian told me, "until you see it with your own eyes. The speed, the discipline, the organizing ability. The Chinese have such enormous quantities of labor. And everyone is working so hard. Nothing we

* An official census gave China's population as 601,900,000 as of June 30, 1953. If this figure is correct China's population should exceed 700,000,000 in 1960.

ever did in Russia was anything like it."

Another Russian strongly urged me to go to China. "It is another world," he said. "You must know what is happening there. To understand the world today you must see China."

And one said: "The speed of development in China is terrifying. When you think of the future . . ."

A neutral businessman, returning from China, said: "China is a terrible threat to the world. The Russians recognize this threat, they understand it is a threat to Russia as much as to the rest of the world."

A Western diplomat who has watched the Russians carefully for a number of years said he felt the key factor in the timetable of world relations today is the date on which China obtains the atomic bomb. When that moment occurs, he pointed out, the world balance of power will change irrevocably. China henceforth will be a member of the atomic club with full rights and privileges.

"And how will you and Russia like that?" he asked. It was his conviction that this prospect was already affecting Khrushchev's policy. The world does not know when China will become a nuclear power. But Khrushchev should be in a good position to find out.

Not that Russia is helping China to arm herself with atoms. There is no evidence that Russia is assisting China with anything more than experimental nuclear laboratory facilities. She is not even building the Chinese a nuclear power plant, so far as is known. But China's possession of atomic weapons is only a matter of time. Chinese physicists study in the great Soviet nuclear center at Dubno and in the Soviet physics institutes. So far as China is concerned, the atom bomb presumably is not a matter of know-how—it is just a matter of allocating facilities to make it.

There is never any public quarreling between Russia and China. But there are some obvious differences of principle, most notably on the subject of the Chinese communes. Mr.

Khrushchev pointedly commented on the commune question during a trip in July, 1959, to Poland. He brought up the subject in the course of an address in which he was trying to convince Polish peasants that they should try collective farming.

Communes, he said, were organized in Russia shortly after the Revolution. But the proper material and political conditions were lacking and the result was failure. The Communist Party abandoned them and went over to farm co-operatives, which provided the basis for the present collective-farm system.

He repudiated the commune idea and also the idea of force or pressure to get peasants to give up individual farming. Thus, without publicly mentioning China, he put himself on record as against the most publicized of Chinese Communist achievements. In so doing, he merely repeated sentiments expressed privately by other Russian Communist leaders. One of his closest associates said to me, months before, that the communes were old-fashioned and would never work. "The only way you can get people to work," he said, "is to give them some kind of incentive."

Mr. Khrushchev has also criticized another Chinese Communist technique—but also obliquely. The Chinese have been mobilizing city workers by the hundreds of thousands and sending them to the countryside to help with sowing and other agricultural tasks. It is a method often used in the Soviet Union as well. Mr. Khrushchev, however, called for an end to it. He said this kind of labor was inefficient. To send city people to the country disrupted both country and city. What was needed was rationalizing of farm jobs and better use of the existing labor force.

The Soviet press studiously neglected mentioning the "backyard iron foundry" campaign, which the Chinese Communists launched in 1958 and abandoned in 1959 with the admission that it hadn't worked. Again privately, the Russians shook their heads sadly at so primitive and naïve an approach to problems of economics.

One aspect of the Chinese commune has gone quite without notice in the Soviet Union. This is the strategic implication of subdividing China into thousands of self-contained social and economic units.

"These are units for survival," an English traveler told me on his return from Peking. "The Chinese told me that if nuclear war came, the rest of the world might be wiped out. But China would survive. Even if two or three hundred million Chinese were killed, the nation would endure. Whole provinces could be wiped out. But each commune would be independent and some would be bound to survive."

Such thinking is alien to the Soviet philosophy that there would be no survival on either the Russian or the American side if nuclear war broke out between them.

The most notable contrast between Moscow and Peking, of course, arose in the sphere of policy toward the United States. In contrast to Mr. Khrushchev's gestures of good will, the Chinese line continued to be firm and unyielding. Although not a word of criticism of Moscow appeared in the Peking press, there were innumerable straws to indicate that the views of the two countries were not the same. Three days passed before the Soviet press was able to quote any Chinese reaction to the Eisenhower-Khrushchev exchange of visits. And Peking's comment was merely a collection of clichés. When Mr. Khrushchev went to Peking after his trip to the United States there were further indications of coolness.

As if to emphasize her aloofness, China had turned her back on the United States. She refused to admit Americans to China. News correspondents were banned. So were political figures and even Americans known to be friendly to Communist China.

A few American Communists or Americans with Communist sympathies occasionally were admitted. Once in a while a specialist or a scholar got in. But no one else.

There was no sign of any amelioration of artificial tensions.

The press continued to rail against the United States, often in terms more savage than were employed by the Soviet press in the worst cold-war days. The Chinese refused to shake hands with Americans on neutral ground.

A succession of threats to the peace emanated from Peking—first to the offshore islands, then elsewhere in Asia. The Tibet rebels were brutally crushed. Fighting suddenly flared up in Laos. Menacing moves took place along the Indian frontier. It was not accidental, I thought, that the Moscow press repeatedly censored the Peking communiqués on the border dispute or that Moscow offered to mediate in the Indian-Chinese quarrel.

Speaking of China's attitude of belligerence toward the outside world, a neutral diplomat stationed in Peking said to me: "It is a fixation. Perhaps the leaders feel that there has to be an enemy to make the people work harder. Whatever the reason, you are the enemy."

Other diplomats from Asian countries spoke of growing hostility toward themselves and their countries, of an increasing tendency by Peking to lump them all together as "Western forces." "The Han people again think of themselves as a master race. They expect to dominate the world by sheer weight of numbers," one said.

There seemed to be no sign that the situation would change. Thousands of foreigners were invited to Peking for the tenth anniversary of the celebration of the Communist Chinese regime in October, 1959. Few Americans were there. An indication of how the wind was blowing was given by the preparations. A program for training a thousand interpreters was set up. Only seventy were trained in English.

An observer in Peking who is well acquainted with the Chinese Communist leaders said to me that so far as Chinese-American relations are concerned: "Definitions of normalization differ so sharply that real agreement cannot be approached for a decade or two. China sees normalization in the return of

Taiwan and I doubt if Peking would exchange embassies until that occurs. So I think they have put off thoughts of the United States for the present.

"I think they believe not only as Communists but also as Chinese who have seen empires come and go that the days of Western capitalism are ending, that the United States with its bases all over the world is overextended and will have at last to pull in. I think they have waited a lot of centuries and can wait a decade or two without pain, especially when they have so many other countries to deal with.

"You should have seen the Latin-American delegations this summer—women, youth, parliamentary groups, capitalist politicians—who want to see how China gets industrialization without dependence on the United States."

This view was supported by Asian diplomats stationed in Peking. They said that China was pressing an active diplomatic and propaganda offensive, not only in Asia but also beyond the frontiers of Asia into Africa and South America.

"These campaigns for international influence are being conducted quite independently of Russia," one diplomat said. "The Chinese want to build international prestige and international relations of their own which are not dependent on Moscow."

Should China win admission to the United Nations, this observer felt, she would seek to put herself at the head of an Asian-African bloc of states.

In this circumstance, is Russia really seeking to help China get into the United Nations? Many experienced diplomats for years have been skeptical of the sincerity of Soviet desires on this score. The longer China is kept out of the UN, they noted, the longer the Soviet will be able to maintain some kind of veto power over China's international relations.

One evening when I was in Ulan Bator I encountered a diplomat from Southeast Asia who had just come over from Peking.

"It is curious," I said, "how warm I feel toward Russians here; and I must say they are equally warm to me."

"I do not find that so strange," the diplomat said. "I think you are merely experiencing a sensation which will be far more common in the future. To those of us who watch the world from Peking there seem to be far more grounds for accord than discord between America and Russia. What you and your Russian friends feel today in Mongolia will tomorrow be experienced in Gorky Street, Moscow, and Pennsylvania Avenue, Washington."

XVII

Accentuate the Positive

ONE DAY during Anastas Mikoyan's trip to America a group of us sat talking with him in the lounge of the DC-7B which was taking us from Los Angeles to Washington. It was not an interview, just an informal conversation; and the talk ranged over many subjects. Finally we got to talking about news, propaganda, and reporting.

Mr. Mikoyan defended the Soviet information policy. He said it was not as propaganda-ridden as we thought. Many abuses of government policy, he said, were brought to light through "Soviet self-criticism."

But, said one of the reporters, doesn't the Soviet policy of reporting everything according to a certain propaganda line—reporting, as we would say, with a certain distortion—doesn't this sometimes lead to misjudgment? Take the case of a high official. Presumably, he has access to supposedly unbiased information. Even so, doesn't he find himself affected in his conclusions by the propaganda slant of the press?

A slight smile played about Mr. Mikoyan's lips. Yes, he said. This does happen sometimes. He was thinking, I felt certain, of himself and of his impressions of the United States. He had last seen America in 1936, when he spent several months studying American consumers industries and public services. He is a remarkably alert man. He had absorbed a broad and detailed picture of the United States during that trip in the thirties. In the more than twenty years that followed, he had been the Kremlin's chief expert on the United States. When any difficult question arose it was submitted to him. He knew. He had been there. He had seen it firsthand.

Only a few weeks before his sudden decision to take his "vacation" in America in the winter of 1959, Mr. Mikoyan was talking in Moscow with an American guest who urged him strongly to come and have a new look at the United States.

Mr. Mikoyan shook his head. No, he did not think he would come. He had a wonderful image in his mind of America and the American people—warm, friendly, dynamic, vigorous. He didn't want to change that picture by coming back to the country now. America today was cold, unfriendly, hostile. It was wracked by unemployment and economic ills. The old America had vanished. No, he would rather keep his warm memories.

Now, here he was in the United States in spite of everything. Khrushchev had insisted that he come. What did he find? He found that the image he had of the dying America, the hate-riddled country, the decadent society sinking into the last stages of economic destitution, was completely false.

He found changes—changes galore. There had not been these magnificent superhighways, these superarmies of automobiles, these startlingly clean, bright, and cheap highway motels, this torrent of consumer goods, this unbelievably efficient system of supermarkets and shopping centers, this rank growth of cities which had changed them beyond recognition.

Materially, America had diversified beyond Mr. Mikoyan's wildest guess. Nor had the people changed in the negative fashion he had supposed. Today as in the 1930's they were warm, hospitable, friendly to a stranger.

Even among the great businessmen of Wall Street, the bankers, the bosses of the titanic American corporations, the masters of international finance, he found that he could talk and discuss and argue in the same vigorous, open way that had always been characteristic of Americans.

He went to Washington. Instead of being treated as a pariah he sat down with the late Secretary Dulles and talked for hours about questions of America and Russia. He came away from his meeting with the Secretary with a feeling that here too he had found a man with whom he could meet openly and honestly, a man who would listen to his arguments, who understood what he was talking about, and who was himself not a clamshell of a statesman but a man who was seeking, torturously and patiently, to find a way toward the solution of international problems.

It was the contrast between such realities as these and the picture of America that had been in his mind before he arrived which, I was sure, had raced through Mr. Mikoyan's mind that day on the airplane. For there was no doubt, as he could realize only too well, that long before the year 1959 Soviet leaders had encountered increasing difficulty in comprehending the reality of the world. It had become a shadowy outline, confused and obscured by the distorting lenses of years and years of propaganda.

There were, in actuality, two sources of this distortion. One was that which occurs in any highly structured system. (It occurs in the American government as well.) This is the tendency of weak or ambitious men to report events in the terms which they believe their superiors want to hear. This built-in bias is the most deadly enemy of diplomatic or news reporting, for it renders impossible transmission to the decision makers of that accurate information which they must have on which to base those decisions. This kind of bias becomes extreme when the penalties for reporting "bad" information, or information which goes contrary to built-in prejudice or preconception, are excessive. In Stalin's day he would not permit men to tell him bad news. For example, he would not permit motion-picture

makers to depict life in the collective farms except in terms of
a rosy, never-ending harvest festival. The first concern of every
diplomat was not what had happened in the capital to which he
was assigned. It was how shall I report the news to Moscow?
What does Moscow want to hear? And as for news correspondents—they hardly bothered to go to the scene of a story. Why
should they? Only when the Kremlin decided what had happened was it possible to write it up. The Tass news agency transmitted more words to Moscow than any other news agency in
the world—hundreds of thousands a day. But most of them
were the raw texts of statements, the unedited reports of other
news agencies. The whole mass was sent back to Moscow.
There it was picked apart. The Party line was decided. The
Kremlin told Tass what to put out to the domestic press—how
much, what words, what headlines. There was a small internal
bulletin circulated among, perhaps, five thousand top officials.
This was supposed to be "informational"—a report of what was
really happening in the outside world. Inevitably, it too grew
highly distorted and censored.

In addition to the built-in bias of the dictatorship there was a
second and formidable barrier. The Communist government
works on a theory of world affairs—the Marxist theory. This
theory dictates in advance the general course of world events.
Thus, the progress of the Communist states is basic, inevitable.
Nothing can impede it. The deadly decline of the Capitalist
world is equally inevitable. Nothing can impede it. Down,
down, down goes the West. Up, up, up climbs Moscow.

So, naturally, all news and all diplomatic reports must fit that
pattern too. It was as if the whole world must be fitted by
Moscow into a double straitjacket.

The practice of fitting all news into a predetermined propaganda pattern is a two-edged sword. I found, for example, when
I returned to Moscow after five years' absence, that the Soviet
press had failed completely in conveying to me any sense of

the real depth of the changes and improvements in Soviet life. Since the press for years had presented life in terms of perfection there was no way for an outside reader to determine when actual progress occurred. The picture never had the depth of contrast; it simply went on from one rosy triumph to another.

Small wonder that a smile flickered on Mr. Mikoyan's lips. Did the distortions ever affect high officials? How could they help but affect them!

This was one reason, of course, for Khrushchev's insistence on the policy of see for yourself. See with your own eyes. Get out and look. It was one reason why he was ever on the go, constantly traveling like a spinning top over the surface of Russia, and not only Russia—getting beyond its frontiers as often as possible to see for himself what lay across those high barriers.

This was what lay behind Mr. Mikoyan's trip to America. Khrushchev had insisted that he come and spy out the land, determine for himself whether the image that he had was still valid after twenty years and ten million words of propaganda. Mikoyan had just found out how wrong the image was.

An awareness of this dichotomy between the real world and the image world in which the Soviet Union has encompassed itself, much as a silkworm encompasses itself in a cocoon, is one of the most striking results of Russia's emergence from behind the security screen where she has hidden herself for nearly a quarter of a century.

This emergence is no accident. It is one of the key policies of Nikita Khrushchev; and without it, of course, there would be no exchange program between the United States and the Soviet Union. It is this program and the whole complex of events connected with it which have brought so forcefully into the forefront of Soviet consciousness the conflict between reality and propaganda.

The consequences have been widespread, and they have pro-

voked results of the most varied character. Not all the steps
have been forward ones. There have been violent and determined efforts by the entrenched bureaucrats, the vested interests of secrecy, cant, and propaganda, to preserve the *status quo*.
There have even been deliberate and dangerous efforts to sabotage the whole new tendency.

There was an immediate and tangible result of Mr. Mikoyan's
illuminating discoveries. The Soviet Vice Premier was struck
with the vigor, objectivity, and resourcefulness of the American
correspondents who covered his trip. He was equally displeased
by the fact that Soviet correspondents seldom put in an appearance. Russian press coverage was following the traditional pattern. It was secondhand and inadequate. Halfway through the
Mikoyan trip several Soviet reporters suddenly showed up.
They had been given rush orders to start reporting. They did
their best but it was not easy. As one confessed: "We are not
used to this kind of reporting. We ordinarily stay in the office
and write our articles there."

But a new day had dawned for the Soviet press. A few months
later, when Mr. Nixon went to Russia, there were half a dozen
Soviet reporters who had learned the slogging, bulldog techniques of American campaign reporters. They stayed at the
Vice President's heels, fought with the Soviet and American
security men to be on the scene, and comported themselves in
the tough, hard-working style that has made American journalism unique. They struggled to get down Mr. Nixon's quotations.
They fought for the names of local citizens he spoke to. And
they sent back to their papers running accounts which resembled very much those of their American colleagues. True, their
editors did not print these materials just as they sent them in.
But that is another matter.

Nor did this prove to be a flash in the pan. When Mr. Khrushchev came to America the new Soviet journalism was again
on display. A former Tass executive came along to study

U.S. news-gathering techniques. Soviet newsmen and camera-
men could not be distinguished from American professionals by
their tactics. It was a shoulder-to-shoulder battle. When I saw
a pint-sized Soviet cameraman ducking under swinging sides
of beef in an Iowa packing plant in order to get a closeup of
Khrushchev in a butcher's apron, I knew that the Front Page
tradition had carried the day.

And for the first time the running accounts which the reporters telephoned back from every city were published with
a literalness which probably had never been surpassed in the
history of Soviet journalism. Even when Mr. Khrushchev was
breaking with the Party line—conceding the fruitfulness of the
U.S. economy, admitting he had found no split between "ruling
circles" and "toiling masses"—his words were reported verbatim
in *Pravda* and *Izvestia*.

It was a triumph for objective reporting, for letting the Soviet
citizen read for himself just what had happened. And this was
as revolutionary a development as I could imagine in the field of
press and propaganda.

This may seem like a very small thing. Why should not the
doings of Mr. Khrushchev be reported correctly and fully to
the Soviet people? The answer is that this never has happened
before.

Unless you have long lived in Russia and become inured to
the control of the printed word which the Party has insisted
upon, you cannot realize the depth of this revolution. Russian
people simply have not been able to read about what was happening in their own country.

For example, after I returned from Russia in 1954 I wrote a
book about my experiences there. I had put together a fairly
detailed account of the events in the last Stalin years. Much of
what I wrote was hearsay. Some of it was sheer deduction.
But it fitted into a coherent whole for the first time the grim,
terrible years from 1949 to 1954. There were errors in the

book. It was written two years before Mr. Khrushchev's famous speech on Stalin's crimes. There was little in it that a well-informed or thoughtful Russian could not have pieced together for himself.

But when I returned to Moscow last summer I found that *American in Russia* had had a very broad readership among those Russians who had a chance to gain access to it. Copies of it were available among the foreign colony, and some of these got into Russian hands. The book was widely known. It was greatly prized by young Russians, who said that it gave them the first real knowledge they had had of what was happening in their own country. Even last summer I still found it being read with avidness.

The book, of course, had been violently attacked by the official propagandists, and I had been refused a visa to return to Moscow. When news of my arrival in Moscow in 1959 spread among the younger intelligentsia, it was taken as a favorable sign that times were becoming more liberal.

Perhaps times were getting better. I believed they were, myself. But not without a bitter fight. The old line Agitprop bureaucrats were going to have to be dragged into this new world kicking and screaming.

A few days after I arrived back in Moscow I ran into Mr. Mikoyan at a reception at the Japanese Embassy. I thanked him for his help in making my new visit to Moscow possible. He said that he had not known when he told me I could come that I had written "bad things" about Russia. I asked him whether he had any complaint about my reports of his trip to America. No, he said. Those reports were excellent. Well, I said, I will write about Russia in the same way. You will not always agree with what I say, but the reports will be as objective and fair as I can make them. That's good, he said. At that moment I heard a voice say:

"Mr. Mikoyan, beware! You don't know to whom you are

talking. That man has written slanderous things about the Soviet Union."

I looked up in surprise. So did Mr. Mikoyan. It was one of the Foreign Office men who deal with the press. He came closer and repeated his remark. There was an awkward silence. Then Mr. Mikoyan said quietly that he did know me, that my reports of his trip to America had been objective, and that, in general, he had a very high regard for the reporting of American correspondents. They were, he said, a hard-working group. "Real proletarians, capitalists without capital," he had called them.

This was not a single, isolated incident. It was typical of the attitude of those Soviet bureaucrats whose connections led up to the director of Communist propaganda, L. F. Ilyichev.

This meant that, for all practical purposes, Soviet propaganda policy was being made on two different levels. The line emanating from Mr. Khrushchev and Mr. Mikoyan was for a new-style objectivity, reporting the facts (or pretty close to the facts) and letting the chips fall where they may.

But at the other level a sinister campaign was being carried out, one whose inevitable consequence would be to negate the new look in Soviet policy.

For example, the Press Department of the Soviet Foreign Office was being run, as I soon discovered, like an Oriental bazaar. Its basis of operation was a bland mixture of blackmail, intimidation, and bribery (in the form of travel permits, special interviews, privileges in transmission of copy, etc.).

In the old Stalinist days the Press Department had a simple principle. Do nothing for anyone. There was universality of discrimination. No correspondent, whether he was a devoted Communist employed by *Humanité* or the correspondent of the Czech news agency or of the *New York Times,* got anything. Everyone had to go through censorship. No one was permitted to interview anyone or take a trip around the country. If anyone in the Press Department ever bothered to read a correspondent's dispatch there was no evidence of it. It was a rough system. But it was, at least, equitable.

Not so today. The new Press Department watched the correspondents like hawks. It was quick to call men in if it did not like their stories. It was not reluctant to point out that the way to get along well was to "write good stories." And it demonstrated this by offering favors to correspondents who pleased the Foreign Office. Communist correspondents no longer had to bother with censorship. They could telephone their stories to their papers from their homes. Special junkets were organized for them. They were taken for flights over the North Pole or to see the wonders of the latest big dam or atomic station.

Western correspondents were prodded and chivvied. Threats of expulsion or other dire punishment were constantly held over their heads. If they didn't write very much, this was quickly brought to their attention. The department pointed out that it was "very expensive" to have foreign correspondents in Moscow. Perhaps it would be better to reduce the corps in numbers.

My own experience was fairly typical. Thanks to Mikoyan's intervention, I had gotten a visa that bore no time limit for my stay in Moscow. The Press Department promptly limited my stay to two months. Twice I had to go back to Mikoyan to get my stay prolonged. And his intervention was required a third time for the most outlandish of reasons—the Press Department refused to vet my son's visa so that his passport could be registered with the Moscow police. This bureaucratic nastiness, but for the intervention of Russia's No. 2 man, would have prevented Michael from staying in Moscow although he had a valid visa legally issued by the Soviet Embassy in Washington.

But there was a much more sinister aspect of this Agitprop activity than the hazing to which the foreign correspondents were subjected.

This was the deliberate fabrication and distortion of reporting in a fashion designed to undercut the new liberalism. This was best seen, perhaps, during the Nixon visit. There was an undercurrent to this trip which was almost lost sight of in the general aura of success which surrounded it and in the great furor which arose over the Khrushchev trip immediately thereafter.

The key incident concerned a visit by Nixon before breakfast on his first morning in Moscow to the Danielevsky market. He made the trip with a friend from California and without his regular interpreter. The visit aroused a lot of excitement. In the course of talking to the people in the market, Nixon heard it said that they could not get tickets to the American Exposition. Nixon understood them to mean they had no money to get the tickets and asked his friend to give them some. The friend pulled out a 100-ruble note. No, no, the people said. The trouble wasn't lack of money. We just can't get the tickets. Nixon said he would see that tickets were obtained for them. He arranged to have two hundred tickets sent to the manager of the market.

The next day several papers published an item saying Nixon had deliberately tried to hand 100 rubles to the people so his friend could take a picture. Nixon insisted on talking to the poorest-dressed citizens, the story said. It was a nasty, evil-tempered item. Its intention was obvious—to put the Soviet people on guard against Nixon, to create an unpleasant atmosphere about his trip.

This was not the end of it. It was kept alive. Letters were written and published, particularly in the newspaper *Trud*. The incident was built up as much as possible.

Now, it was obvious that an honest misunderstanding could have occurred at the Danielevsky market. Nixon could have misunderstood (as he did) what the people wanted. They could have misunderstood what he was up to. But regardless of misunderstanding, the item could not have been published without a deliberate desire on the part of someone in the Soviet government to poison the atmosphere of the Nixon trip. That

the Soviet account was believed by many in the Soviet government became apparent when at least one Presidium member
asked why Nixon did such a thing.

This nasty approach was carried further in the course of the
visit. The Agitprop sent hecklers out to ask Nixon questions:
why didn't we agree to Soviet disarmament, what about the
military bases, etc. These men often did not learn their lines
well. Sometimes they had to be prompted. Sometimes they
lost their heads and talked wildly and angrily. All of this was
then dutifully reported in the Soviet press—that is, the questions were reported. Mr. Nixon's answers often were not. After
about four days it was suddenly suspended—probably because
Nixon was making fools of the hecklers in their public debates.

Georgi A. Zhukov, the man who was supposed to be acting
as Nixon's host, blandly announced that when Mikoyan was in
America people threw tomatoes at him (this was not, incidentally, true) and he thought asking a few questions was not such
a bad thing.

There were other incidents. There was a calculated effort to
create a row over the joint and simultaneous release of TV
tapes showing the Nixon-Khrushchev debate. There was a
consistent violation of promises that no dispatches or photographs of the Nixon visit would be censored. Glavlit, the censorship agency, said, probably with complete accuracy, that it
had no instructions to pass Nixon copy without censorship.

In addition to this, there was at least one deliberate attempt
to create a very unpleasant incident involving correspondents.
This was squelched only by the direct intervention of the Vice
President.

It might be said that all this was not incompatible with a
policy of more objective reporting in the Soviet Union since
most of these measures affected foreign correspondents. But
this would not be the whole story. All of these things had a
playback effect on the Soviet government. They were constantly

being reported to Khrushchev as examples of what happens when you begin to let the barriers down. And, since they had the effect of irritating and outraging the foreign press, there was the constant likelihood that there would be repercussions in the foreign press, an undercurrent of reciprocal nastiness. Thus, the over-all effect of these measures, as anyone who knew the Russian scene was aware, was to create a condition directly contradictory to Mr. Khrushchev's policy, to create conditions in which it would be easy to slip back into the comfortable polemics of the old cold-war days.

In all of this, the real attitude and the real role of Georgi Zhukov was ambiguous. Zhukov is the Soviet official in charge of the cultural-relations program. He formerly was foreign editor of *Pravda*. When Shepilov left the *Pravda* editorship to become Foreign Secretary, there were two candidates to succeed him, Pavel Satyukov and Yuri Zhukov. Zhukov was supposed to be close to Shepilov. In the sandwichlike arrangement of Russian politics, the man who was supposed to be close to you usually turned out to be your worst enemy. It was hard to know what was the truth of the situation.

But Zhukov did not get the editorship. Satyukov did. Zhukov then stepped down, or so it seemed, into the Cultural job. But no Soviet bureaucrat has ridden to the top more rapidly than he. He has taken more and more of an empire under his control. He has practically put out of operation all other organizations for contacts with foreign countries. He has even taken bites out of the jurisdiction of the Foreign Office and the Foreign Trade Ministry. He has become a Soviet bureaucrat par excellence, a past master at effrontery and bland rudeness. (When a group of *New York Times* editors visited him, he said that the reason why the *New York Times* was not sold in Moscow was that it was "an organ of war-mongering propaganda." In a farewell call I paid on him last summer, he attacked me for

having "shed tears over the fate of Beria" in my articles for
the *New York Times!*)

No man was more responsible for the exchange of expositions
between the United States and the Soviet Union last year. Yet
no man did more to throw about the U.S. Exposition a blanket
of unpleasantness. It was Zhukov and Ilyichev who came to the
American Exposition on the eve of the opening and began
pulling books off the shelves—books which they did not want
the Russian people to be exposed to, such as the *World Almanac,*
any book in Yiddish or Hebrew, and Russian classics translated
into English.

Why? There were two explanations. Either Zhukov was carrying on the classic Soviet trick of trying to sabotage his own
creation (having been put in the job for precisely that purpose)
or he was attempting to appease the powerful faction led by
Ilyichev which makes no bones about its cold hatred for the
new policy of objectivity.

When it was proposed that the two countries exchange
reading rooms, each setting up its own facility in the other's
capital, Zhukov burst into print with a denunciation. He said
that the exchange program could not be employed as a "cover"
for smuggling subversion into the Soviet Union.

And here, it seemed to me, he had finally made obvious the
dilemma of the whole new program. Khrushchev and Mikoyan
are not worried about "subversion." They know very well that
it is not going to be easy to substitute the new kind of reporting, the new kind of exposure of Russians to facts and objective
statements, after the years of conditioning to propaganda. They
are probably well aware that the process has reached the point
at which many Russians say: "I read it in *Pravda.* It can't be
true."

But they are insistent on going over to the new policy because it is integral to the whole program of putting Russia
into the twentieth-century world, of tearing down the great

wall of ignorance with which Stalin and his bureaucrats tried to surround Russian minds.

But to the men who have made a career of manipulating information, of building up the smoke screens which constituted the real Iron Curtain, this is desperate news and a policy dangerous beyond imagination. It would not only deprive them of functions and careers; they undoubtedly believe it would leave Russia naked and exposed in a hostile world. They sincerely regard all foreign journalists, just as did Stalin, as spies. They tolerate them in the Soviet Union because only in this way can they send their journalists abroad. They view the whole exchange program with deepest suspicion. But they cannot oppose it openly. They are aware of this. So at every occasion they try with all the ability of their clever minds to twist things—just a little. To sow just a needleful of suspicion in the minds of a Khrushchev or a Mikoyan. To show that you cannot really trust the Americans. They seize on the incidents—of which there are bound to be many—of misunderstanding or even of deliberate anti-Soviet policy (and it must be remembered that the United States *does* have intelligence objectives and does back intelligence attempts in Russia) to try to drive the point home.

They have a whole mechanism of elaborating this kind of information. If possible, they always start with a little nubbin of truth—an actual occurrence like that at the Danielevsky market. They build on that.

But it seemed to me that the Ilyichevs, the Satyukovs, the Pospelovs, the Suslovs were betting on a horse that was bound to lose. At best they were conducting a small rear-guard action. They could poison a particular incident. They could throw out a particular correspondent. They could muddy this little pond or that. But the whole course of the relationship of Russia to the outside world, and particularly toward America, was going against them.

There was a little incident during Mr. Khrushchev's trip to America which seemed to me to support this in the most positive kind of way. One of Mr. Khrushchev's entourage, one of the most important men, was reading to him from the American press. He had found a paragraph taking a mild dig at Mr. Khrushchev. He started to read it as an example of the "objectivity" of the American press.

Khrushchev interrupted him rudely.

"Don't read that. I don't want to hear about it," he said. "Tell me what they have to say about the success of the trip, about how well things are going."

That, I thought, is the new line. And it extends right down through every aspect of Soviet life. There were going to be more exchanges, more and more objectivity, more changes. It was going to be a difficult time for the dug-in bureaucrats of Agitprop and Glavlit. At least I hoped so. Mr. Khrushchev had decided to accentuate the positive and minimize the negative.

XVIII

The Shape of the Future

On AUGUST 31, 1907, Sir Edward Grey brought to an end more than three-quarters of a century of conflict between Russia and England. The two countries signed an agreement which shifted their relationship from a state of cold war (which not infrequently had flared into hot war) to a condition of friendship and alliance. Thus, the great power struggle which had dominated the last half of the nineteenth century was liquidated and the balance of Europe was shifted.

Grey did not find it easy to bring the long Anglo-Russian enmity to an end. There was violent opposition from many quarters. Some said that Russia could not be trusted to keep any agreement. Others contended that it was akin to making a pact with the devil. There was indignation that England should be aligning herself with Czarist tyranny and thus, even indirectly, giving comfort to the leading police state of the day. The *Times* of London refused to give its blessing to the new arrangement until the Russians had formally apologized for the expulsion of the *Times'* correspondent from St. Petersburg some ten years previously. Many in London felt that a rising tide of protest and revolt was likely to overwhelm the Czar at any moment. England should not be lending encouragement to the forces of black reaction in their dying hour.

It has long seemed to me that this episode of past history was well worth recalling for the light which it casts upon present-day great-power relationships.

In a sense, the postwar conflict between the United States and the Soviet Union had been a revival and extension of the continuing Anglo-Russian rivalry which was the major political fact of the latter part of the Victorian era and the early Edwardian years.

Like the American-Soviet contention, that of England and Russia had been global in its aspect. It had broken into open war at the time of Crimea, and there had been countless "brush fires" along the periphery of the rival spheres of influence. Nor was the enmity confined to strategic and military spheres. Strong moral issues had been aroused—the absolutism, the censorship, the penal system, the suppression of personal liberties, the absence of parliamentary guarantees in Russia had aroused hatred and revulsion in England. On the Russian side there was equally violent feeling against the dangerous doctrines of liberalism and democracy which England was fostering, doctrines which were seen in St. Petersburg as designed to overturn the sanctity of divine right, the absolute power over his empire which was the foundation of the Czar's throne.

There is no need to labor the comparison between the situation of England and Russia in 1907 and that of America and the Soviet some fifty years later. However, the two situations are by no means entirely parallel. The catalytic agent which produced the *rapprochement* of 1907 was the rise of Germany. When Germany began to be viewed in Whitehall and in the City as a more dangerous and aggressive rival than Russia, prudent statesmen began to seek a rearrangement of the chessboard to balance the threat of emerging German might.

Without that real and viable threat it is not likely that London and St. Petersburg would have swallowed the harsh, bitter words that long had been bandied back and forth or agreed to settle their equally bitter imperialist quarrels along the spine of Asia from the Bosporus to the China Sea.

The clear and present danger of a rival power whose rise might prove more menacing to either the United States and the Soviet does not yet exist. However, such a power has appeared on the horizon. It has become increasingly obvious to objective students of foreign affairs on both sides of the Atlantic that the *de facto* two-power world which emerged from World War II will within the foreseeable future be a three-power world.

For this reason it is useful, I think, to keep in mind the statesmanship of Sir Edward Grey. He did not agree to deal with Russia because he had decided that the Czar's tyranny was no longer reprehensible. He did not suddenly find the Imperial Court cleansed and purified. He acted from the motivation which always guides the prudent statesman—the basic security interests of his country.

Sir Edward was forced to act contrary to the moral prejudices of the England of his day which viewed Russia as evil and the Czar as an antideluvian monster who had survived beyond his time. Not only was Russia a police state, run on a basis of prison, execution, and Siberian exile; it was a citadel of fierce, uncompromising anti-Semitism—the home of the pogrom, the pale and the yellow ticket.

In our present-day preoccupation with the moral obliquities of Communist Russia, most of us have long since forgotten that the Czar's Russia was an object of hatred and indignation as fierce and relentless as that which we have visited upon the Czar's heirs.

We have now entered a period of questing, of re-examination of the premises of our postwar relationship to the world. My thousands of miles of travel behind the long-since-riven Iron Curtain was motivated by this questing impulse, by a desire to find new, hard facts on which to erect the structure of a coherent and effective viewpoint toward the world problems which press inward on us and explode outward, simultaneously, and with such protean force in this transatmospheric world of the latter half of the twentieth century.

The strongest conviction which I brought back with me from the wild, undreamed-of borders of Mongolia, the turbulent new empire of Siberia, and the capital-in-transition which Moscow has become—a conviction freshened by arms-length observation of the formidable leaders of the Communist camp—was that the time had come to examine the world with a surgeon's piercing, impartial eyes, freed from the prejudices of the past and wishful thinking about the future.

The time had come to think of the world in terms of geopolitics and not in terms of adolescent emotionalism. We must strip ourselves of an anthropomorphic tendency to plaster adjectives onto nations and to dress up power motivations as moral principles handed down from Sinai. Nothing, I thought, could be more perilous than to continue to view world politics as a kind of global struggle between "good guys" and "bad guys" in which, of course, our side was always the "good" side and, therefore, as we had been taught from nursery tale to TV story, bound to win.

We must, I was confident, begin to view the world in terms of the ebb and flow of forces, the emergence of new states, the acquisition by older powers of new weapons and technology of a range and scope that beggared the imagination and, sometimes at a single stroke, rendered obsolete static military concepts of several generations.

When, I wondered, would we begin to realize that the rocket-nuclear warhead had long since made obsolete the whole painfully established Word War II doctrine of strategic bombing and, along with this, the fantastically expensive multimechanical aviation world created by the followers of General Douhet.

I could not but agree with the statement that war was far too important—and expensive—a matter to be left to the generals.

What we now needed, above all things, it seemed to me, was

the depth and perspective to analyze long-range trends—those
factors so difficult to evaluate when looked at closely but which,
when we turn to history, suddenly emerge with the clarity of
sunlight burning through a morning mist.

Take the Russian problem, for example. Where was Russia
going to be five years from now? Or ten? How far would the
oscillation toward more liberal policies at home and a more
beneficent attitude toward the West carry Moscow before the
inevitable countervailing tendency toward rigidity at home and
harshness abroad begin to set in?

For nearly a hundred years before Czarist autocracy began
to break up early in the twentieth century, a fierce and un-
quenchable thirst for liberalism had fired the minds of Russian
intellectuals. No tradition of idealistic striving for man's rights
was stronger than that written in the hot blood of every generation of Russian young people from 1825—the year of the Decembrists—onward. The traditions of the literary mostik dominated Russian thought from Pushkin to Mayakovsky.

When revolution finally came in 1917, it was hailed on every
hand as the fulfillment of nearly a century of national striving.
That the Revolution fell into the hands of the Bolsheviks was
an historical accident. That the Bolsheviks themselves were
steadily driven into the repressions which had characterized
the Czarist regime was also more accident than design—for all
the talk of the Communists about historical "necessity" and
dialectic determinism.

George Kennan, who understands Russia far better than
most Russians and who is one of the most thoughtful of Americans, feels that the whole Bolshevik episode—from 1917 down
through the death of Stalin—constituted an aberration in Russia's national trend. It was, in his view, a little like an earthquake
which temporarily diverts a river from its course by thrusting
a chain of hills in its path. The river is forced into a long,
meandering detour that takes it in just the opposite direction of

its natural flow. But, eventually, the stream wears a path through the unnatural obstacle and resumes its former course.

In the Russian scene today I found much to support this thesis. There was the persistence of liberal ideals in art and thought which survived every measure of suppression and oppression at the command of the Party. There was the persistence of idealism in the younger generation, the persistence of a spirit of dedication to humanitarianism. True, the Party had often harnessed these fine young people to its shady ends. But the tradition of idealism survived. It could be found among older intelligentsia; they had nothing but cynicism for the Party, but for Russia and the Russian ideal they still dreamed.

Nor was the least important factor the Party's own fight for liberalization—its struggle against itself. For the Party was Dr. Jekyll and Mr. Hyde. It was Agitprop on the one hand and Khrushchev liberalism on the other. I did not think Khrushchev was indulging in cynicism in his effort to run the state without resort to the police power. I could see, as the Russians could too, that there was divided opinion on this subject. It was obvious that the pulling and hauling behind scenes was intense.

But I did not think the reactionaries would succeed in once again shifting the bedrock course of Russia, now that it was beginning to flow once again toward long-familiar goals. After all, Russia had been deprived, by the artificial time lag introduced into her calendar by the conquest and long rule of the very Mongols whom I had seen out on those endless grass prairies, of that golden era of internal leisure and good will which had been the pleasant fate of western Europe during the nineteenth century. She had had to work like a slave into the twentieth century to achieve her industrial revolution. Now she had attained it. Not only had she her industrial revolution, she had her technological breakthrough into new ground, just as England had in the 1870's. The fruit of this evolution invariably would be to bring comfort and leisure to the middle class and an end to the sweating labor of the proletariat which always accompanied the industrial revolution.

Would Russia, now that she had achieved her industrial revolution, not follow the characteristic history of all states?

It seemed very strongly to me that this was what she would do. You could not find in the Communist society of 1959 any stronger motivation than those very motivations to a more comfortable way of life. This was what Russia was striving for. This is what she had in sight. This, I felt certain, was what she was going to get.

And this required a new relationship with the West. I took Mr. Khrushchev with the greatest seriousness in his proposals for a *détente,* for a standstill in the arms race, for negotiated settlement of the cold-war quarrels.

Khrushchev, I felt, had cast himself in the role in which he hoped history would cloak him. He was the man of peace. This was the part he had set out to play. He knew it was a difficult task, but it suited the necessities of his nation and of his times. He would not be easily diverted from this role. Indeed, I did not think he could be diverted from it. I had listened to the solemnity with which he told a frivolous California audience of the deep seriousness of his mission to America. I was confident of that serious purpose before he had come to the United States. It was obvious in his every act while there. And if added emphasis was needed, it had been given when he returned to Russia. There an incredible thing happened. All the vast resources of the Soviet propaganda machine were turned loose to demonstrate to the Soviet people two things: the success of Nikita Khrushchev's mission to America in search of peace, and the feasibility of the new relationship with the United States.

Whatever the United States might be doing, Nikita Khrushchev was preparing his people for that golden era in relations with the Western world for which they had so long yearned.

I did not believe it credible that Khrushchev or any other responsible statesman would stake his every chip on such a gesture, would put the full force of his political career behind it, unless he was completely confident of his ability to achieve his objective and to maintain his course.

Khrushchev could be wrong. He had made political errors; he probably would make them again. But if he had made an error this time it was one of tremendous consequence both to himself and his country. If I analyzed his position correctly, he was going to fight for his objectives. And those objectives were the achievement of a *détente*—an effective *détente*, not a paper one. It had to be real—as real as that of 1907.

Anyone familiar with the working of Khrushchev's mind well knew he was striving for a goal which had been the objective of the late Joseph Stalin. This goal was the two-power world— the world run by the United States and Russia, acting in concert. Stalin had always thought this a logical idea. He had expanded on it to Roosevelt, who was not entirely opposed to the concept.

In recent years Khrushchev had mentioned it to many of his American guests, particularly the political guests like Stevenson, Humphrey, Nixon, and Harriman. The concept was not without its attractive side. It was founded on the present reality of world power: the fact that there were only two powers with global potentiality. The Russian idea was that the world be divided roughly into two spheres. In each sphere Russia or America would be dominant and would have the decisive voice in settling conflict and maintaining order. There would, of course, be twilight zones—particularly in the Middle East and Asia. Or perhaps a settlement could be negotiated here, too. This would instantly reduce the possible areas of conflict. It would mean, for instance, that the United States would recognize the stability of regimes and borders of the whole Communist world from the Elbe to the Bering Strait. At the same time Moscow would recognize the *status quo* in the West.

This would mean that the United States henceforth would take upon itself the task of acting as spokesman for the Western bloc. Russia would do the same for the Eastern bloc. Conflict within the United Nations would be eliminated at the top because the two great powers would resolve matters, not in debate in the Security Council or in the Assembly, but in private over the green baize tables of diplomacy.

This would not solve the problem of central Europe—of Germany, specifically. But it might create an atmosphere in which conflict over Germany could be isolated and, particularly, it might limit the ability of Germany to draw other nations to her side in any renewal of a *Drang nach Osten.*

For when all the outer superficialities were stripped away, this was what seemed to lie at the real core of Russian security forebodings—German *revanchism,* the re-emergence of German military power.

To anyone who recalled the 1907 *rapprochement* of England and Russia, the idea of drawing a line across the map and dividing the world had a curious nostalgia. For this was precisely the way the British and the Russians in 1907 settled their power rivalries in Asia—by drawing a line straight across the continent. On one side, Russia; on the other, England.

The naked idea of a two-power world was hardly likely to prove acceptable to the United States, although, I thought, it was considerably more attractive in reality than our statesmen were willing to admit publicly. After his long Camp David conversations with Mr. Khrushchev, President Eisenhower began to talk a great deal more like a two-power statesman than he had before. But, of course, such a policy could not be publicly proclaimed because the United States was a party to an alliance of equal powers—the NATO pact. She was a supporter of the principle of the equality of nations in the UN charter. And while any realistic person would have to concede that it was the United

States' voice which was decisive in these councils, he would also have to admit that a single power such as France under De Gaulle or Germany under Adenauer could and frequently had defied U.S. dictates successfully.

In any event, it was obvious that, whatever their private inclinations, American statesmen would be compelled to reject the two-power thesis publicly. It was not without certain difficulties for Moscow as well, for China was demanding her equal right to be heard in international issues. Had not China placed a veto over Mr. Khrushchev's attempt to turn a UN Security Council meeting into a summit conference at the time of the Lebanon crisis in 1958? Had not Peking forced Mr. Khrushchev to cancel his plans to come to New York?

It was quite evident that the concept of the two-power world, attractive as it might be both in Moscow and in Washington, could not be placed into effect without serious damage to the underlying alliances on which each great power now based its security. The two-power concept would undermine NATO, long a short-term objective of the Russians. And it might well have an equally devasting effect upon the Sino-Russian alliance.

But just because the two-power concept could not be officially established did not mean that it might not provide a basis for unofficial understanding.

The great political obstacle to any *modus vivendi* with Russia arose from the fact that it would give recognition to the validity of the Communist regimes of Eastern Europe and, presumably, to those of Asia as well.

This crossed one of the basic shibboleths of American policy. We had never conceded that the Communist states of Eastern Europe had come to stay. Indeed, we sometimes even challenged the right of Soviet rule over the Baltic States. This was an element now deeply rooted in American domestic politics. It was held to be a master factor in mustering the votes of many minority groups.

Our argument, however, had long seemed to me to be founded on the blandest and most dangerous kind of hypocrisy. We had long since demonstrated in Hungary that in fact, as opposed to word, we had accepted Communist rule in Eastern Europe. The words were simply bandied about for domestic political purposes. They had no validity in Eastern Europe. And this had had tragic consequences in Hungary. Hungarians relying on what we had said convinced themselves we would come to their aid. But the brutal truth was we never intended to lift a single finger, send a single gun, or aid in any way any kind of revolt behind the Iron Curtain. It was nothing but a glittering panorama of words.

This had cost America dearly in the lands behind the Iron Curtain. And to go on professing our dedication to the cause of "liberty" in these countries was merely to add cubits to our stature as hypocrites.

If we truly hoped to help the peoples of Eastern Europe, there was another route open to us. This had become evident to me in a long swing in 1957 through all of these countries, beginning with unhappy little Albania and winding up in provocative Poland. We could help these countries to move toward greater freedom by reducing tensions in the world; by helping them economically and culturally; by placing our relations with the satellite peoples on as warm a basis as possible; by helping the governments selectively (many of the Communist leaders also wished to move west but could do so only with the greatest caution); and, above all, by negotiating a settlement with Russia which would reduce the military threat in Central Europe.

If we could make an agreement with the Russians which would call for a pullback of forces on both sides and a neutralizing of the Central Zone, then we would place these countries in a position in which they could begin to edge toward the West again. After Hungary, with its demonstration of the ease and certainty of Red Army intervention, no East European country was going to try revolt again. But if we could get the Red Army off their backs, these states would again begin to move in the direction of their natural historical and cultural inclinations. You could halt the progress of history for a year or ten years with guns. But the moment the guns were withdrawn, the states would begin to move again in the direction of their natural inclinations. And the nations of East Europe—with one or two exceptions—inclined west, not east. Communism was not going to change that—any more than Communism was going to keep Russia from inclining west, not east. This was the way the twig was bent. It would stay that way.

And, of course, we would have to end the ostrich attitude of pretending that some states do not exist. Finally after ten years we had re-established diplomatic relations with Bulgaria in 1959. But Albania was still beyond the pale and had been since 1939 when the mountain-fierce, mountain-poor little kingdom of Zog fell victim to Mussolini. Il Duce long since had been hung by his heels. But Albania remained in limbo—not recognized, not unrecognized—with no diplomatic contacts. And no one in the State Department could begin to explain why this was so. The truth, I felt, was that it was small and Communist, and why bother. There was the paradox of the very alive, very present, very rambunctious, very difficult East Germany—another state which we did not credit with existing, although we stubbed our toes against it each day. Yankee horse sense dictated an end to the see-no-evil, hear-no-evil policy of diplomacy.

This, then, would be a program which might offer hope to the peoples of East Europe—if we really cared about their fate, and not just about the way the election went in Hamtramek or Yorkville.

In discussing any accommodation with Russia the question arose, of course, of the American bases. You could not talk long to any Russian, official or unofficial, without coming up against this question. Why did we need the circle of bases? There was a good answer to that. We needed the bases desperately at the time when we invoked the policy of containment to prevent the thrust and push of Communist aggression from smashing across the Soviet borders in the early years after the Second World War. Did we need them now? The truth was they were rapidly becoming obsolete—much more rapidly than our military men, with their investment in jobs, their deep involvement in procurement of outmoded essential weapons, and their rigid mentality, were capable of comprehending.

So far as "deterring" Russia was concerned, what we needed were intercontinental missiles as well as mobile forces based in the U.S.A. If close-up positions were desired, they could be provided with much more security and secrecy through nuclear-powered rocket-launching submarines which could cruise unseen at the key points of contact, safe and secure from counterattack. There were no more easy targets in the world than our air bases and strong points around Russia's perimeter. Every one of them had long since been zeroed-in by Soviet rocket-launchers. This was true not only of advanced posts like Turkey and Germany. It was true of every single installation in Europe, every installation in the British Isles. One push of a button, and every forward base on the map would disappear in a mere matter of minutes.

In the Russian demand for withdrawal from our "bases," the Russians were only asking us something which common prudence, both military and economic, should long since have caused us to do.

The only justification which could now be maintained for these installations (with, perhaps, a handful of exceptions) was that they provided some military support to the existing regimes which we supposed were friendly to us (a contention which grew more and more dubious as the years went by). And they did afford some economic support for ailing and spavined states. The savings to the U.S. Treasury and the gain to these countries if we were to liquidate the bases and use the money for intelligent economic and fiscal aid would come to a staggering sum.

Thus, to an extent much greater than was widely realized, what the Russians were asking us to do was only what our own best interests dictated.

Behind all these questions, of course, loomed the larger and larger question of China—the question which, it seemed to me, was the real issue of our times.

I could not and did not doubt that China presented a problem more difficult, more menacing, more frightening than any other in the world. It seemed apparent that Russia was having persistent and increasing difficulty in maintaining her own relationship with China. It seemed beyond doubt that these difficulties inevitably would grow in the future. It was easy to say that this was fine for our side. In a limited sense it was. But it did not remove the threat of China to world peace or to the continuance of the Western way of life. It merely underlined this threat.

If one could postulate—and this did not seem to be an exaggeration—a China with close to a billion population before 1975; if one could postulate that the China of 1975 would have an industrial potential approximating that of the Soviet Union in 1950; if one could postulate that this China would be armed with nuclear weapons and long-range means for their delivery —rockets, for example; and if one could postulate a continuance of the present Chinese tendency to supernationalism, jingoism, and aggression—where then would the world be?

Was it reasonable to suppose that Russia would find it any more comfortable to live with this colossus of the East than we did? Was it reasonable to suppose that the ramshackle states of Southeast Asia would not topple like tin soldiers as Chinese legions marched and countermarched along the frontiers of jungle and mountain? Could we be certain that India would be able to stand up against the juggernaut of Han?

I wondered. I wondered very deeply. I could see in Siberia the mighty and magnificent programs Russia had for creating a new world in this northern land. I knew of the plans the Russians had for joint development of the power of the Amur River—joint development with the Chinese. I had read of the "friendship" bridges Russia proposed to construct in that wild and tangled country.

But I had seen the statistics of the northward march of the Han people. I knew how rapidly they were moving up into all the areas facing Russia. I could see no possible plan whereby Russia could create more than a thin skirmish line of settlement in that area as contrasted with the surge of millions of Chinese.

Common sense dictated that Russia would to the last moment seek to work with China. But the hour of decisions lay not far ahead—the question of the atom weapon, for example. I presumed the Chinese had asked Moscow for atomic weapons and military nuclear know-how. I presumed that Russia had refused to provide it. What did this mean? Obviously China would develop her own bomb. She would do it herself, as France had done. And once she had the bomb, who could say that she would not use it as a threat against her neighbors—against Taiwan, against South Korea? Where would she not use it?

If today Russia sought to play the middle role of mediator between aggressive China and neutralist India, what would or could Russia do in the event of a new ultimatum from Peking to Taiwan?

These were questions on which the fate of the world was going to hinge in the next decade. I did not doubt that, if we wanted to get along with Russia, we could. The outline of that could even be spelled out. But could we get along with China? To ask the question was to answer it. There was every indication that we could not get along—that we would not even be able to establish diplomatic relations with her. The minimum demand that China would make would be the corpse of Taiwan. And this we would never give.

Once India might have been a mediator between ourselves and China. Not so today. Russia still might be. But for that we would have to pay a price. Was it worth offering a price to see what would happen? This, I thought, was a hard and close question. To me one of the most scandalous outrages against U.S. national security which had been perpetrated in the past decade had been the failure to establish diplomatic relations with the Peking regime at the outset. It might well have prevented the Korean war. If my theory of conflict between Stalin and Mao was correct, it might have changed the whole course of the past ten years. In any event, we would have established a corps of expert observers, trained to understand the development of the Chinese Revolution. We would have first-class firsthand information on every step of the strange and unusual development of Chinese Communism—instead of being compelled to peek over the high wall, to rely on secondhand reports of the dubious diplomatic missions of the West in Peking, the occasional reports of travelers, and the intermittent accounts of British and French journalists.

Here, if I had ever seen an example, was something which came close to the ultimate blunder. We had deliberately blindfolded ourselves to the reality of the China menace, deliberately deprived ourselves of information on which to form intelligent judgment. If there was a crime to be charged against Truman and Acheson, it was not for the failure of their China policy in the years before 1948. It was in their failure to establish diplomatic relations immediately with the Chinese Communist regime. This, I was confident, would be the true verdict of history.

But looking backward did not solve the problem of today.

I was convinced that China would reject any proposal made by us for establishment of diplomatic relations. Nonetheless, it might be useful to make such a proposal—but make it with eyes open and with public warning both in the United States and in Asia that we realized that it probably would be refused. This would at least place on public record the extreme intransigence of Communist China.

If the Chinese replied with a demand for the extermination of Taiwan, this too could be placed on record. We might well be advised to pursue the same course in the United Nations. Certainly, China would demand the Security Council seat held by Chiang Kai-shek. And certainly, by any rule of logic, she was entitled to it, regardless of what we thought of her as a world power. But could not this demand be utilized as a bargaining counter? Might it not be possible to negotiate something with Peking? This seemed dubious, but it could at least be explored. The important thing was not to lose sight of the real objective from the standpoint of U.S. security. This was certainly to unlock the gates of Peking, to open up the country to mutual observation and inspection, to give ourselves the opportunity of trying, at any rate, to influence the course of China policy.

The experiment might be a dismal failure. It would be necessary to go into it with our eyes open, coldly and coolly, understanding what were our true objectives, cutting out sleazy sentimentality as a surgeon cuts away rotten tissue from a festering wound.

Our relations—or lack of relations—with China were a festering wound. Any change would bring outrageous cries from the supporters of Chiang Kai-shek. Certainly we had our moral obligations to an ally. But this did not give the tycoons of Taipei any right to run U.S. policy. If mistakes were made they would be ours, not those of our Taiwan friends. If the world went up in flames, the responsibility would be ours, not that of our allies on Formosa. Too long we had been ducking under comfortable contrivances of fiction about China which had only prevented us from carrying out our own responsibilities.

There were little things which might be done. We had never established diplomatic relations with Mongolia. This was another state whose existence we did not recognize. It was not on the maps of the State Department. This was another of those cruel jokes of the Department. It deprived us of a chance to influence events in the very heart of the Asian continent. It deprived a small nation of acquiring a little leverage in its relationship with the great-power neighbors. And it deprived us of a window into the Asian heartland. There was every reason to recognize Mongolia, and none for keeping it in purdah.

Beyond this lay the difficult and dangerous questions of Korea and the jerrybuilt structure of Southeast Asian states. Unless we made some genuine and intelligent effort to establish a truly viable regime in South Korea, it would simply fall apart as soon as the viciously reactionary Syngman Rhee passed on to his ancestors. The situation in Southeast Asia was even more desperate. The crumbling of these states under Chinese pressure would leave India even more wantonly exposed. We had a similar problem in the Middle East, where it was obvious that the Arabian oil kings were going to play the old bazaar game between ourselves and the Russians for all it was worth.

These were problems of urgency. Behind them lay the question of Africa. And here, too, we were not becoming any more forehanded.

But, it seemed to me, the intelligent approach to and solution of all of these problems depended on how we handled the key piece in the whole world puzzle—Russia. It rested on our own utilization of the opportunities of the moment to negotiate a new and more soundly structured world system.

Everything I had seen in Russia convinced me that this now lay within our power. But it would not come without effort and it would not come for nothing.

There is a rhythm of world affairs which the experienced diplomat can hear. It can be caught and utilized to a nation's advantage. Opportunities in world politics, like opportunities in life, come and go. The Russian situation for the moment was favorable. Khrushchev was pressed by restless internal forces and by his own emerging difficulties over China. He wanted to go down in history as a man of peace and he wanted to deal with the United States.

But this moment could pass. Moods change. Great powers reach accommodations. China was well aware of the mood of her Russian partner. She could put a spoke in Khrushchev's wheel again or approach Russia with enticing offers. Or something might happen to Khrushchev. There was no assurance that his successor would be as able or as willing to deal with the United States. There was no real certainty that another terrible power struggle might not ensue. The question of Russia's orientation might become a key point of internal conflict between neo-Stalinists and Khrushchevites. The successor would have to prove himself, consolidate his power, as Khrushchev did. Years would pass—perhaps five or six. The whole aspect of the world power situation could change. China would have nuclear weapons by then; this was certain. She would be on her way toward obtaining Asiatic hegemony. The continuance of the arms race could well start Russia back down the trail of constraint, terror, and rule of fear. The West, in turn, would be driven to resume the policy of no peace, no war, of arms and reliance upon the global warning systems.

But by this time the West might not even be equal to Russia in military power. By this time Russia might have perfected her satellite systems in space. Her landing stages could have reached the moon. There was no telling what these changes might be and how fast they could come in this never-never land of science.

Khrushchev now was speaking and acting in the mood and in the main current of popular Russian feeling. He was in this sense moving from a position of force. So was Eisenhower.

There was, I strongly felt, a conjunction of interest and in-clination which could well serve our mutual cause. Whether each power would find it possible to take advantage to the full-est of this moment, I could not say. But I hoped that if they did that this would not lead the American public to suppose that we had finally settled our international questions or even our Russian problems.

All this, really, was opening the way to the next new stage. We had the great, positive challenge from Khrushchev of the peaceful economic and social competition of the two systems—a competition which I felt confident we would win with ease. But we could win it only in a peaceful world. We could not win it in a world in which the threat of war rose higher and higher in the East. We could win it in a state of peaceful rela-tionship with Russia. We could win it in a state of peaceful relationship with China.

I firmly felt that we had a chance of achieving that state with Russia. Perhaps we might through Russia reach better relations with China—but of this I had no confidence whatever. However, I did believe that the United States and Russia could, if they joined together, provide a counterweight to China. But not for all time—not by any means.

Looming over the world for the next century clearly lay the shadow of the Han people, rising once again to the position of superiority, the Middle Kingdom between heaven and earth, the Han people at the head of the camp of Asia's hundreds of millions. It seemed to me that we were going to need Russia badly and Russia was going to need us. The time for serious talk was here and now.

Index

Index

DATE DUE

MAR 4 '84			
MAY 1 '69			
FEB 25 70			
FEB 27 '70			
F			
MR 21 77			
AP 9 '85			
MAY 5 '85			
GAYLORD			PRINTED IN U.S.A.